EDUCATION

PART I.

HISTORY OF EDUCATION,

ANCIENT AND MODERN.

PART II.

A PLAN OF CULTURE AND INSTRUCTION,

BASED ON CHRISTIAN PRINCIPLES, AND DESIGNED TO AID IN THE RIGHT EDUCATION OF YOUTH, PHYSICALLY, INTELLECTUALLY, AND MORALLY.

"A sound mind in a healthy body."

BY H. I. SCHMIDT, A.M.,

PROFESSOR OF THE GERMAN LANGUAGE AND LITERATURE IN COLUMBIA COLLEGE, NEW YORK.

NEW YORK:

HARPER & BROTHERS, PUBLISHERS,

329 & 331 PEARL STREET,

FRANKLIN SQUARE.

1876.

PREFACE.

The writer of the following work can, he believes, truly say, that he has been induced by no idle cacoëthes scribendi to prepare it for the public. The subject is one of the very highest interest in itself, and of special interest in our day and country; and so regarding it, the writer has long considered such a work as he has here aimed to produce, a desideratum in the English language; for while the Germans possess voluminous works of the greatest merit from such authors as Jean Paul Friedr. Richter, Niemeyer, Schwarz, and others, no work, covering the whole ground of education, has, within our knowledge, appeared in the English language. To translate, entire, one of the extensive works of the Germans on pedagogics, would probably, from various reasons, have proved a thankless undertaking; and the shorter, but profound and sparkling work of Richter is scarcely susceptible of an English dress. In order, therefore, to make an attempt to supply a desideratum in our literature, the present writer ventures to offer to the public, in the second part of this volume, a work, in which it has been his object to present a complete system of pedagogics, its principles, and its methods, in a compass as narrow as might be consistent with clearness and due copiousness of detail. To a candid and indulgent public it is left to decide to what extent his object has been attained.

He ventures to flatter himself that the history of education, which constitutes the first part of this book, will be acceptable to the friends of education and the public in general, as he is not aware that any similar attempt is extant in the English language.

The writer makes no pretensions to originality as regards the general plan and matter of his work. Its history is briefly the following: In the days of his academic study he heard a few lectures on pedagogics and the science of method from one of his German professors. Of these lectures notes were taken at the time, and these notes constitute the groundwork of the present attempt, furnishing both the plan and a great part of the matter here presented. They have been very considerably expanded receiving various modifications and numerous additions, to adapt the work to the wants and peculiar circumstances of the American public, and to the character of American institutions. The extracts, inserted from the large and excellent work of Schwarz (Erziehungslehre, in drei Bänden), will be found acknowledged wherever they occur. These also have been modified in various ways, in order to accommodate them to the peculiarities of our country.

The history has been taken substantially from the work of Schwarz, which (*i. e.*, the historical part alone) consists of 1058 closely-printed large octavo pages. This statement will also show the extent to which the present writer has been obliged to condense and abridge. While, therefore, he has, in the main, translated from the above-named author, he has been under the necessity of taking great liberties with his work, in order to reduce it to such dimensions as seemed suitable to the present design. Hence, as the work assumed an entirely different character, it became necessary to give it, in various respects, a different form; to introduce, occasionally, original observations in bringing forward some new personage or subject, or in passing from one period to another. Some few additions have also been made, especially at the close. These statements are made merely in order to show that, although the train of narrative, as given by Schwarz, has been closely followed, he is not responsible for the form in which this abridgment of his history of education appears before the American public.

The reader will find the substantive pedagogics (frequently, and, as we think, incorrectly written pedagogy by English writers) and the adjective pedagogic employed in the work, because they are the only words that adequately convey the idea which it was here intended to express, viz., the science of education, in its whole compass. In this sense the

Germans have long used the words "pædagogik" and "pædagogisch," and it is time that the terms were domesticated among us also.

If the writer knows himself at all, his sole object is to do good; and his prayer to God is, that this humble attempt may, in some measure at least, subserve the interests of his country, the welfare of the rising generation, and the praise of his Maker's name.

Columbia College, New York, July, 1848.

CONTENTS.

PART I.

HISTORY OF EDUCATION.

I. THE OLD WORLD.

SECTION I.

EASTERN ASIA.

SECTION II.

CENTRAL ASIA.

SECTION III.

WESTERN ASIA.

SECTION IV.

AFRICA.

SECTION V.

SECTION VI.

THE CLASSIC NATIONS: OR, THE GREEKS AND ROMANS.

SECTION V.

SECTION VI.

PART II.

A PLAN OF YOUTHFUL CULTURE AND INSTRUCTION.

DIVISION I.

INTELLECTUAL AND PHYSICAL EDUCATION.

SECTION I.

CULTURE OF THE UNDERSTANDING AND THE SENSIBILITIES.

CHAPTER I.

CHAPTER II.

CHAPTER III.

DIVISION II.

MORAL EDUCATION.

CHAPTER I.

CHAPTER II.

CHAPTER III.

PART I.

HISTORY OF EDUCATION.

INTRODUCTORY REMARKS.

No subject can be more important to enlightened man than the education of his race for time and for eternity—none more attractive and interesting than its history from the earliest ages, and its gradual development down to the present time.

Some sort of education must have existed among men at all times and in all places. It would not be difficult for one intimately acquainted with human nature, and conversant with the hints given in the Scriptures with regard to the character of human life and the condition of society in the antediluvian world, to advance plausible conjectures respecting the state and methods of education during that remote period. But, as such conjectures are not likely ever to be authenticated by the publication of hitherto undiscovered monuments of antediluvian literature, we shall not, in this, follow the example of others, but abstain from them altogether. Yet there cannot be a doubt, that in the earliest ages of the world the religious instruction and education of their children was a prominent object with parents. That such education had not entirely ceased, though nearly so, before the Deluge, is attested by the piety of Noah and his family. It were needless here to argue the necessity and importance of religious education, from the degeneracy and corruption which, in consequence of its total neglect and abandonment by almost the whole human family, caused the earth to be swept of nearly all its inhabitants.

It is equally obvious that antediluvian education must have occupied itself mainly with the necessary pursuits, the practical purposes and duties of life. It had regard, doubtless, to the immediate and more imperative wants of common life; and necessity, as it arose, dictated its rules and its methods.

The same remark is in a great degree applicable to all popular education since the Flood, of which we have any knowledge, down to the invention of the art of printing. The mysteries of Egypt and her colonies, the philosophic schools of Greece and Italy, were not for the people. The facilities of an intellectual education belonged to a privileged few.

The invention of Faust threw wide open the avenues of learning, and bid come, and take, and enjoy, all that would and had leisure. Yet, though the vast multiplication and wide diffusion of books, through the intervention of printing, tended to the greater equalization of education and the extension of its benefits, little attention was paid to principles, and to a judicious and wise development of suitable and effectual methods. The universities of Europe were, and of necessity are, jealous mothers of the learned professions. In respect of popular education, therefore, things remained very much at loose ends until, in the eighteenth century, the learned began to set up theories on this important subject, and to propose and advocate systems; enterprising and benevolent men established schools with specific, large, liberal, and worthy objects in view; and at length governments began to interest themselves, and to provide for the intellectual and moral training of their people. Since then a new day has arisen upon schools; education has become a science; its methods have been reduced to a system, which the progress of intelligence and wisdom continues to improve. The interest thus excited has led men of profound learning to examine with minute research the monuments of classical lore, with a view to read and point out the history of education in ages long since past, and to follow its thread down to our day. Of the more or less successful results of these efforts we shall here, in the first place, present a compendious view.

THE OLD WORLD.

SECTION I.

EASTERN ASIA,

COMPREHENDING INDIA, CHINA, AND JAPAN.

I. HINDUS.

It cannot be doubted that the inhabitants of ancient India were among the first civilized nations of the earth. The limits which we have prescribed to ourselves will not permit us to present the proofs of this unquestionable statement. They are found in the divisions of society, in the religious and civil institutions and usages which still exist among the Hindus, as they have come down from time immemorial; in the philosophical, or philosophico-theological systems of the Brahmins, the Buddhists, and the Dshainists, and, more than all these, in the Sanscrit monuments of Indian literature, which, though but recently made known to Europe, belong to hoar antiquity; the Shastres, the institutes of Menu (collected, probably, 1280 A.C.), the epic poems Ramajana and Mahabharata, and many other works which it would be superfluous to mention. We must suppose the reader to be acquainted with the character of East Indian society, and in some measure, at least, with the recent discoveries of Sir William Jones and others, or refer him on this subject to sources whence information may be obtained, while we proceed to give a brief view of what is known respecting the education of this remarkable people.

It must be borne in mind that the Indians have always been divided into four distinct tribes or castes: the Brahmins, or priests; the Ketri, or military class;

the Vaisaya, or labourers, comprising husbandmen and mechanics; and the Pariahs, "the outcasts of all the rest," employed only in the lowest and meanest offices, and scarcely treated as men. The distinct privileges, and the insurmountable barriers, presented by fixed social arrangements, which separated each of the higher castes from that next below, and these three from the despised and abhorred Pariahs, precluded everything like a general system of education for the whole people; and, indeed, little more can be done than to infer the nature of their education from the degree of culture which the character and ancient literature of this nation exhibit.

The Sanscrit poems represent the matrimonial relation as one most intimate and sacred; so much so, that we can regard the right of polygamy, granted to the three higher classes, only with surprise. The Brahmins were required to marry; and that the procreation of children was regarded as the important end, appears from the law of Menu, which allowed the husband to repudiate a barren wife in the eighth year of wedlock. In their religious system the father was the representative of permanent existence. He not only saw himself renewed in his son, but might improve or perfect himself in him. If he had sinned, the devotional exercises and good works of his son could release him from punishment. If, then, the character, the piety of the son could benefit the father, even in the next world, what greater concern could the latter have had than that his sons should become as good and virtuous as possible? If the daughters partook less of this interest, passages in the Sacontala show that they also were embraced by it. These views are sufficient to show that religious and moral education must have employed the careful attention of parents.

It is probable that the education of the Hindus was almost entirely limited to the family training. We say "almost entirely," because the popular schools of the modern Hindus are perhaps to be regarded as a remnant of ancient institutions. In these schools, which are often described in our common schoolbooks, reading, writing, and some arithmetic are taught.

A custom still prevails in India which has probably come down from remote antiquity. An old man, occupying an elevated seat in some public place, assembles the children of the village around him, to instruct them in the principles of a virtuous life.

The present schools of the Brahmins, or the learned caste, bear evident marks of great age. The students are divided into exoteric and esoteric. To the privileges of the former even those are admitted who do not aspire to Brahminical consecration. It has been stated that no Hindu was excluded: this is improbable; but it may be regarded as pretty certain that all the three higher classes were admitted to exoteric privileges. The studies of this class were language and sciences, poetry, the doctrines of the popular religion, philosophy, history, astronomy, jurisprudence, and medicine; doubtful are the higher mythology and mathematics.

The esoteric instruction was confined to native Brahmins after they had received the second consecration of their order, and this instruction constituted their third and final consecration as priests and sages. Among the esoteric students the highest rank is held by those who devote themselves to the exposition of the religious books, *i. e.*, by the theologians. From these same books, which to the Hindus are the source of all the sciences, others study jurisprudence, or medicine, &c. This mode of procedure appears to be as old as the nation. They still make use of the ancient text-books, which, comprehending even the Sanscrit lexicons, are written in verse. Nor is the mode of communicating instruction less ancient in its character. During five years the pupil can be only a hearer, without having permission to speak. He listens merely to the conversations of two teachers. In the exercises of divine worship he is also bound to silence, being allowed only the language of gesture. During this period he is probably also required to engage in ascetic exercises. At the end of these five years he is permitted to communicate his thoughts and doubts to the two conversing teachers, and therefore to take an active part in the disputation.

The time of study continues from twelve to twenty years. During this time the pupil dwells in the house of a teacher (Guru), to whom he must be entirely devoted, like a son to his father. The teachers, whose general designation is Pundit, are exclusively Brahmins. Each one receives from ten to fifteen pupils, for a period of ten or twelve years, into his house. They possess large revenues, but their indolence is much complained of. Those living in a state of celibacy are said to enjoy the largest incomes. Their principal institution is at Benares, or, rather, in the suburbs Kasi: instruction is there given in the gardens or in the temples. There are elsewhere two other high schools of this description.

No Brahmin is permitted to establish a household of his own, and to marry, before he has completed his studies. All this, even the tediousness of the course of instruction, serves apparently to fix their mode o. thinking, their doctrines, and their art of disputation, and thus to establish the people in their usages, and their devotion to the Brahminical caste. For to this highest caste alone belongs the privilege of expounding the religious books or Vedas; the second and third are allowed only to read them, and to the fourth, as the unclean, even this is denied.

II. THE CHINESE AND JAPANESE.

We deem it unnecessary to consider these two nations separately, because in every point of view they are of kindred character, and have similar institutions; and because, while we know little of the Chinese, we know still less of the Japanese.

With the civilization of the Chinese, their literature and arts, their political and civil institutions, we are pretty well acquainted. A great variety of books, giving information respecting the character and condition of this people, as far as it can be obtained under existing circumstances, are before the public. On these points, therefore, we shall not dwell, but proceed to give an account of their education.

Respecting the manner in which children were in ancient times educated among this people, we can only form conclusions from what has become known to us concerning the present state of things in this particular.

In the Melanges Asiat., par Abel Ramusat, Paris, 1825–26, ii., p. 317, an interesting extract is given from the commentary of Young-tching, in which a Chinese emperor expatiates with much depth of feeling on the love of parents to their child. The emperors and their vicegerents in the cities are the highest moral instructers of the people ; and this, and similar passages, authorize the belief that parental affection is warm, and religiously cherished among the Chinese. That medical science is employed in the proper physical treatment of children, may be conjectured from the fact that they possess many works on medicine, in which, among other things, there specific rules with reference to this point.

There are a great many elementary schools through out the Chinese empire, for which, however, the government is said to make no direct provision. The children are sent to school in their fifth year, and very closely confined to their lessons, which employ chiefly the memory, and communicate little beyond what was conned over, a thousand years ago, by their predecessors. From early times the Chinese have practised printing from stereotype blocks of wood, whence instruction in China differs from that of all other nations of antiquity in this, that the pupils learn mostly from books. Besides reading thus taught, they are instructed in writing, and the Chinese attach much importance to calligraphy. It is not certain whether arithmetic is taught in these schools ; but, besides the general information which the pupils must derive from their exercises in reading, they are specially instructed in divers matters connected with practical life. They recite twice a day.

It appears that only the boys enjoy the privilege of

attending the schools; and among this people, also, the female sex is in a degraded state. Yet the custom prevails of employing private tutors in families, for which office the more wealthy select a man of learning who has obtained the degree of doctor.

Besides these elementary schools, there are common schools of a higher character for the people, and high schools for the nobility and gentry. In the former the course of instruction comprises four classes, to each of which a particular book is assigned. The first is the Pe-kia-sing, a book of names, in which the members of a hundred families are mentioned by name; and these names the children are required to commit to memory. The second is the Tsa-tse, containing a collection of things necessary to be known in common life. This is succeeded by the Tsien-tse-ouen, a combination of a thousand letters. The fourth, the San-tse-king, contains verses of three syllables, in which are taught the first principles of morals, and the rudiments of history. We have not been able to ascertain whether this closes the course of the common schools, and leaves the pupil to commence the higher course with the study of the Sse-chou, *i. e.*, the four classic books, nor have we any information respecting the relation in which the elementary schools of the Chinese stand to their higher seminaries of learning.

These higher seminaries, which are designed only for the sons of the nobility, are under the immediate direction of the state; and a college, enjoying great reputation, has been established at Pekin by the government. Persons desiring to attend these schools, who probably are always grown-up young men, are sent to the governor of a city of the third magnitude, whose business it is to examine the applicants, and to confer on those who pass a creditable examination the title of Hien-ming. The applicant, who has obtained this distinction, now calls on the governor of a city of the first magnitude, by whom he is examined a second time. The competitors are here required to prepare their exercises in a building devoted to this purpose, and those who are selected for advancement are called Fouming. Into the highest seminary of learning, the above-mentioned college at Pekin, every Mandarin of superior rank enjoys the privilege of sending one of his sons, who, after pursuing his studies for three years, receives some inferior office with a salary.

Among the learned there are different grades, which may be compared to our academic honours. A Mandarin of Pekin is appointed to hold, annually, an academic visitation in all the larger cities, in order to examine those who aspire to the inferior honours (or the first degree in the arts), of whom it is always necessary that there should be four hundred. Each competitor is required to pass through ten trial-exercises. The Mandarin selects fifteen of the most deserving, and bestows on them the title of Lirou-tsay. This title exempts them from chastisement with the bamboo, and marks of honourable distinction are conferred upon them. The title is of considerable value in the state; whence the title of Kien-song, which is about equivalent to the other, and which the chamber of finance disposes of for about seven hundred and fifty dollars, is purchased by many, who stand in awe of the above-mentioned ten contests for promotion.

Persons who have obtained one of these two inferior academic honours, are at liberty to present themselves among the competitors for a higher degree, at the intellectual contest held every three years at Pekin. This second degree is also obtained only by passing successfully through appropriate exercises of trial. The successful candidate has the right to apply, in the following year, at the capital, for examination in view of the highest academic honours; and if he sustains it with credit, he receives the title of Tsin-tse, or doctor, which is highly esteemed in China. The relatives and friends assemble around him with joyful festivities, and bring him presents: he enjoys great consideration everywhere; can expect to be appointed to the most important offices, and may receive from the emperor a rank still higher—that of Han-lin.

All this proves, indeed, that the Chinese hold intellectual culture in great esteem, and that the learned enjoy a sort of rank, and are appointed to the highest offices, so that they not unfrequently acquire great wealth. Yet external circumstances are too much regarded, and the natural consequence of this is, that titles are purchased in order thus to obtain offices. Riches, and the rank of birth, secure exemption from onerous exertion; and the Mandarins of the first and second rank have even the right to propose their sons, without titles or examination, for offices, so they be not the highest.

Why the Chinese, after reaching so respectable a degree of civilization, should nevertheless have so long been stationary, is an interesting question, which the philosopher is still at a loss to answer satisfactorily.

Respecting the education of the Japanese, who in national character and civilization so much resemble the Chinese, very little is known. That their literature is quite respectable, that they print books, and are fond of reading, is certain. The history of their country, and other sciences, are much studied.

Their education is probably not inferior to that of the Chinese, and there are said to be many schools in Japan. At the high school or academy, established at Miako, the capital, the faculty cultivate the sciences and instruct the students in them. The inaccessible seclusion of this nation leaves us utterly ignorant of the development of its civilization, and its ancient methods of education.

We possess some interesting information respecting the state of culture enjoyed by the nations living contiguous to the Hindus and Chinese: the Siamese, the Burmese, the Malays, and, in the north, the inhabitants of Thibet and Mongolia; but, as we know nothing of their education, we must pass them by.

SECTION II.

CENTRAL ASIA,

COMPREHENDING THE BABYLONIANS, CHALDEANS, MEDES, AND PERSIANS.

I. BABYLONIANS.

THIS people are remarkable as the first after the flood of whose fixed civil organization and established government we have any knowledge. Some centuries after Nimrod, their prosperous empire fell into the hands of the Assyrians, who greatly advanced its prosperity. However fabulous the accounts which we have concerning Semiramis, there can be no doubt as to the early magnificence of Babylon, the splendour of its court, the elegance and grandeur of its architecture, and the luxury that was rife within its walls. About 600 A.C., Nebuchadnezzar, at the head of his Chaldeans, a northern and warlike tribe, conquered the kingdom; but this united monarchy was soon after taken possession of by the Medes, who, like the Chaldeans, were merged in the native population. At this time, however, the Babylonian, the Median, the Lydian, and the Persian monarchies had still a distinct existence; but about 550 A.C. the Persian monarchy had already incorporated within itself all the others.

These nations appear to have been intimately related in culture and religion, and in the use of one language, the Semitic, which was, however, diversified by several different dialects. The peculiar culture of these nations proceeded from the Medes, from whom it extended to the Chaldæo-Babylonians, who had themselves attained a state of high civilization. With them also originated the division of the people into the four classes of the Magi, or priests and sages, the warriors, the husbandmen, and the mechanics.

Babylon was emphatically the abode of idolatry and its abominations. The religious system of this people is so well known, that an account of it here is unnecessary. Its priests, as has been said, were the Magi, of whom there was a well-organized institution at Babylon, under the direction of their superior, the Destur Mobed, or Grand Magus. In number about seventy, they were divided into classes, of which each had its superior. They studied nature and astronomy, mathematics and history. The Babylonians or Chaldeans were regarded as the inventors of astronomy and astrology.

The state of culture attained by these nations authorizes the belief that the education of their youth, however little certain knowledge we have of it, was in some measure provided for. The doctrines of Zerdusht do not, indeed, recognise monogamy, but they insist on domestic virtue and order, condemn unchaste and unnatural vices, and represent a numerous family as a good greatly to be desired. Yet this people sacrificed their male children to idols, and the innocence of their daughters in the pyramid of Belus. Children were sacrificed in the temple of Astaroth at Hierapolis. Sometimes their parents tied them into a sack, and, exclaiming that they were not human beings, but beasts, hurled them from the rock on which the temple stood. Practices like these augur very unfavourably respecting the state of education among them.

II. THE PERSIANS.

In the ancient kingdom of the Medes we find, under the name of Persians, a distinct race, inhabiting Mount Taurus to the south of the Caspian Sea. They were divided into twelve tribes, had their own kings, and were far from being uncivilized. Although the civilization, and hence the system of the Magi, doubtless influenced them at an early period, they did not, therefore, renounce their own peculiar manners. As we do not become acquainted with them until we find them established in Babylon, it is impossible to decide what must be regarded as original in their culture, and what as adopted. But in the account which Herodotus gives of their religion and manners, we find various indications of original development. They were a powerful and warlike race of mountaineers, and conquered Babylon under Cyrus, who there established the Persian throne. From this time forward the Persians are found at Babylon in connexion with the Magi, whose religion and authority were recognised by Cyrus. But with the religion, they adopted the voluptuousness and luxury of the Babylonians: having soon sunk into effeminacy and corruption, their expeditions to Greece resulted only in disaster and disgrace, and the vast Persian monarchy itself became, 333 A.C., the easy prey of Alexander the Great.

For valuable information respecting the character and civilization of the ancient Persians, we refer the reader to Herodotus. We hasten to give an account of their education, concerning which we are better informed than that of any other nation of antiquity. On this subject the principal authority is Xenophon. While the learned have nearly ceased to doubt that this eloquent writer wrought out, in his thoroughly Grecian mind, an ideal of what education ought to be, instead of presenting a mere matter-of-fact statement of what he witnessed among the Persians about two generations after Herodotus, his account is yet unquestionably founded in truth; and, treating of a period about 400 A.C., presents us with one of the most valuable contributions to the history of education. And while we admit that the master-pencil of Xenophon may have drawn a picture more beautiful in many respects, and more perfect, than the reality, the ingenuous reader can nevertheless scarcely entertain a doubt of the general truthfulness and accuracy of the account which he gives, with so much minuteness of detail and beautiful simplicity, in the second and third chapters of his Cyropædia. Leaving the scholar to turn to the simple and elegant language of the original, we here give, for the benefit of the general reader, a version, as literal as possible, of the second chapter.

"The father of Cyrus is said to have been Cambyses, the king of the Persians, who was descended from the family of the Persidæ, and these derive their name from Perseus. Mandane, the daughter of Astyages, king of the Medes, is universally named as his mother.

"The stories and songs of the barbarians still celebrate Cyrus as a man of the most beautiful figure, and the most humane soul; as most eager for knowledge, and of the strictest integrity; as submitting to every species of hardship, and encountering all manner of dangers, for the sake of fame. As such he is described both in respect of the nature of his soul and of his personal appearance: as regards his education, he was brought up in the laws of the Persians. But these laws proceed very differently from the laws of most states: they set out with provision for the common good. Most states allow every citizen to educate his sons as he pleases, and then suffer the more advanced youth to shape their conduct according to their inclinations; and after that, they command them not to steal, not to rob, not forcibly to enter a house, to beat no man unjustly, not to commit adultery, not to disobey the magistrates, and other like things. If any man then offend, they visit him with punishment. The Persian laws, on the other hand, anticipate, and take care that, from the very outset, the citizens be not such as to incline to any evil or disgraceful deed. And they make such provision in the following manner: They have a public place which they call the *ἐλευθέρα ἀγορὰ*,* where the royal dwellings and other state-buildings stand. From this place merchandise, and the market-people with their clamour and rude bearing, are excluded, and sent elsewhere, in order that their noisy proceedings may not interrupt the good order and conduct of the well-educated.

"This forum, thus situated at the state buildings, has four divisions; one for boys, one for young men (*εφη*-

* We do not translate this word, because the literal version, "free place," does not give its full meaning: it signifies a place of meeting, secured against the interruptions of common public business.

βοι), one for men of mature age (τελειος), and another for those who have passed the age of military service. The laws now require that each class repair to its appropriate place—the boys at daybreak, as also the men of mature age; but the aged, whenever each one finds it convenient, except on certain days, when they are required to be present. The young men sleep round about the governmental buildings with their training-arms; those who are married are excepted, and are not expected to attend except when they receive special orders; but they are not favourably looked upon if they absent themselves frequently. Each of these divisions has twelve rulers (or presidents), for the Persians also are divided into twelve tribes. And to preside over the boys, such of the old are selected of whom there is reason to expect that they will be most successful in training them. Over the young men, such of the men of mature age are placed as are likely to turn out the best young men. With authority over the men of mature age, those are invested, of whom it is believed that they approve themselves as eminently prepared to execute whatever is commanded, and to obey the mandates of the highest authority. The old, also, have their rulers selected from among those who give evidence that they themselves perform their duties. We shall now set forth what things it is prescribed to each age to perform, that it may become the more obvious in what manner provision is made that the citizens may be as good as possible. The boys attend the schools where they are employed in learning justice, and they declare that they go for this purpose, just as with us they go to school, in order to receive elementary instruction. Their rulers spend the greater part of the day in judging them; for it happens among the boys, as well as the men, that charges are mutually brought for theft, and robbery, and violence, and fraud, and slander, and other things which naturally occur. Upon those whom hey ascertain to have been guilty in any such point, they inflict punishment. They punish those, also, who are found to have alleged unjust accusations.

But justice is administered also with respect to a crime, on account of which men indeed exceedingly hate each other, but are not apt to go to law, namely, ingratitude. And when it is found that any one, who was able to render thanks, neglected to do so, he is very severely punished; for they are of opinion that the ungrateful care nothing at all about the gods, nor their parents, their country, or their friends. It is indeed found that impudence is the companion of ingratitude; and impudence, it appears to me, is the greatest promoter of everything shameful. They also teach the boys self-government (temperance); and the acquisition of temperate habits is greatly promoted by their seeing the old passing all their days in the most discreet manner. They teach them also to obey the magistrates; and what greatly contributes to the attainment of this object, is that they see the aged themselves strictly obedient to their rulers. They also teach them to be temperate in eating and drinking; and this is the more easily effected, because they see that the old do not go to their meals until their rulers dismiss them, and also because the boys do not eat with their mothers, but with their teacher, and not until the ruler or president has given the signal. They bring their food with them from home; bread, and no vegetable but cresses or nasturtiums: for drinking, they bring only a goblet, in order, when thirsty, to take their drink from the river. Besides these things, they learn the use of the bow and the javelin. In this they are practised to the sixteenth or seventeenth year of their age, but after this they are advanced among the young men (*εφηβοι*). These also have their prescribed mode of life, as follows: Ten years from the time of the expiration of their boyhood, they are lodged, as has been said above, about the state-buildings (palaces), both in order to guard the city, and to preserve their habits of self-government; for this age appears to stand most in need of careful attention. During the day, also, they are required to be ready to assist, especially when the rulers require it, in any duty connected with the common good; and when such occasions are likely to arise, they all remain about the state-buildings. But when the king goes out hunting, which he is wont to do frequently every month, he takes with him the half of this guard. When they go out with him, they are required to be furnished with a bow, quiver, and a sword in a scabbard, or a battle-axe; and, besides, with a shield and two javelins, in order that, if one have been thrown, they may have another at hand, in case of necessity. But the reason why the chase is thus made a public matter, and why the king himself is their leader in the chase as well as in war, and urges on the others as well as hunting himself, is this, that the chase is regarded as the most suitable training for war; for it habituates to early rising, and the endurance of cold and heat; it exercises in walking and running, for it is necessary to pursue with bow and javelin any wild animal that may show itself. And the exercise of courage is often necessary in the chase, in case one of the more powerful animals should offer resistance; for when the animal is encountered, it must be struck down, and if it attacks, it must be contended with; so that the qualities required in war are not easily dispensed with in the chase.

"When they go hunting they carry their breakfast with them, being, of course, a larger portion than that given to the boys, but the same in kind. But while out hunting they would not eat breakfast, but they take this to serve for supper in case they should tarry longer, on account of some animal, or otherwise prefer to prolong the chase; the following day they continue hunting until supper-time, and thus they count these two days as one, because they consume food only for one day. But this they do in order to accustom themselves to such privations, so that, if required in war, they may be able to do the same. The only additional dish which these young men have, consists of what they take in the chase; if they capture nothing, they have only their cresses. If any one should consider cresses with bread but meager fare, or complain that he has nothing but water to drink, let him remember how sweet broth and bread are to him who eats with an appetite, and how sweet water is to him that is thirsty.

"The divisions which remain at home are meanwhile engaged in those other arts which they have learned as boys, in shooting arrows and hurling the javelin; and in these practices they strenuously contend for pre-eminence. There are also public games of this kind, in which prizes are proposed, and the division which can show the greatest number of the most expert, manly, and prompt in obedience, earns praise and honour from the citizens, not only for themselves for the time being, but for him who instructed them as boys.

"The rulers also employ the young men who remain behind, either when there is anywhere need of a guard, or when malefactors are to be discovered, or robbers to be taken, or in any other service demanding strength and speed. This, then, is the business of the young men. When they have thus completed their term of ten years, they are advanced among the men of mature age.

"These, from the time when they cease to be ἔφηβοι (young men), spend twenty-five years in the following manner. In the first place, they, like the ἔφηβοι, are required to be in attendance upon the rulers, in order to render any service called for by the common good, and requiring men of prudent mind and tried ability. When a military enterprise becomes necessary, then those who have been educated in the manner prescribed, no longer carry bows or javelins, but arms for close conflict (called ἀγχέμαχα): a cuirass on the breast, a shield in the left hand, as the Persians are represented in paintings; in the right hand a sword or a dagger. From among these are also taken all the magistrates, the rulers of the boys excepted. After they have spent five-and-twenty years in this manner, they are somewhat more than fifty years of age, and they now enter the class composed of those who are old, and are so designated. These aged men no longer render military service out of their country, but, remaining at home, they administer justice in public and private matters. They also decree capital punishments, and act, in general, as magistrates; and if any one, either among the young, or among the men of mature age, offend against the laws, the ruler of the respective division, or any one else that thinks proper to do so, informs against him. The old men now give him a hearing, and pass sentence upon him; and the person condemned becomes infamous for the rest of his life.

"But, in order that the whole constitution of the Persians may be clearly before us, I must go back a little; for, in consequence of what has been said, a concise view may now be presented. The Persians are said to number about one hundred and twenty thousand, and none of these is excluded, by law, from honours and offices; but all Persians have the privilege of sending their sons into the public schools of justice. But those only send their boys who are able to maintain them, without requiring their labour; those who cannot afford this, do not send theirs. Those who have been instructed by the public teachers have the privilege of advancing into the class of ἐφηβοι; but this is denied those who have not enjoyed this instruction.

"Those who have, as ἐφηβοι, well performed what the law prescribes to that class, are privileged to advance into the division of the men of mature age, and to receive honours and offices; whereas those who have not spent their time among those boys, or those ἐφηβοι, do not enter the class of mature men; and, in the same manner, those are ranked among the old men who have passed with credit through all the previous classes. This is the constitution adopted by the Persians, with a view to becoming the best possible citizens.

"They still enjoy the reputation of taking food with moderation, and of using such exercise as is necessary for the digestion of their food. And it is still disreputable among the Persians openly to spit, to blow the nose, and to give evidence of flatulency; it is considered disgraceful to be seen going aside for the purpose of making water, or for any such purpose. All this they would be unable consistently to observe, if they did not eat moderately, and consume those fluids by labour, so that they pass off in some other way."

Thus far our author treats of the general subject of Persian education, and certainly the picture which he presents to us is a beautiful one. It has one feature which deserves special attention, and that is, that education in Persia took up man at an early age as an active member of society, to whom his appropriate sphere was assigned, and that this education consisted, in a great measure, in the practical training which he received in the duties of his respective sphere of life. It appears to us that our age might learn an important lesson here.

SECTION III.

WESTERN ASIA.

This division of Asia comprises the Phœnicians, the Carthaginians (who belong here, as the principal colony of the Phœnicians), the Lydians, the Phrygians, and the Scythians. Among these, the Phœnicians sustain the most important relation to ancient civilization; and the Scythians are particularly interesting, because of the account given, in connexion with them, by Herodotus, of a distinct tribe or people, whom he calls "*Μελαγχλαινοι, ἀλλο ἐθνος, και ὀυ σκυθικον*," and who were probably, in part, our Teutonic forefathers. But we know nothing, except by inference, respecting the education of these nations

SECTION IV.

AFRICA.

I. ETHIOPIANS (MEROE).

These, according to the account of Herodotus and the allusions of Homer, were a highly interesting people. Their culture resembled that of the Egyptians, but never reached the same eminence. Modern travellers have introduced us to a nearer acquaintance with the country which the Ethiopians inhabited, and which comprehends the present Nubia and Sennaar. These travellers all speak, with the highest admiration, of the past magnificence of this people, the traces of which remain, after the lapse of thousands of years. And it is much to be regretted, that besides these monuments, we have received no information respecting their ancient culture and history.

II. EGYPTIANS.

The Egyptians are one of the best known and most important of the civilized nations of antiquity. The earliest inhabitants of the Valley of the Nile were so-called Ichthyophagi, and in a completely barbarous state. A race of foreigners brought civilization among them. These were of a light complexion, and, though originally, it is supposed, from India, they entered Egypt from the south, from beyond the cataracts of the Nile, probably from Meroe, and, settling in Upper Egypt, in the progress of time occupied and cultivated Middle and Lower Egypt: and thus arose successively the separate states of Elephantine and Thebes, This, Heracleopolis, Memphis, and subsequently several in the Delta, especially Sais. They were independent of each other, each having its own divinity and worship, its own temple and peculiar sacred animals, &c. Yet certain divinities they had in common, such as Osiris and Isis, which were worshipped throughout Egypt.

After this arrangement had subsisted for many centuries, Sesostris, about 1300 A.C., united the separate states in one kingdom, yet so as, on the whole, to retain the authority of the priesthood, which had held the government from the beginning. The aborigines had partly emigrated, and in part been incorporated with the immigrants. The civilization of Egypt dates from the remotest antiquity, at least 2000 A.C.

We must suppose the reader to be acquainted with the history of Egypt, with its religious system, and the character and privileges of the priesthood; with the permanent division of the people into castes, and the strictly hereditary nature of all secular occupations, as well as other matters, which, however important, cannot be detailed here. We proceed to give a succinct account of their education.

The very respectable degree of civilization attained by the Egyptians leads us to infer, that their education, however different in the different castes, was in the main well regulated and effective. There has, however, little certain information respecting it come down to us.

The three principal institutions for the education of the priests were at Thebes, Memphis, and Heliopolis. Into these institutions it is probable that none but young men were received, who passed through a long course of graduated studies: for we find here the same divisions as among the Brahmins, into exoteric and esoteric students. Among the former, pupils were admitted who did not belong to the priestly caste, so that it is uncertain to what extent strangers could be initiated into the higher mysteries.

Here were studied the different sciences, in which the Egyptians excelled all their contemporaries: astronomy, mathematics (geometry and arithmetic), chemistry, of which, as their skill in embalming and in mixing colours proves, they possessed much practical knowledge; architecture, sculpture, painting, music, medicine, &c. It is obvious that some of these could, without danger to their mysteries, be communicated, at least to a certain extent, to the uninitiated. Among other methods of instruction in arithmetic, they made use of the ἄβαξ, a counting-table furnished with small stones. The teachers were priests, of whom each had his particular department.

As in Egypt the common people could read, and write, and even cipher, without which latter acquisition the women could not transact their market business, the children must, of course, have received instruction in these branches of knowledge, and hence the Egyptians cannot well have been without com mon schools. This seems to be attested by Plato, who says, De Leg., 6, fin., that the children of the Egyptians learned reading *together*. This is all the information we have on this point. In the mechanical trades, the fathers were the instructers of their sons. Gymnastics were also practised in Egypt: and in warlike exercises, the young men of the military caste were instructed by their fathers.

The children of the priests, both sons and daughters, were much better educated than those of the other castes. The education of the king's sons received the utmost attention. Their instructers were the priests, and their only companions were the best educated among the sons of the priests, who were over twenty years of age. These companions of the young princes were not only chosen on account of their rank, but according to the degree of culture which they had attained: a wise measure, which was adopted also in the Asiatic monarchies.

In general, education was, among all classes, domestic; pre-eminently so among the priests. For among them monogamy prevailed, while in other castes the men might take as many wives as they pleased. The wives of the priests were undoubtedly better educated than the women of the other castes, and had more leisure for attending to the early education of their children. The state of degradation to which all the nations of antiquity had, more or less, reduced the female sex, was doubtless a great injury to the children, and gave to their education a widely different character from ours. The fixed institutions of the Egyptians, which gave to each caste its sphere, and made occupations hereditary in families, no doubt greatly facilitated the process of education; but, at the same time, it greatly cramped and narrowed it down. In the education of the Egyptians we find all the benefits peculiar to such an organization—the steadfast adherence to a peaceful life during centuries of prosperity; but we see also all the evils of it, in its arresting the development of the intellect, crushing the aspirations of genius, and imposing adamantine chains on the freedom of thought.

Respecting the other African nations, we know so little that we can merely suppose that, through commercial intercourse, and the oracle of Jupiter Ammon, they were, to some extent, made partakers of the civilization of the Ethiopians and Egyptians. The latest discoveries in the civilized countries of Central Africa, *e. g.*, of the kingdom of Sudan, confirm this conjecture, although their present civilization is derived from the Mohammedans.

The civilization or culture of those nations of whom we have hitherto treated, may be described as having been fixed or stationary. That which remains is free and progressive in its development, or was so as long as the nations to whom it belonged had a political existence. The people, which here first claims our attention, is the ancient covenant-people of God, whose distinct national (not political) existence, even to the present day, under circumstances the most extraordinary, is one of the most remarkable phenomena in the history of mankind, to be accounted for only by acknowledging that Divine Providence has miraculously provided for the fulfilment of prophecy, and the attainment of infinitely wise and good purposes.

SECTION V.

THE ISRAELITES OR HEBREWS.

INTENSELY interesting as is the history of this people, of their civilization and religion, we cannot here dwell upon it, both because it would not be much to our present purpose, as we know little of their education, and because the same source of information from which we could draw, is, or ought to be, in the hands of all.

The civilization of the Hebrews had a peculiar character of its own, not without a considerable admixture of Egyptian culture. It owed its peculiarities, in a great measure, to the character and mode of life of their great ancestor Abraham, and of his immediate descendants, and to the patriarchal government that prevailed among them, and gave a peculiar complexion to their social system; but, above all, to the mighty influence of their glorious religion, of their holy law, in which they were instructed by men divinely commissioned, and of their theocratic polity. Their religion, derived directly from heaven, was the inherited means or instrument of this nation's culture. Their glorious literature, rich in the most magnificent compositions in prose and poetry, presenting the only authentic and true account of the origin of the world, and the early history of our race; constituting, in its history, its revealed truths, its devotional productions, its moral precepts and discourses, and in its wonderful prophecies, the basis of that religion which it was designed to introduce, whose influence has regenerated a great portion of mankind, given a new impulse and direction to human culture, and which is carrying its noiseless and peaceable conquests to the uttermost ends of the earth: this literature requires no discussion here; it is in the hands of the high and the low, the rich and the poor, and, accessible to all, invites all to receive its divine instruction.

We proceed, then, to give a brief account of Hebrew education. The subordinate position of woman, so characteristic of the East, was among the Hebrews also a great hinderance to education. Yet among them, as the readers of Scripture know, powerful religious influences, which gave to wedded life, and to the relation between parents and children, a sacredness not known among other Eastern nations, greatly contributed to the melioration of this evil. The absence of castes was also favourable to the free development of mind, and of character, among the Israelites.

Although it was usual for mothers to suckle their children themselves, it was not uncommon to employ wet-nurses, even as early as in the time of the patriarchs. They also had male attendants for their children. We find, therefore, that among the Hebrews, as with us, persons were employed to assist the parents in the business of education, and in some cases, to supply their place. In the time of David, already there were educators, or superintendents, or governors for the king's sons, who were men of distinction, such as Jehiel Ben Hachmoni, with David's sons, and especially the prophet Nathan, to whom Solomon's education was intrusted, and who called his pupil, the future wise king, by the name of Jedediah, the beloved of the Lord.*

After the children were weaned, which was usually done in their third year, they grew up and were educated in the bosom of the family, and their education took its character more from domestic usage, and national custom, than from regular institutions. Their physical education was not exactly calculated to render them hardy, but their moral discipline was strict and vigorous. The rod was in common use, and this rigid discipline was made the duty of parents; and an indulgent father, like Eli, was accounted responsible for the evil conduct of his children.

The education of the Hebrews was thoroughly religious, and in the father, who acted in the name of God, supreme authority was vested. Respect and reverence of old age was a religious duty, expressly inculcated in the divine law. See Levit., xix., 32.

The father's authority over his children continued as long as they remained in the parental home. The obedience of children towards their parents was rigorously enforced, and disobedient sons exposed themselves to the sanctions of the law. The punishments for the violation of filial duty were very severe. He who had cursed father or mother, *i. e.*, grossly reviled or contemned either, received a public malediction and sentence of death. The same punishment was incurred by those who gave a blow to either parent. Children were bound to support their parents,

* See 1 Chron., xxvii., 32. 2 Sam., xii., 25. 1 Sam., i., 22, sqq.; ii., 11, sqq 2 Kings, x., 1, 6.

when these were unable to maintain themselves. A son addicted to strong drink, or otherwise dissolute, was subject to stoning.

It was, therefore, the father's great concern to educate his children in the law of Jehovah, and adapt to this end the arrangements of his household. He was required to impress on their minds the general commandments, frequently to call them to their remembrance, and to enjoin especially the fundamental commandment of love to God. At the same time, special laws were to be inculcated on every suitable occasion. The observance of the ceremonial law habituated the children to cleanliness and wholesome diet, which had, not only physically, but morally, a happy influence. Self-pollution was guarded against by a special statute. In general, the customs and arrangements of the family were calculated to promote love to the law, to the whole nation, and to the only true God.

This religious education was rich in instruction, which exerted an influence on the Hebrew's entire mode of life; for this instruction was historical, not only communicating oral information respecting what Jehovah had, in times past, done and commanded, but initiating, by its practices, rites, ceremonies, and feasts, the young in the national culture. The education of the Israelites was truly national.

The oral instruction of children in the law was commenced as soon as they could repeat the words pronounced in their hearing. In the fourth year they were taught the alphabet, and began in the fifth to learn to read. This early instruction in reading, in which the father was the teacher, appears, however, to have been introduced at a later period of the Jewish history, for the express purpose of accustoming the young to the sacred language, and enabling them to read the word of God.

There is, indeed, mention made of writing (Deut., vi., 9, et al.), but not as a subject of domestic instruction, and it is not probable that the people generally were able to write. Still less reason is there to believe, that in ancient times the boys were instructed in arithmetic. Nor is there any evidence that there were schools for boys, or that the Levites gave instruction in families. The father appears generally to have been the teacher, and to have instructed his sons by his own example, and by practical illustrations, in those attainments which they were required to make, among which was vocal and instrumental music.

At twenty years of age the young man was enrolled among the warriors; and all the men, with the exception of the Levites, were required to render military service until their fiftieth year.

The education of females was not exactly neglected, yet they received less than the other sex; and even the daughters of the priests could neither read nor write; but they enjoyed the common privilege of growing up in the bosom of the family, in which kindness and affectionate solicitude watched over the development of their character, and trained them up in habits of cleanliness, piety, and modesty. They were not only educated to be faithful and skilful housewives, but to appear respectably in public. They wrought in flax, hemp, wool, cotton, camels' and goats' hair; possessed great skill in spinning, weaving, fulling, and dyeing; in making garments for themselves and their families; in working tapestry and tents; and were perhaps as skilful in embroidery as their neighbours, the Sidonian women. They learned to cook and to bake; and although females of rank or wealth left the affairs of the kitchen to female slaves, the daughters of kings did not regard the art of cookery as beneath their dignity. Instructed in music and dancing, the young Hebrew women may be said to have received some measure of aesthetic education; but these accomplishments were valued chiefly on account of their connexion with religious rites and festivals.

The education of the Hebrews was not, in the strict acceptation of the term, a national education; but it was in the strictest sense domestic, and thus also national, and its good fruits often became manifest in the course of their checkered history. They were wont often to repeat its fundamental principle: "the fear of the Lord is the beginning of wisdom."

It is scarcely necessary to say that the consideration of the schools of the prophets would here be out of place, especially as their real character cannot be ascertained. The later schools of rabbinical learning, however interesting in many respects, we also omit, as they are not exactly embraced by our present plan.

SECTION VI.

THE CLASSIC NATIONS: OR, THE GREEKS AND ROMANS.

I. THE GREEKS.

The important relation which the culture of the Greeks and Romans sustains to modern education; the mighty influence which their literature exerts upon that of Europe and our own country, and the intense interest with which every man of liberal education must regard those nations, with whose great minds he has been in delightful intercourse, and cultivated an ever-growing intimacy, from the early days of his academic studies, demand that we should consider, somewhat extensively, the influences which produced their peculiar culture, so long the admiration of the enlightened world; or, in other words, that we should give as extended a view of their education as our limits will permit. While, therefore, we begin with the Greeks, we request the reader to impress anew upon his mind their history from the earliest times, as our limited space would, at best, admit only of a meager outline of a great historic picture, which ought to be viewed in all its fulness of detail, and freshness of colouring.

The ante-Homeric era of the Greeks presents to our view their culture rather in masses, like the confluent light of the nebulæ; and we discern less the education of youth, than certain influences which operated on the whole body of the people, and on a grand scale; and among these, next to religion, music and poetry are prominent. We therefore turn to particular stars of that ancient world, whose light comes down to us from a distance less remote. These are framers of states, legislators, and, at the same time, educators; or they are distinct institutions, promotive of national culture; or they are entire states, in which we find the Grecian idea of education brought to a high degree of development, and offering instruction even to our age. In following the current of time, the following periods present themselves to our consideration. The Homeric era; the Dorians in their principal seats, especially the Spartans; the philosophic schools; Athenian education; the Athenian educators, and the Grecian culture of their, and subsequent, times. These cycles of culture will be classified under the names of men who are worthy to be placed at their head, as follows: 1. Homer. 2. Lycurgus. 3. Pythagoras. 4. Solon. 5. Socrates. 6. Plato. 7. Aristotle.

1. *Homer. Achaians and Hellenes.*

Homer, acquainted with the manners and countries of the people dwelling about the eastern portion of the Mediterranean, shines, by his intellectual culture, which he probably acquired by travel, perhaps even in Egypt, as a great and brilliant star of that ancient time. The knowledge which he acquired, assumed with him a Grecian form. All his collected treasures were remodelled by the creative power of the genius of beauty. From the gods which he found, he formed the Grecian Olympus, and the world to which it was sacred, and his poems became the schoolbooks of the Greeks; his mythology, his historical narratives, his moral precepts, his geography, and his ethnology, became the substratum of whatever was spoken or taught in the Greek language.

Glorious are the ideals of Homer, not only as subjects for the plastic arts, but also on account of a certain moral power and grandeur: male and female characters of lofty conception, comprising the twelve higher divinities; and they have thus always exerted a powerful influence, even upon our culture. For the history of education, Homer's works contain, in multiplied hints and portraitures, a mine from which we shall offer a few gems. Achilles, his principal hero, was at a tender age intrusted to the care of the faithful Phœnix, who educated him, and was in his old age highly esteemed by his pupil.—See Il., ix., 485. His friend Patroclus was educated with him, in the palace of Peleus.—Il., xxiii., 84, sqq. Homer's second ideal is Ulysses, a man of refinement and extensive culture, which appears in his moderation and calm discretion, in his rigid self-government, and his comprehensive knowledge of the world and of men. In his son Telemachus we see a well-educated young man, whose prominent traits of character, filial reverence, youthful ardour and enterprise, and artless modesty, are depicted with evident delight by our poet.—See the Odyssee.

Hector, who, in our estimation, is the noblest of the Homeric heroes, was humane, generous, and exemplary in his relations to gods and men, towards parents, brothers and sisters, wife and child. A beautiful repose characterizes this picture of the Trojan hero. There are many allusions in Homer to the educational practices of his time. From Od., xv., 262, it appears that persons of rank sometimes educated the children of others with their own. An aged man, Phylas, is represented as educating the orphan child of his daughter as his own son.—Il., xvi., 191.

Beautiful and instructive are the following passages: Il., xxii., 490–508. Od., ix., 34, sqq. Il., xvi., 7–10. Il., vi., 466, sqq. Il., xxiii., 588.

Homer's female characters are far from being destitute of knowledge and good culture; witness Penelope, Arete, and her admirably-educated daughter Nausikaa.

From the time of Homer down to the period in which we behold the Grecian states in a clearer historic light, various institutions of an educational character appear to have existed. Such were the medical schools of the Asclepiades in Cos, at Crotona in Magna Græcia, at Cnidus, and at Rhodes. No doubt there were other schools for boys, as they were instructed in vocal music, for which purpose they were necessarily, in some way or other, associated under a teacher. The common schools which, at the time of the Peloponnesian war, existed even in Bœotia, lead us to infer that similar institutions were established at an early period. This inference is sustained by the traces found, at a very early period, in Magna Græcia, and in other regions of Italy settled by Greeks. Nor was the influence of the gymnastic institutions, the several public games, unimportant in respect of mental and moral culture.

2. *Lycurgus and the Spartans.*

The peculiar culture of the Spartans, which was originated by Lycurgus, is less interesting or important to our age than that of the other Grecian states. For this reason, but also because there are many things connected with Spartan education, nay, essential features of it, which would be offensive to the modesty of the well-educated reader, we shall forbear entering much into detail. The prominent characteristics of the culture of the Spartans may be readily ascertained from any good work on general history; *e. g.*, the larger work of Tytler, to which the general reader is referred.

It must be conceded that the idea of Lycurgus, though it embraced little more than the physical culture of man, was a grand one. It was clearly conceived, admirably developed, consistently carried out, and invested with permanent authority by an extraordinary example, on the part of its author, of self-consecration to the attainment of some great purpose. The fundamental principle of the national culture which he originated, and of the education which, in subserviency to it, he established, was, that all children belong to the state immediately, and not merely because the parents belong to it.

It was the desire and glory of Sparta to possess a beautiful and brave race of people, healthy in body and soul, blooming sons and daughters. While war was the great business of the state, to raise, to educate a vigorous race of warriors was its great concern. To train up hardy citizens was the aim of Spartan education; and to the attainment of this, all its provisions and methods were admirably adapted. Immediately upon the birth of a child, the state asserted its paramount right over it; for it depended on a public decision, whether it should be permitted to live. The father was required to bring his new-born child to the older inhabitants of his ὠβὰ, or quarter of the city, who met in a hall (λέσχη); these inspected the child, in order to ascertain whether it was well-proportioned and healthy. If they found it to be so, they ordered that it should be raised; but if it was weakly or deformed, they caused it to be cast into the chasm of the Taygetus. From early infancy the children were subjected to treatment, and habituated to diet, calculated to render them hardy.

In early childhood already they were required to submit to the annual διαμαστίγωσις, or scourging; when small boys, together with older ones, and young men, who had allowed themselves to be detected in stealing, were scourged even to blood. Under this infliction they were not permitted to utter cries, and their parents stood by to administer encouragement. If they held out without giving signs of suffering, they were crowned, as victors, with a wreath; but many perished under the operation.

Unlike the Persians, the Spartans intrusted children, during the first seven years of life, to the affectionate care of their parents, and besides them, only the nurse had any charge over them. After the seventh year the boy was surrendered to the public education, in which he passed through a number of different grades or stages until he was thirty years of age, when he was accounted a man, and belonged entirely to the service of the state and of war.

The aged stood in high respect, and reverence for the old was strictly inculcated upon the young.

When the boy entered on the public course of education, the principle was laid down, that the Spartan must learn, from his early youth, to govern and to be governed; and therefore the young must, above all things, learn to obey. At the same time, they were required to engage in athletic exercises; and their minds were trained to prompt activity. Even the boys were thus intellectually exercised, and practised, daily and rigidly, in thinking clearly, in judging correctly, in speaking the truth, and in expressing themselves briefly; from which latter practice, for which the Spartans were noted, we have the word laconic. These exercises were often introduced at meals.

When the young commenced their course of public education, they were required to go barefoot: their hair was closely cropped, and they received a sort of cap, and were made to clothe themselves lightly. At twelve years of age they exchanged their χιτων for a cloak, which had to last them at least a year.

The black soup was as yet considered too strong for them; their own meager fare they were compelled to prepare themselves. If, in addition to it, they could steal anything from the gardens or the tables of the men, this was permitted, as a practice in artifice and skill; but they were punished if they allowed themselves to be detected. Their couches were rushes, just as they pulled them up at the Eurotas. On these they slept in companies, and were not, in winter, allowed any additional comfort, except a portion of a certain other plant, mingled among the rushes.

Their instruction was limited to gymnastics, music (vocal, and on the lyre and flute), orchestics, *i. e.*, severe athletic exercises, and dancing. Reading and writing were not required, and therefore much neglected; grammar was, therefore, not thought of, and still less rhetoric, as the art of oratory was despised in Sparta. A little arithmetic, especially mental, was taught for the uses of common life. This whole course of education was managed by the public teachers; yet the parents had considerable influence in the training of their children. Notwithstanding the decided one-sidedness of Spartan education, it was often much commended, and even sometimes preferred to that of the Athenians. Ruddy and rugged health and bodily vigour, and severe self-government, were its principal results; yet, as it strictly inculcated love of country and a certain sort of piety, sharpened the understanding and communicated some degree of æsthetic culture, the claims of the mind were not totally neglected. It continued in operation during several centuries, until, after the Peloponnesian war, and still more, after the reign of Alexander the Great, the genius of Greece departed, and everything external perished that was not founded in intellectual culture.

3. *Pythagoras. Pythagoræans.*

Pythagoras, born on an Asiatic island in the Mediterranean, became the founder, among the westernmost Greeks of Magna Græcia, of a philosophic sect, and the lawgiver of the Doric colony at Crotona. He was the first Greek in whom the spirit of the East was united with that of the West, and in whom the culture of Babylon, Egypt, and westernmost Asia combined to develop that of the Greeks in a new and glorious form.

This great sage and educator of men was born on the island of Samos about 600 A.C. Respecting the history of his education there are various reports, which, after all, leave us in uncertainty. But certain it is that Pythagoras, who early lost his father, attracted, already in his youth, the observation of all, by his extraordinary excellences of mind and character: there was something highly dignified and sage-like (σεμνότατος και σωφρονεστατος) in his appearance, so that he was accounted a son of Apollo. At the age of twenty-two he left his native land, and sailed to Syros, where he visited the celebrated Pherecydes, and, finding him in ill health, took care of him till his death. From here he went to Anaximander, and afterward to Thales, who found his expectations respecting him more than realized. Thales, one of the most profound and learned thinkers, was then suffering of the infirmities of old age, and therefore advised his young visiter to proceed to Egypt, in order to enjoy the instruction of the priests. He first visited Sidon, where he was initiated in the sacred mysteries of the Phenicians. Arrived in Egypt, he visited the temples and the priests, whose esteem and love he everywhere gained, and who admitted him to privileges which no foreigner before him had ever enjoyed. He studied (according to a highly exaggerated statement, during twenty-two years) the geometry, astronomy, and theology of the Egyptians. Carried into captivity by Cambyses, who had invaded Egypt, he became acquainted with the Magi, and soon obtained their friendship and learned their sciences. After a sojourn among them of twelve years (probably exaggerated), he at length returned to Samos, enriched with all the learning of his age, and familiar with the profoundest regions of thought. Hampered in his educational efforts in his native land, he commenced his travels anew; visited Delos, and afterward the different oracles; then proceeded to Crete, where he was initiated in the mysteries of that island; and thence he went to Sparta, made himself acquainted with the manners and customs of the Dorians, and studied the institutions of Lycurgus. After returning for a short time to Samos, he left it finally for Italy, where he arrived at Crotona, in Magna Græcia, in the sixty-second Olympiad. Here, having been received with great respect, this extraordinary man found, at length, an extensive sphere of action, in which his powerful and opulent mind could put forth all its energies, and apply its hoarded wisdom. His influence in education and politics was immense, and the institutions which he founded were productive of the most extensive and happy effects. But, persecution having driven him to Metapontus, he incurred here also the rancour of faction, and is said, among other reports concerning his death, to have been slain in the disturbances which had arisen. Some authorities say that he died nearly one hundred years of age: according to Diogenes Laertius, he had reached his eightieth year. The Crotonians consecrated his house as a temple of Demeter, and in memory of him called their port Μουσεῖον. His philosophy continued to flourish in the celebrated Italic school.

After this brief sketch of this true sage's life, we proceed to give an account of his system of education, selecting from a vast amount of interesting and delightful materials only what is most essential, and present, in the first place, the prominent features of that culture of man which he aimed to exhibit in himself, and to realize in society through his pupils.

Harmony in all things was the aim. This exists in the universe (hence *κόσμος*), and is to be also in man (whence he is styled *μικροκόσμος*). The harmony of the spheres finds its echo in the well-cultivated mind. To this we are brought by purification of the soul (*κάθαρσις*), by self-knowledge (*γνωθι σαυτον*), and by devotion. Man, attaining thus to the perception of pure relations, of good order, and of heavenly beauty, is admitted also to constant converse with God (*ὁμιλειν τῷ θεῷ*), and in this he finds his highest good. Purification advances through a succession of exercises, in a well-regulated life, both contemplative and active; for sensual gratification (*ἡδονή*) defiles, conducts merely from one desire to the other, and plunges us into the torments of passion. But the human soul performs also a transmigration through different bodies (or human beings), in order to attain, when at length purified, to a higher state of being.

Self-knowledge consists not only in our forming a correct estimate of our gifts and defects, but in obtaining a more penetrating view of our minds, and in judging of them according to the relations of eternal order; but as this could be done by him only who had perfectly seen through the order of the universe, the effect of this will be that modesty, which will permit no man to esteem himself a *σοφος* (sage), for wisdom is only in God, and the highest that man can pretend to is to love and seek after wisdom, and to be a *φιλόσοφος*;

and thus he is the true philosopher who meditates upon God and the world—the cause and the nature of things—the order of the universe—and the highest good.

Whatsoever is good comes from the Divine Being (the gods), which rules over all, and orders all things. Man ought, therefore, to inquire after the will of the Deity; to do what is pleasing to that being, and to aim, by truth and morality, more and more to approximate his character. Prayer and good actions, and finally death, bring us near to God. The divine government is therefore the pattern for human government, both in the state and in the family; internal discord is worse than fire and sword, and anarchy is the greatest evil. As God notes all our actions, and regards nothing as beneath his notice, we ought to be watchful of ourselves, and careful of everything committed to our management. Man, being a *ζῶον ὑβριστικόν*,* requires guidance and rigorous control by means of laws and education. But justice is more important in its legislative than its judicial character, for it must so arrange matters that every man may be treated in the manner which is suited to him, so that every one may, from free impulse, obey the laws; nay, that every one may acquire that inward harmony, which everywhere strikes upon what is right and fitting.

The highest aim of culture is to know things in their nature and pure relations, and to live and act accordingly. And this is the nature of music: she perceives the harmony of the universe; she copies it in the soul, and causes it to resound throughout the whole of life (*μουσική παιδεῖα*).

Thus was the life of Pythagoras one of music; of harmony between the life without and that within; an echo of the music of the spheres. He needed no earthly tones, for that music resounded in his ear. He saw in the laws of the planets those pure relations of the beautiful and the glorious, and he felt himself irresistibly impelled to exhibit or represent in human life what was thus present to his lofty mind: and thus he conceived the idea of education as no sage

* Inclining to evil, or under the influence of strong passions.

had ever done before him. He had profoundly and maturely developed this idea. He aimed at the good of the community, which he sought to attain, by political institutions, the education of youth, and the culture of men in general. Religion constituted the basis of that harmony which he sought to promote. He desired to make external order dependant on that which is inward; civil liberty on nobleness of soul; the administration of state-affairs on the intellectual culture of the citizens; the prosperity of the city on purity of morals. He wished to cultivate excellence of character in all, and the rulers were to be the most excellent. More immediately he educated young men at an institution of his own, but also adults, by lectures; and lastly children, by leading parents to the adoption of his principles of education. His institution at Crotona was designed for adults, and he assembled around him a large number of young men, who, living with him, became his particular disciples. Each one was required to submit to a certain preparation and initiation, to regulate his daily life according to certain rules and prescribed exercises, and to devote himself, as it were with body and soul, to his master. Thus his disciples led a common life, whence they were called *κοινόβιοι*.

It is with extreme reluctance that we omit a great deal that is valuable and delightful in the practice of this extraordinary man, in order to describe the order of things at his institution, which was as follows: In the morning, all dressed themselves in a clean white robe, sang to the accompaniment of the lyre, and addressed a prayer to the rising sun. Hereupon they repeated the instructions of the preceding day, and prepared themselves for what might happen to them on the day which had just begun. Then each pupil took a solitary walk, in order to bring his mind into a calm and placid state for the day. After this, they all assembled to receive instruction, to which succeeded bodily exercise. At noon they partook of a little bread and honey: no wine at all was allowed. After dinner, business was resumed: towards evening, particular friends took walks together, and discoursed on what they had learned. Thereupon each one went into his bath, after which they partook of another meal, never more than ten eating in company. They began with a libation and scattering incense, and then ate moderately of the food which was allowed them, being chiefly vegetables, and the meat of those animals only which they could offer in sacrifice. At this meal they also took a little wine. It ended with another libation, after which one of the younger pupils was required to read something under the direction of one of the older ones, and, at separating, the senior pupil pronounced some precepts; for example, that no useful animal or plant should be injured; that pious thoughts should be cherished towards gods, demons and heroes, parents, and good men; and the like. And now each one laid himself down on his couch, and ended the day with serious communion with himself. Many articles of food were forbidden them, and of meat they ate but little; and, in fact, they were not to drink wine, from which Pythagoras himself abstained altogether. Music was with him a prominent means of culture, and he employed it for the purification of the mind, and the subjugation of the passions. Hence, with song and instrumental music, especially of the lyre, began and ended the day. His pupils had particular songs against particular excessive emotions and passions, as also peculiar metres and tunes. He made use, also, of choice verses from Homer and Hesiod, to awaken good thoughts and cultivate right feelings.

A certain discipline (παιδαρτάσις) was introduced among his pupils, which required the older ones affectionately and tenderly to counsel the younger, to instruct them without envy, and kindly to assist them: it was the duty of the younger ones to submit to the authority thus given to their seniors. Good morals were rigidly enforced; friends were not allowed to speak untruths to each other, even in jest. The influence of friendship in the culture of man was highly estimated; through it, the disciples of Pythagoras were to elevate each other mutually to the divine. His principle was, "friends have everything in common;" and "our friend is our second self, our alter ego." The tone of their whole associated life was unity and harmony: contention and ill-will were positively interdicted: love prevailed throughout. To their master they were devoted for life and death. They were expected to accustom themselves to maintain friendship with the whole universe, and to be in communion with the gods, waking and sleeping. Even between men and beasts a friendly relation was to subsist. The depths of the mind were to be the abode of purity, undisturbed by passion, untainted by aught that was rude or base, so that its inward eye might be opened, which was valued more than a hundred outward eyes.

That these doctrines of Pythagoras were not merely speculative, that his method of education was profoundly and pervasively efficient, was abundantly attested by the high, the exemplary character sustained by his pupils. They everywhere obtained the respect and esteem of all. In the Grecian cities of southern Italy (or Magna Græcia), the happy effects of his institution soon manifested themselves, in the revolution which it effected in all the relations of life, in all the institutions of society, to the admiration of all the neighbouring states.

Such was the system and the activity of Pythagoras, a phenomenon equally important for politics and for pedagogics.

But he was not merely a legislator, limited to the city in which he lived, or to the confederated cities of Magna Græcia. He was the founder, also, of a sodality, or association, or sect, which extended itself farther under the name of the Pythagoræan, and possessed a sort of secret or esoteric doctrine, in which he was, of course, the teacher. He taught the sciences of that period, particularly those of Egypt. These were mathematics, astronomy, natural science, and medicine, in their different branches. Astrology he appears to have discarded

Unlike many who are great in their systems, he was truly a philosopher in his capacity of instructer. He exercised the minds of his pupils, and gave them a direction and impulse, which prevented their merely learning his system, or repeating his words, but led them to think for themselves, and with freedom to cultivate the intellect. In this process of culture, he insisted on three requisites: ὀξύτης, ἀγχίνοια, μνήμη: acuteness and versatility of mind; desire and resolution for prosecuting inquiry; and memory for retaining. His pupils were required firmly to impress and appropriate whatsoever they learned, before they were permitted to take another step forward. Hence they were expected, before rising in the morning, to repeat in their minds what they had learned the day previous, or even at an earlier period; and that even in the very words in which it had been communicated. At the same time, they were, in various ways, stimulated to farther reflection and independent development of thought. The mode of teaching thus adopted by this great master is highly instructive to educators of our own day. Collections of the sayings, the maxims, and aphorisms of Pythagoras, are to be received with caution, as great liberties have been taken with his name.

Many of his pedagogical principles and rules will be found in writings of several of his pupils; among others, of Ocellus of Lucania, and Aristoxenus. Stobæus gives (Serm. 96) a fragment from the work of Teles, concerning human life, which is interesting.

Among his pupils were also females, who distinguished themselves as authors. To his wife, Theano, is ascribed a work on Piety, περὶ ἐυσεβείας. Letters from her to female friends are extant, which contain much that is beautiful and excellent on various human relations, especially on education.

The entire picture of Pythagoras, and his school, is one of the most delightful to look upon in the whole ancient classic world.

4. *Solon. The Ionians. Athens.*

Solon, a descendant of Codrus, was born at Athens, 638 A.C., and was one of the wisest and most learned men of his age. Elected to the archonship of his native city, he was called upon to prepare a new code of laws, as the severity of the laws of Draco had become intolerable. He drew up a milder code, and introduced, at the same time, a system of education for the people. After the Athenians had adopted his laws, he absented himself for ten years, and travelled to Egypt and Crete, receiving distinguished honours wherever he went.

The immediate results of his new constitution were not as favourable to Athens as the effects of the legislation of Lycurgus had been, three hundred years before, to Sparta. When he returned, he found everything in confusion. The people received him as though he had been a god, who would restore perfect order in the state. But his sagacious and wily relative, Pisistratus, succeeded better than he in remedying the existing evils. Solon died 559 A.C., at the age of eighty years.

Athens, founded 1600 A.C. by Cecrops, did not attain to complete civilization, or acquire a regular municipal constitution, until the time of Theseus, about 1250 A.C. The regal government ceased after the noble Codrus had sacrificed himself for his people; and under its aristocratic constitution, administered by archons, Athens enjoyed almost uninterrupted peace, during nearly five centuries. But the want of a new constitution being felt, two distinguished legislators appeared: first Draco, 600 A.C.; soon after him, Solon, 594 A.C. The results of Solon's legislation have been hinted at; for farther information, the reader will consult historical works; as also for an account of the rise and progress of art and science at Athens, which were already beginning to flourish in the time of Solon.

Solon's legislation comprehended, as we have said,

a plan for the education of youth. Here also, in Athens, the principle was recognised that the child belongs to the state, and is to be educated by and for the state. But there was not here that unity of popular life, which we find among the ancient Persians and at Sparta; and the multiplicity of forms, in which life developed itself at Athens, did not admit of any fixed, uniform mode of treatment for the young: hence the public education of Athens was by no means as uniform, or as one-sided, as that of the Lacedemonians. The Athenians were, therefore, the first among whom culture was free, and the education of children open to experiments and improvement. Free development prevailed in all things. The dominion of the priesthood, the hitherto sacred authority of ancient institutions, perished; and superiority of intellect, and of fortune, and arbitrary ambition, had unrestricted scope. But as men had now reached that point in which this stage of development had to be passed through, we should do injustice to the wisdom of Solon, if we censured him for not preventing the evil and disorder, which were the inevitable concomitants of this state of transition.

The laws which Solon enacted respecting marriage and succession, were promotive of well-regulated domestic life, and of good education. The father was required to have his son taught some useful occupation; and the son was, in turn, obliged to maintain his parents in old age, or when incapable of providing for themselves. Every Athenian citizen, whether rich or poor, was required by law to teach his son at least to read and to swim; and for instruction in these, the public institutions, of course, made provision. But Solon had also made it a law, that every man should educate his sons in a manner suitable to his rank and property.

But, passing by these general arrangements, of which an outline may be found in every good work on general history, we proceed to the particular methods of instruction employed in the education of the Athenian youth.

From early times the Athenians had given their

children a twofold education. Their παιδεία required the culture of the mind, and that of the body in pure harmony, ἐυρυθμία; the former was attained chiefly by grammatical studies, the latter by gymnastics. The latter, in accordance with the spirit of the ancient Greeks, took precedence of the former; on this branch of education the state bestowed the greatest attention, and from it the public place of instruction was called Gymnasium.

The gymnastic training of Athens was very similar to that of Sparta. Some of its distinctive peculiarities will be mentioned. One of the most honourable offices in Athens was that of the gymnasiarch, or president of the Gymnasium; he was usually elected for a year, and had not only to superintend the gymnasia of the city, but to furnish, at his own expense, the oil that was used in them. Each of these institutions had several teachers and overseers, whose business it was to provide for order in all things. These officers were the παιδοτρίβης and the γυμναστής. The one unlocked the Gymnasium at sunrise, and locked it at sunset; chastised the tardy, prescribed the diet, and, during the whole day, watched the boys and young men closely. His instrument of chastisement was a slender stick (ῥάβδος), which he plied industriously; he was a formidable character, like our pedagogues of olden times. He conducted the gymnasiasts to their public contests; at the Olympic games they had a separate place assigned them. This officer was probably the γυμναστής, who farther instructed the αθληταί. There was another officer, the ἀλείπτης, who anointed the bodies of the gymnasiasts with oil, and administered medical aid to those who had been hurt.

The Gymnasium itself was a large open space, surrounded with walls, containing shady spots, and furnished with a building having corridors, so that the exercises might continue at all seasons, and in every sort of weather. In the Gymnasium was also a particular place for the contests, called παλαίστρα, which was strewed with fine sand.

The laws concerning the conduct of the gymnasia

ran as follows: "The teacher of the boys shall not open the schools before sunrise, and close them before sunset; and no one beyond the age of boyhood shall be allowed to enter while the boys are within, except it be his brother or son-in-law: if any other person enter, he shall be punished with death. Nor shall the gymnasiarchs at the Hermaia (a place in the Palæstrum), on any account, allow any one beyond the age of boyhood to enter: if he should, nevertheless, permit others to enter, or fail to prevent them from so doing, he shall be subject to punishment, according to the laws which relate to the crimes of free citizens." From all this it appears how sacredly these places were guarded against moral pollution. The object aimed at was general good culture; the bodily exercises were designed to render the young hardy and athletic, that in peace they might be good citizens. and in war stalwart defenders of liberty and their native land. By these exercises each pupil was to gain for his body, beauty, ἐυρυθμία, and strength; and therefore exertion was interrupted by suitable recreations. The gymnastic rules provided for moderation in living, self-government, and especially chastity; the system aimed at suitably combining moral culture with μουσικῇ, or elegant education. It was the duty of every youth to frequent the gymnasia.

When the boy had left the reading and singing school, and was, therefore, about ten or twelve years of age, he began the course of the Gymnasium, being required to attend daily from sunrise to nearly sunset.

Grammar, or instruction in language. In early times the Athenians appear to have had but one elementary teacher (the γραμματιστής) for this branch of instruction: in later times, another of higher pretensions, the γραμματικός, or, as he was at first called, the κριτικός, was employed. The former taught the alphabet, spelling, and writing (τα γραμματα); with the latter, the pupils read the works of the writers of Greece, and committed poems to memory, while the teacher made explanations, and gave other instruction.

The schoolhouse (το διδασκαλεῖον), a building totally different from the Gymnasium, comprised one large room, furnished with benches for the boys. The teacher probably occupied a chair (κάθεδρα). The law required all the boys to attend this school, which they entered, not before they were seven, according to Plato, ten years of age. The course of instruction probably embraced several years. Afterward they were sent to the music-master, κιθαριστής, who taught them to sing and to perform on the lyre. This instruction must either have been synchronous with that of the grammaticus, or the office of the latter was altogether of later origin. Some also learned the flute from the ἀυλητής, whose charges were high.

The pupils of the παιδαγωγεῖον were probably not taught to write, until they had made some progress in reading. In writing, they made use of tablets covered with wax, and a style: in later times they wrote with ink. Much importance was attached to elegance and rapidity in writing.

The higher studies, which succeeded this elementary instruction, consisted in the reading of the poets, and the memorizing of suitable passages, as has already been stated. The author most generally read was Homer, who was so thoroughly studied that many Greeks could, even in their old age, repeat memoriter the entire Iliad and Odyssee. Besides Homer, Hesiod was read, as well as other prose writers, and for this purpose Chrestomathies were prepared. Every pupil was required to be acquainted with Æsop's Fables. All this supplied the mind with an abundance of beautiful figures, excited in the soul admiration and love of whatsoever was noble, gave the thinking faculty an exalted impulse, and produced that pure and enthusiastic love of the beautiful, which characterizes the Greeks in general, but pre-eminently the Athenians.

Every variety of popular instruction, in mythology, ethics, and politics, was combined with this course of reading, and was fruitful, in proportion as the teacher performed his duties with intelligence and zeal. It rendered unnecessary any special religious instruction, which was farther superseded by the observances of domestic life and the popular festivals.

5. *Socrates.*

Socrates was born 469 A.C. (Olymp. lxxvii., 3); his father, Sophroniscus, belonged to the middle class of citizens, and was a skilful sculptor. He passed through the Athenian schools in the prescribed order, and learned his father's art, in which he acquired considerable skill. He continued daily to practise gymnastic exercises to his old age, and to this custom he was indebted for the regular health which he enjoyed. The grammatical course he had so thoroughly accomplished, that nothing remained for him but to become acquainted with every public teacher, who arose at his time in Athens; and he so completely assimilated in his own mind the philosophic views of Anaxagoras, Parmenides, and Zeno of Elea, whose personal intercourse he enjoyed at Athens, that his mind, stored with intellectual wealth, rapidly developed itself. Through Anaxagoras he became acquainted with the philosophy of Pythagoras and of Thales, and therefore with the Italic and Ionic schools; made himself familiar with their theories respecting the universe, and practised himself in the use of their dialectics; but, as it becomes every independent thinker and teacher of philosophy, he connected himself with no particular sect. The unity of God, the divine omniscience, justice, and foresight; the dignity and immortality of the soul—these exalted truths were firmly fixed in the living conviction of his mind. But the mind of Socrates was thoroughly practical, and he seemed born to advance the culture of man. The idle speculations, and especially the arrogant vanity of the so-called sophists, which he perfectly saw through, and which seemed, at that time, to have reached their pinnacle in Gorgias, were utterly disgusting to him. All this convinced him of his duty to instruct; not, however, in a school of his own, but in the midst of his fellow-citizens, in order to overthrow the false wisdom of the sophists, to show men what they ought to be, and to save his native city from the increasing corruption. And in all this he exerted himself to the utmost of his ability.

As, at his time, the splendour and the culture of Athens were at their height, after the Persian war, and as he witnessed, also, the excitement of the Peloponnesian war, which brought the heaviest calamities upon Athens, no man could easily have better opportunities of enriching himself with valuable experiences of life, than had this wise and good man, in whose life and character are exemplified all the virtues that we can conceive attainable among a pagan people. He was the friend of the great statesman Pericles; of the tragic poet Euripides; and, in a measure also, of the comic poet Aristophanes. He became personally acquainted with the artists and men of talent of his native city, and the distinguished strangers who visited it; and the circle of his studies daily extended its compass, in the most intellectual intercourse with men.

We have said that it was his desire and aim to arrest the growing corruption of Athens: a difficult undertaking, which demanded the interference of one greater than Socrates, and something better than human wisdom. Yet he made the attempt; and while we admire the wisdom which he displayed, we cannot blame him for not succeeding better than he did.

Initiation in the Eleusinian mysteries, in which, probably, a sort of Deism was taught, was at that time so common at Athens, that no one any longer seriously believed in the gods. Socrates sought to infuse into what was left of external religious institutions and rites, more of a pious and moral spirit. The accusation of revolutionary designs, of a desire to overthrow existing institutions, could proceed only from a total misapprehension of the character and the principles of Socrates.

His peculiar method of teaching presents itself under a twofold aspect. In the first place, it was, undoubtedly, antagonistic, subversive, or polemical in its tendency. But in this tendency it was directed against the absurdities, the self-conceit, and the selfish policy of the sophists, whom he completely unmasked, by treating them with that happy irony, which is from him called the Socratic.

The positive direction of his pedagogic philosophy induced him to select his pupils, but to avoid establishing a school or sect of his own. Athens was not, at that time, the place for a Pythagoræan consociation; yet, in so far, the ancient customs still prevailed, that pupils congregated about their teacher, to learn from him both in doctrine and practice. Such followers were his three most distinguished pupils, Xenophon, Plato, and Æschines, all of whom wrote concerning him, and in the spirit which they had imbibed in their intimate intercourse with him. A compensation Socrates accepted from none of his pupils, although such as were rich, for example Crito, cheerfully offered him all they had. He would not even accept presents from them; and when Æschines gave himself to him, he said, "Very well; but I shall spare no pains to return you to yourself, better than I have received you."

He had few wants, and self-government (σωφροσύνη) was not, with him, a mere doctrine; he rigidly practised it in all things; and his humane and benevolent disposition, which manifested itself in all his relations of life, endued him with a certain grace, for which, known as the Socratic Χάρις in his conversational intercourse, he was noted to his old age. Notwithstanding all his distinguished excellences of character, he was arraigned of crimes of which none could be more innocent than he, and condemned to die by poison. His noble defence, his last conversations with his friends, the calmness and greatness of soul which he manifested in his last hour, are familiar to every reader of history. He died 399 A.C., in the seventieth year of his age.

This great educator's history in this city presents, in itself, a picture of the manners of that age: and when, in addition, we consider that his own sons turned out badly, we have strong evidence of the growing degeneracy of the youth of that day. Of what avail was it, that he taught, and illustrated by example, that self-government, which was, in the education of the ancients, the paramount object aimed at? The good seed which he scattered was choked by the rank growth of the corruption of morals. The two most eminent disciples of Socrates, Xenophon and Plato, did indeed diffuse abroad the most valuable doctrines and precepts; but neither they, nor the entire school of the so-called Socratics, effected a reformation in Athens. But of so much the greater importance is the relation sustained by these two distinguished men to the pedagogics of modern times, so that they belong, pre-eminently, to the present historic sketch. With Xenophon we became acquainted in connexion with Persian education; and it remains for us, therefore, to communicate the pedagogic views of Plato.

For a picture of Athenian education of his day, we refer to his Protagoras.

Lucian also exhibits, in his Nigrinus, characteristic features of Athenian education, which belong, however, to a later period. Nigrinus was wont to exhort his pupils to that practical virtue, which was contradistinguished from that asceticism, which then prevailed in the philosophic schools, and he directed the attention of educators to the individual temperament and capacities of their pupils. Thus some noble plants yet remained in that city, through which, even when its constitution and good morals passed away, it handed down to posterity the seeds of genuine culture. The doctrines of Socrates, Plato, and Aristotle were sustained, in some measure, by some good qualities which the Athenians had inherited from their ancestors. Such were their love of country, their political enthusiasm, the honourable distinction enjoyed by truly noble citizens; also, the daily observation of the beautiful in the statues of the gods, and the like; the national songs, the works of their great poets; in short, the influence of the fine arts and the sciences. Everywhere something would strike the eye or ear of the youth, which held up to him the most glorious ideals, and tended to excite in his breast enthusiasm for the freedom of his native land. Thus, in Athens also, domestic and public education could readily combine to educate the son, through the family, for the state, and through the state for the family, and that without prejudice to genuine human culture. What a glorious work of education might the idea of Solon have effected! But there were not sufficient safeguards against the corruption of morals. The good habits of early times were put to flight by the evil ones of later days. Formerly there had been rigid discipline and a severe mode of life; the boy wore light clothing, even in rough weather, and received simple and spare diet; and the youth also retained his modest deportment: with downcast eyes, and without ever crossing his legs, he sat in the presence of his elders, before whom he was not allowed to speak. But it was widely different at the time when a Socrates was compelled to drink the poisoned cup, and the lamentation of a Plato over the corruptions of education were indeed heard with approbation, but died away without effecting a change. At that period children were indulged and spoiled in every possible way: witness the dainties which little boys received to reward them for writing handsomely, while their punishment consisted in the withholding of such gratifications. Wine was given to them, which the parents justified by saying that Achilles had drunk wine when a boy; they had shoes, and gay dresses, and warm beds, in which they were allowed to sleep as long as they pleased. The young men were particularly encouraged to acquire a pleasing exterior, a polished deportment in company: in short, the same state of things prevailed, which characterizes fashionable society in modern cities. Thus the young men, beardless as they were, and more of boys than men, obtruded themselves into the circles of adults, had much to say on all subjects, carried about theatrical news, visited the ladies, and even the ἑταίραι, and indulged in ridicule at the expense of good and honest citizens. They sometimes endeavoured to entertain company with performances on the flute or harp (κιθ αρα)

They patronised the new style of music, whose object was entertainment, and were always ready to retail the latest arguments in favour of it, and against the ancient grave and solemn musical style. Even in their carriage and gestures, they betrayed their intolerable presumption and pride. They became addicted to every sort of dissipation, and even boys gave themselves up to drunkenness. The most exemplary citizens were unable to save their sons from the prevalent corruption; for the sons of such men as Themistocles, Aristides, Pericles, Thucydides, and even Socrates, turned out badly. Yet, notwithstanding all this, the coryphæus of that corrupt youth, Alcibiades, exhibited the invincible vitality of Athenian energy, and the almost indestructible proclivity to καλοκᾀγᾰθια.

Aristophanes, one of the closest observers of that age, presents to us, in his Clouds (960, sqq.), a scene, in which the good old time of Athens, and the corrupt age in which he lived, appear as persons speaking: and the pedagogic picture which he draws, not only affords us a view of what was then the state of things in Athens, but exhibits strikingly many features, in which our own age may discover a strong resemblance to itself. The two styles of education are represented as presenting their rival claims to the youth, and respectively contending for their favour. The following is the address of the ancient discipline, as translated by Mitchell.

"Thus summoned, I prepare myself to speak
Of manners primitive, and that good time
Which I have seen, when discipline prevailed,
And modesty was sanctioned by the laws;
No babbling then was suffered in our schools:
The scholar's test was silence. The whole group
In orderly procession sallied forth
Right onward, without straggling, to attend
Their teacher in harmonics; though the snow
Fell on them thick as meal, the hardy brood
Breasted the storm uncloak'd; their harps were strung,

Not to ignoble strains, for they were taught
A loftier key, whether to chant the name
Of Pallas, terrible amid the blaze
Of cities overthrown, or wide and far
To spread, as custom was, the echoing peal:
There let no low buffoon intrude his tricks,
Let no capricious quavering on a note,
No running of divisions high and low,
Break the pure stream of harmony; no Phrynis
Practising wanton warblings out of place—
Wo to his back that so was found offending!
Decent and chaste their postures in the school
Of their gymnastic exercises; none
Exposed an attitude that might provoke
Irregular desire; their lips ne'er moved
In love-aspiring whispers, and their walks
From eyes obscene were sacred and secure;
Hot herbs, the old man's diet, were proscribed;
No radish, anise, parsley, decked their board;
No rioting nor revelling was there;
At feast or frolic, no unseemly touch
Or signal, that inspires the hint impure."

The more recent style having here objected that this was "oldfashioned stuff," the ancient discipline proceeds:

"Yet so were trained the heroes that imbrued
The field of Marathon with hostile blood;
This discipline it was that braced their nerves,
And fitted them for conquest. You, forsooth,
At great Minerva's festival produce
Your martial dances, not as they were wont,
But smothered underneath the tawdry load
Of cumbrous armour, till I sweat to see them
Dangling their shields in such unseemly sort
As mars the sacred measure of the dance.
Be wise, therefore, young man, and turn to me:
Turn to the better guide; so shall you learn
To scorn the noisy forum, shun the bath,
And turn with blushes from the scene impure.
Then conscious innocence shall make you bold
To spurn the injurious, but to reverend age
Meek and submissive, rising from your seat
To pay the homage due: nor shall you ever
Wring the parent's soul, or stain your own.
In purity of manners you shall live
A bright example; vain shall be the lures
Of the stage-wanton, floating in the dance;
Vain all her arts to snare you in her arms,

And strip you of your virtue and good name.
No petulant reply shall you oppose
To fatherly commands, nor taunting vent
Irreverent mockery on his hoary head,
Crying, 'Behold Iapetus himself!'
Poor thanks for all his fond parental care."

The recent style having again replied in self praise, the other once more proceeds:

"Not so, but fair and fresh in youthful bloom
Among our young athletics you shall shine;
Not in the forum loitering time away
In gossip prattle, like our gang of idlers,
Nor yet in some vexatious, paltry suit,
Wrangling and quibbling in our petty courts,
But in the solemn academic grove,
Crowned with the modest reed, fit converse hold
With your collegiate equals; there serene,
Calm as the scene around you, underneath
The fragrant foliage where the ilex spreads,
Where the deciduous poplar strews her leaves,
Where the tall elm-tree and wide-spreading plane
Sigh to the fanning breeze, you shall inhale
Sweet odours wafted in the breath of Spring.
This is the regimen that will ensure
A healthful body and a vigorous mind,
A countenance serene, expanded chest,
Heroic stature, and a temperate tongue.
But take these modern masters, and behold
These blessings all reversed; a pallid cheek,
Shrunk shoulders, chest contracted, sapless limbs,
A tongue that never rests, and mind debased
By their vile sophistry, perversely taught
To call good evil, evil good, and be
That thing which nature spurns at—that disease,
A mere Antimachus, a sink of vice."

6. *Plato.*

This illustrious sage, descended from Codrus and Solon, was born at Athens on the 17th of May, 429 A.C. In his early boyhood, his extraordinary talents manifested themselves in various ways, and the productions of his youth betokened the future genius. When not far from twenty years of age, his education was intrusted to Socrates. Under the instruction and guidance of this true philosopher, his mind received that mighty impulse which carried him into the highest regions of thought, and made him the prince of philosophers. In his mature age he travelled, and even tried himself at state-affairs; but he found his most congenial employment in study, and in communicating instruction to others. His personal instruction gave the world a number of excellent men, and his writings have an undying value to the culture of man. His life was pure and truly noble, healthy in body and soul, and thus he died in a green old age of eighty-one years, 347 A.C.

He has written much on education, and our present business is to exhibit briefly his educational idea, or his leading thoughts on this important subject, detaching them from the connexion in which they are found, as our limited space forbids our making long extracts from his writings.

His more important ideas are the following:

It is education that makes the man: it belongs to the whole of life. In it are combined cultivating care, and intellectually and physically cultivating discipline, *τροφὴ καὶ παιδεία.*

Education must commence previous to the birth of the child, in the parents themselves: it must supply right habits for the whole life, and, in a certain sense, continue to the end of life.

A city can become a state (*πόλις*) only by taking good heed of culture and education. It will then develop itself from within, and internally, like a circle, extending its circumference. For by good education, internal and external (*τροφὴ καὶ παίδευσις*), excellent characters are produced, and by means of it these constantly become more excellent than their predecessors, and can therefore produce others of still greater excellence.

That training which teaches how to make money, or aims at the development of physical strength, or at communicating skill in any mechanical business or common art,* without intellectual culture and a sense of right, does not deserve the name of educa-

* *Βάναυσος καὶ ἀνελεύθερος.*

tion. A man may thus be brought up to navigation or to the wine-trade, and yet have no true education. Only those who are educated (*i. e.*, by the proper τροφή and παιδεία) become good; discipline alone can make an excellent man. Education awakens the desire of becoming a good citizen, one who accustoms himself both to obey and to rule from right principles; it forms truly noble characters, and impels them to continue in the pursuit of such perfections as they are still destitute of; it is the first thing among all that are best, and must on no account be neglected.

Good and evil exist together in the soul. If the latter gain the preponderance from defective education, or the absence of good example, man sinks beneath himself, degenerates; education, on the other hand, elevates him above himself.

Education is but badly cared for in that state, in which those who have been educated still require great judges and physicians. The excellence of a well-educated man consists in his clear apprehension of the good.

Everything depends on the formation of good habits, and in this, example, familiar intercourse, scientific and practical culture must co-operate; good morals attained by good customs, πᾶν ἔθος, διὰ ἔθος.

The welfare of a commonwealth consists in this, that wisdom, manliness, self-government, and justice prevail therein. For the magistrates of a state which is what it ought to be, the most excellent persons should be selected in childhood, and educated with the utmost care.

There are marks by which we may discover for what future calling children are fit. For example one who at no period of life gives himself up to infatuation, or suffers himself to be diverted from his principles, is fit to administer the laws. Let, therefore, something be given to the boy to do, in executing which he may be tempted to forget his principles; and if he nevertheless continue mindful of them, and cannot be induced to become recreant to them, let him be chosen. But he should be tried also by difficulties, pain, conflict, and excitants; in the same manner as colts are taken to places where a loud noise is made, in order to ascertain whether they be skittish. But let him, who shall be fit for the office of a magistrate, be tested also in the different sciences, that it may be discovered whether he possess energy enough for what is most difficult.

The mark of the future philosopher is an aversion to all untruth, and the most ardent love of truth and desire to learn, manifested from childhood upward. His soul must also pre-eminently possess the gift of recollection (of that which was divine in its former life), and must have a native talent in all things to perceive the idea; he must understand what man is designed to be and to become, to discern his character, and thus, by instructing and exercising him in the sciences, to lead him to the divine. The inclinations of children may also be ascertained from their amusements, for in the plays and the serious pursuits of the boy, we behold the future man: for example, the husbandman, if the boy is fond of digging in the earth; the architect, if he amuses himself with building houses.

Some men possess natural advantages; although all are formed of one clay, some have an admixture of nobler metal.

The first three years of life are the most important in education. Hence it is necessary to exercise special vigilance respecting their first impressions, and at that age already to accustom children not to give themselves up to pleasure, nor succumb to pain; at that period, already, not to grant them everything, for this makes them impetuous and domineering. But be not too harsh and severe with them, as this would make them timid and slavish: they should be carefully protected against fear and alarm. By indulgence, they become peevish and irascible. The nurses should carry them about in the fields, in the temples, and among their kindred. They should handle them cautiously when they are not yet able to stand, guard against every injurious pressure on their limbs, and carry them about until they are about three years old. When the child is to be put to sleep, the mother should carry it on her arms, rocking it gently, and singing; and thus, by the motion of dancing and music, rock it to sleep; for outward motion subdues that which is within.

This mode of treatment should be continued after the third year, until the child is six years of age: *i. e.*, it must neither be indulged, nor treated with undue severity. By inflicting on the child punishments that are debasing, or excite ridicule, you can only exasperate it. At this age they may also be taken by the nurse to the national festivals; but she must provide that their appearance be clean, and otherwise decent.

The young should receive no wine before the eighteenth year, for fire must not be poured upon fire.

The age of adolescence also calls for the most vigilant care of education.

The amusements and games of children may be improved for directing their inclinations to employments in which they may hereafter excel; but they should be accustomed to such plays only as are becoming. Let them not have too great a variety of plays, as this makes them inconstant and discontented, so that they are always wishing for something new.

Children should, from infancy, not hear anything but what is calculated to make them regard as sacred the worship of the gods, reverence towards parents, and friendship. When passages of Homer, which contain anything immoral, are read to them, it should be done with expressions of disapproval. The poets should never represent the wicked as happy, or the good as unhappy; and artists should represent only what is beautiful. In general, the desire of imitation should be directed only to what is calculated to make children manly (ἀνδρεῖος), virtuous, and truly free.

All instruction should be treated in a dignified manner, worthy of the great end aimed at; it must accomplish the culture both of the body and of the mind, so that both may be cultivated for what is most beautiful and excellent. It must, therefore, from the earliest age, secure a healthy development to the body.

We have, therefore, two generic divisions of the subjects of instruction, the physical and the mental. The former are comprehended under gymnastics, the latter under music.*

Gymnastics is again divided into two branches: the one for skill in combats, the other in dancing. The former is designed to exercise the neck, the limbs, the hips, with a view to noble carriage, to strength, and health; the latter is to give grace, agility, and beauty; so that in the whole body, and in all the motions of the several members, a certain ἐυρυθμία (harmony) may be expressed. Pure gymnastics ought to render warlike, and should be practised throughout the whole life.

Children should be accustomed, like the Scythians, to use the left hand with the same skill as the right. Boys ought to become strong in the feet as well as the hands.

Music is intended to bring the soul into a healthy state; only such varieties of music ought, therefore, to be selected, as are adapted to effect this object.

Musical culture comprises the arts and sciences, and its ultimate aim is love to the beautiful and good: hence philosophy is the highest music and the highest manifestation of culture, for it is the love of science and wisdom: it contemplates divine things, exalts to true liberty, and gives to action also a divine character.

Those who would communicate musical culture must first possess it themselves, for they must be able to discern what is greatness, and what is virtue.

The best gymnastics is the sister of pure and simple music. As the former gives health to the body, and the latter self-government to the soul, both co-

* Among the Greeks, music, ἡ μουσικὴ (scil. τέχνη), meant the liberal arts, comprehending not only music, poetry, and eloquence, but designating, in general, the proper and harmonious development of the mind and character.

operate in producing complete culture. Those who practise gymnastics alone become too wild; those who cultivate music alone become too feeble or effeminate (μαλακωτερος). One God has given both to man, in order that body and soul may duly harmonize, both by necessary exertion, as well as the not less needful relaxation; for he who combines these two in his soul in the most correct proportion, may justly be regarded as the most musical and harmonious man (μουσικώτατον καὶ ἐναρμοστατον), much more so than he who understands tuning the strings.

But the knowledge of language, as well as of other subjects, is also necessary to complete culture. Here let the following course be pursued. Let the boy be first exercised in gymnastics. When ten years of age he should learn the alphabet; then reading and writing, and spend three years in this manner: whether he learn to read and write rapidly or elegantly is not, as yet, important. At thirteen years of age the boy will proceed to instruction in music, learning, for the present, the κιθάρα (guitar) in a very simple manner, in order to accompany his song in the same tones and measure; for variety only confuses and renders learning difficult; but the young ought to learn in the easiest possible manner. At the same time, the boy must learn passages from the poets, which ought to be well selected, omitting what is offensive; and these, written partly with, partly without metre, should be committed to memory, including passages from different poets, and of a variety of metres: also, passages from prose writers.

The boys are also to learn the use of numbers; first, calculation (λογισμὸς), which, being the doctrine of proportions, considers and compares what is equal, and what is unequal. This should be made pleasant and easy by distributing among them apples, wreaths, and the like. The second part of the science of numbers is arithmetic.

A principal means of culture is geometry, which teaches the measurement of space, *i. e.*, distances, planes, and solid bodies. For the soldier and the statesman, this science is important; for the philosopher it is necessary, for it leads upward to truth.

The preliminary exercises are followed by dialectics: economy, astronomy, &c.

While the pupil is engaged with these severer sciences, he must be left unencumbered with business. When he has attained the age of twenty, and has learned well, he should, for the second time, be inducted into these sciences, and deeper than was practicable in his boyhood: thus only is permanent knowledge acquired, and only at this age can real dialectic talent be discovered with certainty.

Every subject of liberal learning must be studied with a liberal spirit, not in a slavish manner: not by compulsory methods should boys be instructed in the sciences, but in such a manner that they may take delight in them, as though they were playing. It is thus only that we can discover for what each one has been destined by nature. Do the same as when you wish to excite fondness for martial exercises in boys, by taking them to see soldiers with their horses.

In general, the young should be acted upon by the beautiful and the good, which should, like the pure air of healthy places, everywhere strike the ear and the eye, and incline them to whatsoever is beautiful and good. Youth should reverence old age, especially when it is dignified. The young must learn to obey; for he that cannot obey, cannot rule.

By means of example and strictly-enforced law, the young should be imbued with modesty or a sense of shame (*αἰσχύνη*), and an aversion to everything unchaste (*ἀφροδίσια*). This will have a happy effect, as well on pious minds, as on those that are honourable, or those that strive after beauty of soul. If the athletæ can cultivate chastity for the sake of the desired victory, why should not the youth for the sake of the nobler victory?

Everything should combine to form man, from his youth, to excellence of character: for even as the plant is then most certain to reach perfection, if its first developments are beautiful, so man has indeed his natural destination as an (tame) animal (ζῶον); yet does he most need education, for without it he becomes the wildest animal; but through it he attains his highest destination, and becomes the tamest (*i. e.*, most cultivated), yea, the most divine among all creatures. The first good a child can receive is discipline and culture.

Man is to be cultivated for perfection, both as man and as citizen.

From a vast deal contained in Plato's writings on education, we have thus presented a free translation of those passages which are most interesting and important in our own day, while, at the same time, they afford a tolerably comprehensive view of the great pedagogic idea, by realizing which, this illustrious sage sought to improve his race.

7. *Aristotle, and the later Period of the Greeks.*

Aristotle was the most learned scholar among the Greeks, yet, at the same time, second to none of their distinguished sages as regards brilliancy of genius, and philosophic depth, and acumen. In him the ancient Grecian culture reached its summit, so that in him we already discover its later tendencies, manifested in systematizing scholarship, and establishing the later age of the sciences. Thus he became the first systematic teacher, and the great master in dialectics.

He wrote systematic treatises not only on government and ethics, but on pedagogics, and he may be regarded as the first *scientific* instructer of youth.

He was born at Stagyra, in Thrace, 384 A.C., and inherited considerable wealth from his father Nicomachus, who was physician to Amyntas, king of Macedonia. An ardent love of the sciences, extraordinary talents, combined with indefatigable industry, distinguished him, at least in the later years of his youth. He paid great attention to his outward appearance, by cultivating neatness and elegance of dress. When nearly eighteen years of age he went to Athens in order to study, and became the pupil of

Plato, who was wont to call him "the Mind of his school." With him he remained five years, when he left Athens and went to Mysia. Philip of Macedon invited him, in the most flattering terms, to become the educator of his son Alexander, who is certainly indebted to his distinguished teacher, for any claim which he may really have to the title of "the Great." His royal pupil manifested his gratitude towards him, and his sense of his high merits, by enabling him, in various ways, to prosecute at leisure, and in the enjoyment of the most ample resources, his studies, especially in natural history. After Alexander's accession to the throne, Aristotle established himself as a public teacher in Athens; but, meeting with persecutions there, he removed to Chalcis, in Eubœa, where he died 320 A.C., at the age of sixty-two years, having probably destroyed his health by excessive application to study.

Aristotle brings the science of government, ethics, and the whole of pedagogics, into the closest connexion, and thus exhibits in this, also, the prominent characteristic of antiquity, unity of life. We present a few of his pedagogic principles in a detached form. According to him, the prerogative of man consists in this, that he is able to discern and apprehend something that is higher and better than himself.

Whatever he may become is effected by the combined influence of nature, habit, and instruction. The last two elements together constitute education; and these must always be conjoined, yet so that habit exerts its influence first. Instruction has an internal design, for it does not become noble and liberal minds to inquire after the uses of that which is learned. Education is to prepare the soul for the precepts of morality, just as the soil is prepared for the reception of the seed. Not until the mind has been ennobled, and acquired a proclivity to what is good (*ἦθος ἐυγενὲς καὶ φιλοκαλον*), can instruction in morals be communicated with profit; and only when good habits have been acquired, can principles exert an elevating or ennobling influence. Through the heart the understanding also is to be cultivated.

Good (correct, judicious) education (ὀρθὴ παιδεία) consists in habituating man, from youth upward, to rejoice or to grieve as reason may require; and in general in this, that the inferior elements of the soul be absolutely governed by its higher principle, reason. A healthy and cultivated (rational) soul in a healthy and well-disciplined body.

He that would govern must first have learned to be governed. The education of youth is a principal concern of the state; and with a view to it, the state is bound to establish public institutions.

It is wrong to expose children, except such as are born deformed.

The screaming of children promotes their health.

Weeping is a beneficial exercise for children.

Stays (or corsets) (ὄργανα μηχανικὰ) should never be used.

Warlike nations give their children abundance of milk. Wine must not be given to children, for it aggravates their diseases.

Children must be guarded against all bad examples and impressions; they should, therefore, not be allowed to keep company with slaves: their governor should be carefully selected. Boys ought not to be taken to convivial feasts.

In the first five years of life, the children play, and thus exercise themselves in activity, until they are advanced to their first efforts at learning. Their plays, or amusements, should be the type of their future occupation.

The first stage of youth ends with the seventh year, the second with the twenty-first. All culture must closely conform to the course of nature.

From the sixth year, boys may be gradually inducted into the process of instruction.

Physical education is first in order of time, because the body exists before the soul; next follows the cultivation of the appetites or desires (τῆς ὀρέξεως); and lastly, scientific culture. Yet for the sake of necessary recreation, alternation should be practised. There are, in fact, only three principal branches of instruction: to wit, gymnastics, music, and grammar (the study of language); to these a fourth may be added, namely, the graphic art, or the art of drawing; for this also serves to employ the free in their leisure (Διαγωγὴ τῶν ἐλευθέρων ἐν σχολῇ); but it is otherwise useful in various ways: for example, it trains the mind to judge correctly of works of art. Education is an ornament in prosperity, an unfailing resource in adversity.

As the eye receives light through the circumambient air, so the soul receives it through instruction.

Rapid progress will be made by the pupil, if he strenuously emulates those who are in advance of him, and does not wait for those who are behind him.

Bitter is the root of education (παιδεία), but sweet its fruit.

After he had educated Alexander, Aristotle became the instructer of young men. He was thus experienced in all the branches of practical education. Yet his mind inclined to the scientific mode of instruction, and more particularly in its acroamatic form: so that, in this respect also, Aristotle has shown the lead in the modern methods of study.

In the forenoons he was wont to deliver lectures, on the sciences which he cultivated, to a number of friends: he lectured on ethics, politics, or the science of government; also on rhetoric, accompanied with exercises, especially in the afternoons, which he generally devoted to practical subjects.

The Athenians had granted him the use of the Lyceum for his educational purposes. A number of distinguished men proceeded from his school. Although he adhered to the ancient custom of distinguishing between exoteric and esoteric pupils, we decidedly discover, in his scientific institutions and labours, and in his educational operations, the beginnings of modern culture.

The Grecian education of youth, as regards scholastic instruction, had, especially at Athens, attained its full development in the time of Aristotle. We shall here present a cursory view of the course which prevailed at that period.

The custom of the rich to provide private instruction for their sons, which had become general already in Plato's day, was alone sufficient to procure for the cultivated class a distinct series of studies, while the common people scarcely retained those which have been specified above, at the proper place. Yet the public schools were not altogether destitute of such higher instruction, as it was sometimes communicated by the grammaticus. But it was now that separate branches of study were definitely distinguished; these were the following: arithmetic, geometry, the art of design or drawing; also geography, history, rhetoric, and philosophy.

It would lead us too far to give a detailed account of the mode of instruction pursued in these different branches.

In learning arithmetic, the boys were made to distribute apples among themselves, or exchange places, or transpose letters, attempting the possible combinations, first with three, and then with four, &c. The units were designated by certain letters, the tens either by accented or compound letters.

In teaching geometry, the figures were drawn on a board or in the sand, and, according to the ancient method, the pupil was probably left, in a great measure, to independent thought, being required to seek and to find for himself.

Instruction in the art of design (γραφική) was pretty general in the time of Plato; and Aristotle insists on its being practised, in order to cultivate the sense of the beautiful and the artistic judgment.

Geography was taught in connexion with geometry. Thales had already made use of geographic tablets (πίνακες), on which countries appear to have been marked with great accuracy. Of course, the geographical knowledge of the Greeks was limited and defective. Anaximander (about 570 A.C.) is said to have first described the circumference (περίμετρος) of the earth and sea, to have declared the earth to be spheroidal (σφαιροειδὴς) and the central point of the world, and to have constructed a terrestrial globe.

The following sciences were studied by adults:

1. Rhetoric. This was indispensable to the culture of the statesman (πολιτικὸς). With this study many other subjects were brought into connexion, especially history, in order at once to furnish to political eloquence its necessary materials. Practical exercises were instituted in a certain progressive gradation. Even mnemonics was taught in connexion with rhetoric. The course of instruction usually embraced a series of years. Gorgias of Leontium, in Sicily, is said to have established the first school of rhetoric at Athens, 494 A.C. Other distinguished names are Isocrates, the pupil of Socrates and teacher of Demosthenes; Æschines, the founder of a school of rhetoric in Rhodes, which became highly celebrated, and, as it were, the university for the Roman orators.

2. Politics, or the science of government, which was first taught by Aristotle in connexion with rhetoric. Much information respecting statistics, political economy, and financial matters in general, was introduced.

3. Philosophy, as taught by Pherecydes of Syros, Thales of Miletus, Pythagoras, and others, had received, through Plato, Aristotle, and other great philosophers, a form, as regards the method of instruction, widely different from that of those earlier teachers. The distinction between esoteric and exoteric disciples disappeared more and more. In philosophy, also, Athens continued to be the metropolis of the intellectual world. It was here that great numbers of teachers congregated, who, under the name of sophists, degraded the sacredness of truth by the dialectic arts, and the rapacious avarice with which they everywhere hawked about their intellectual ware; while opposed to them stood, as we have seen above, Socrates, as the free and noble teacher of men.

The ancient usage, according to which the pupil devoted himself, for a long period of time, to one and the same teacher, as did Plato, and Aristotle, and Epicurus, to their respective instructers, was superseded by a new order of things ; the pupil attending the instruction of several teachers, so that now disciples became hearers.

There gradually arose, furthermore, out of the former, more comprehensive instruction, a number of distinct branches : for example, from the study of language proceeded that of the poetic art. Aristotle, by his inventive genius in science, laid the foundation for this transition to the methods of modern times. For example, he originated the distinction of μαθεματική and φυσική : under the former he adopted the following subdivisions : 1. arithmetic, geometry, stereometry ; 2. the φυσικώτερα, mechanics, optics, astronomy, and music ; and with these sciences he farther associated πολιτική, ἠθική, &c., political science, or the science of government, and ethics, &c.

Thus there arose a distinct individualization of the sciences ; but, at the same time, a combination of them into a complete course of instruction, the ἐγκύκλια παιδεύματα : and hence comes 'Εγκυκλοπαιδεία.

We find this course first in the Alexandrian ἑπτάς, or septenary. About the time of the Saviour, there were taught in Alexandria the seven liberal arts : grammar, rhetoric, dialectics, arithmetic, geometry, astronomy, and music : and these composed the complete cycle of liberal learning. But rhetoric, besides the attention which it thus received in connexion with other studies, was separately and pre-eminently cultivated.

From the time of the ancient rhapsodists down to the sophists, of whom we have just spoken, the genius of the Greeks had never entirely disappeared from their culture : and yet this their culture had become essentially changed.

Instruction and study, and the institutions devoted to them, assumed a new form. The state of things, which prevails at the universities of Europe, grew more and more into vogue. Athens itself became such a place of study, after the sophists had commenced to lecture for money. In this practice the example was set by Protagoras of Abdera, a pupil of Democritus. He was an adept in the sophistic art, and realized a fortune by means of it.

Gymnastics also lost its ancient character, being degraded into a mere art by which money was made. In the many different exhibitions of Rome, especially in the gladiatorial shows, we see the extent to which this noble exercise had degenerated.

The Grecian institutions of learning were patronized and supported by the Romans, and the teachers of Athens and Byzantium received salaries from the emperors. Those of the former city subsisted for some centuries after Christ; those of the latter continued for a long time to flourish in that imperial city, until it (Constantinople) was conquered by the Osmanlis, A.D. 1453, who destroyed, with rude barbarism, all the literary institutions which they found there, and thus became the means of sending the glorious intellectual treasures of Greece to Western Europe. Some plants of Grecian culture had indeed been previously transferred, by other means, to Germany, and other portions of Occidental Europe; but the Germans did not become fully acquainted with the rich treasures of that ancient mine, until, in the fifteenth century, many learned Greeks fled before the sword of the barbarian to Italy.

II. THE ROMANS.

It cannot be our office here to discuss the much-disputed question, whence the Romans really took their origin. The history of ancient Italy is buried in impenetrable darkness. That Grecian, Asiatic, and other colonies emigrated across the eastern Mediterranean into this beautiful land; that probably also northern tribes, of Celtic or Germanic origin, were attracted by its sunny plains to settle in its upper part, while the lower was peopled by Greeks; that especially the Etrurians, as a highly-civilized nation, diffused their culture throughout the central portion: all this is historically ascertained. and yet so envel oped by fabulous traditions, that we cannot penetrate nearly as far into the antiquity of this western land, as we can into that of the nations which have been hitherto considered. And thus the origin of Rome itself, although it dates no farther back than the times immediately after Lycurgus, is covered by a mythic cloud.

For such information as is attainable respecting the early culture and probable educational institutions of the Romans, the Etrurians, the Falisceans, the Sabines, we therefore refer the general reader to Livy, as translated by Baker, and published by the Harpers in their Classical Family Library, and to Plutarch's Life of Numa, and hasten, without farther introduction, to present a connected view of Roman education itself, from materials derived from a variety of sources.

The education of the Romans differed in this from hat of other civilized nations of antiquity, that the state took no cognizance of it, made no provision for it: not even in the manner in which this was done in Athens.

Education was, therefore, in Rome a domestic matter; and it was at the domestic fireside, around the sacred Lares, that the children acquired what knowledge was necessary for the purposes of life, in that primitive period, until the state ordered that the young should be exercised in arms.

In the earliest times, Roman life was regulated rather according to established custom (mos) than express law; and, unquestionably, the early manners and customs of the Romans constituted, in themselves, an excellent school for the young, if not in learning, yet in the graces and virtues of domestic and public life. Among these customs was monogamy, which was subsequently sanctioned by law. All the members of the household, including the slaves, belonged to the father of the family (paterfamilias), who possessed a power over his family, almost more unlimited than that of any despotic monarch over his subjects. He was master (dominus) in his house (domus); but among the Romans the wife also had her sphere and authority as mistress (domina) ; for among all nations of the ante-Christian era, the Romans and the Germanic nations were distinguished for the dignity of their matrons, and the generally respectable position of their females; and among them, therefore, polygamy was forbidden.

Hence, among the ancient Romans, both custom and law watched over the purity of the matrimonial relation. Among them, chastity had its home, and everything was done to honour and guard it. If the institution of the vestal virgins furnishes evidence of this, the honour, the high respect which was paid these virgins, the severity of the punishment which they incurred by the violation of their vow, were a public testimonial to the sacredness of female virtue, and a stern rebuke to licentiousness. The earliest kings made provisions for securing the sanctity of wedded life.

In the most ancient times of Rome, marriage was regarded as indissoluble. What were the enactments of the Twelve Tables respecting divorces is not known; but there is no evidence that any occurred until 520 A.U.C.: and although, in the case which occurred in this year, the husband had plausible reasons, which were sanctioned by the censor, he yet incurred the contempt of his fellow-citizens. But, from this time, separation became frequent, on the part both of husband and wife, and took place for reasons the most arbitrary. Augustus endeavoured, by legal enactments, to arrest the increasing demoralization; and subsequent emperors gladly availed themselves of the Christian institutes respecting marriage, especially Constantine the Great, who incorporated them in the civil law, and resisted, with severity, the prevalent frivolity in respect of repudiation.

The father's authority extended only to his legitimate children, who were called liberi ingenui. Various regulations served to limit this patria potestas, and to mitigate the excessive severities of its possible abuse.

If the exposure of infants (expositio infantis)

which prevailed so generally among the nations of antiquity, was not prohibited in Rome, it was yet subject to great limitations; and an express enactment of Romulus made it the duty of parents to raise their firstborn son or daughter. If the child had not been exposed, the parents were bound, by the ancient custom, to its maintenance and education.

The adoption of children, which was not unfrequent, was an important matter of legislation, and carried out with such rigid consistency, that even marriages within this relation were regarded, and condemned, as incestuous.

When a divorce had taken place, the sons usually remained with the father, and the daughters with the mother. As might be inferred from the position and dignity of the Roman matron (materfamilias), the mother's influence in the education of her children was very considerable; greater, probably, than with any other nation of antiquity. History furnishes a number of beautiful examples of the respect and veneration, which the matrons of Rome enjoyed.

Roman education was then essentially domestic, and, to a great degree, influenced by the mother, so that, in this respect, it more nearly resembled our own, than that of either Sparta, or Athens, or any other ancient state. The state, indeed, made provisions for the treatment and education of children, but, as we have already remarked, established no educational institutions. The father was the natural teacher of the son, and the mother his natural educatrix.

Omitting a number of customs and ceremonies, which were observed in connexion with the birth of children, and their subsequent treatment during infancy, we proceed to notice some arrangements which had in view the necessary care of childhood. The boy was furnished with a guide, custos, or pædagogus, who sometimes instructed him in gymnastics, or accompanied him to the exercises, and then he was styled progymnasta. The pædagogus attended the boy to the theatre, where he took his seat at his side:

he had great power over him, and, being always one of the older slaves, he generally grew morose and inflated. It was often his business to instruct the boy in reading; but his office, in general, was to counsel (*monere*) him how to conduct himself. The custos frequently exercised his office, until the boy had reached the age of manhood.

We have seen that it was, in reality, the father's business to instruct his children, and many a distinguished Roman performed this duty faithfully: Augustus assisted in the discharge of this paternal duty, but Cato took the whole of it upon himself. The latter, although he had a slave who was not only competent to act as teacher, but even gave instruction, in the capacity of grammaticus, to other boys, himself instructed his son in reading, swimming, and other necessary attainments, because he considered that the father would treat his child better than the slave. There were, however, many teachers, who instructed boys in reading, writing, and sometimes also in calculation, for which purpose the boys made use of tablets. A common teacher of this description was called ludi magister.

Girls also attended the schools, certainly as early as 450 A.C., as we learn from the story of Virginia, given in detail in the third book of Livy.

The incipient youths or tyros were, for the space of a year, exercised in arms in the Campus Martius, and in swimming in the Tiber. The Romans had, besides, palæstra, in the manner of the Greeks.

It was not as common in Rome, as it was in Greece, to learn music: the flute was even regarded as unseemly for Romans of rank. Yet, by means of the ancient national songs, which, in the earliest times, it was customary to sing at meals, the practice of singing was probably kept up. But when the culture of Greece had become, not only a desideratum, but the fashion in Rome, the city was well supplied with Grecian pædagogi, grammatici, *παιδοτριβαί*, rhetores, and philosophers, as early as 250 A.C., soon after the first Punic war; and, of course, still more abundantly after the conquest of Tarentum and of Corinth. Greeks, who devoted themselves to the instruction of youth, now flocked in crowds to the capital of the Empire, and it was quite common to employ Grecian slaves as teachers. And now the boy and the youth learned to read, and expound, the Grecian poets and prose authors; the literature of Greece was transplanted into the Roman soil, and ingrafted on the Roman mind. Livius Andronicus and Spurius Carvilius are said to have been the first who undertook the duties of grammatici. After the second Punic war, the ambassador of King Attalus, Crates of Mallos, being confined to his room by a fractured leg, delivered lectures on the Greek authors. Not long before Cicero, the greatest of Roman orators, appeared on the public stage, Latin exercises in rhetoric were instituted, Valerius Cato and Varro having already, the former 160 A.C., the latter about 130 A.C., supplied written instruction in the Latin language; while L. Plotius Gallus had himself instructed Cicero, when a boy, in this his native tongue. Julius Cæsar, a man of many-sided culture, and a zealous friend of science, even wrote a Latin grammar, which has been lost. But as the culture of the Greeks, in conjunction with the increasing corruption of morals, effected a change in the habits of the public mind, the philosophers and rhetores were, by a decree of the censors, expelled from Rome 170 A.C. But the effects of this expulsion were shortlived and unimportant. Grecian culture became more and more diffused in Rome, combining with that of its adopted home in the production of a new literary and public life.

The results which grew out of this union of the Grecian and the Roman mind may, to a great extent, be learned from the comedies of Terence, who transferred those of the Grecian Menander to the Roman soil. Not many passages are suitable to be cited in a work like the present.

Juvenal, in his fourteenth satire, contrasts the manners and domestic life of early Rome with the state of things prevailing in his own age, and the picture which he draws of the latter is indeed deplorable. Similar complaints are raised by the author of the "Decay of Roman eloquence," who is thought by some to have been Quintilian, by others Tacitus; it belongs, probably, to the end of the first century of the Christian era. Of the passage here particularly referred to, we give the following translation: "Things are different now from what they were with the ancients. Parents and teachers have degenerated. With the ancient Romans there was severity of discipline. The child owed its existence to chaste parents, and the domestic mother took delight in rearing her young charge. It was not given to a nurse, but a female relative, of mature years and good character, assisted in its nurture. Such noble matrons were Cornelia, the mother of the Gracchi, Aurelia, the mother of Cæsar, and Attia, the mother of Augustus. The design was to cultivate well the good dispositions of the son; and hence he was made to devote himself entirely to some one pursuit, according as his inclinations prompted him, either to the profession of arms, to jurisprudence, or to eloquence. But now the child is given in charge to a female Grecian slave, with whom a male slave, who is fit for nothing else, is associated, and by them the tender mind of the child is immediately crammed with idle tales and divers errors; and these slaves, moreover, indulge themselves, in the presence of the child, in everything that is calculated to make bad impressions. The parents themselves often train their children to vice and shamelessness; nay, it seems as though now the vices of the city, and fondness for gladiatorial shows, &c., were born with children. What room is then left in the mind for noble art and science? Where are the children to hear anything of these better pursuits? They know nothing else to converse about, except those entertainments and the like, when they come into the lecture (or recitation) rooms, and even from their teachers they hear scarcely anything else; for these merely pay their visits to the pupils, talk to them in the tone that suits them, and seek only to please them"

Horace complains in a like manner, but in language still more definite, in his celebrated and indignant ode, "Delicta majorum immeritus lues," &c. —See Carm., lib. iii., ode 6. Yet what Horace says of his own father proves that a better culture was not yet entirely extinct.

Many classical passages, exhibiting the decay of education and morals, might be cited from the poets and the prose-writers of Rome. Thus the writings of Cicero alone would furnish a large amount of valuable matter. This great man approved himself, in various ways, the careful cultivator of his children, and wrote, as is well known, his celebrated treatise "De Officiis" (concerning duties) for his son, besides furnishing instructive writings on various departments of science, especially rhetoric.

To relieve the dark picture which we have presented, we may state, that it appears from several letters of the younger Pliny, that even in the later times of Rome there were yet found exemplary wives and mothers, and worthy fathers and educators. The writings of his friend, the great historian Tacitus, also furnish classical passages respecting the education of youth which then prevailed in Rome.

Rome produced some authors who treated expressly of education. Marcus Varro wrote, about the time of the Saviour's birth, a work entitled "Capys, aut de liberis educandis," which has not come down to posterity. Gellius has preserved a few fragments of it.

But the most distinguished Roman writer on education is Quintilian. His work, Institutiones Orato ris LL.XII., is indeed more immediately designed to form the complete orator; but he begins with the culture of man, and the earliest education of the child; and it therefore falls directly within the scope of the present historic sketch to give the following extracts from this work.

"In the earliest education of the boy, his future destination should be had in view; hence also in that of the orator."

"Much depends on education; its object is to make of the child a good man."

"Every father, cherishing the earliest hopes from the very beginning, should himself undertake the education of his son; and for this, therefore, he ought to possess all necessary attainments. By imitation children acquire good and evil (habits)."

"The child, and especially if designed to be an orator, should be at once accustomed to a correct pronunciation. In grammatical instruction, the Greek language, as the source of the Latin culture, ought to be commenced with, but the Latin language should be very soon after taken up, so as to be studied at the same time with the other. Instruction may be commenced even before the seventh year, but it ought to be made agreeable to the boy: there is thus much gained for the age of youth."

"Even for elementary instruction, the most skilful teachers ought to be selected."

"I cannot approve of the practice of causing the names, and the alphabetic succession of the letters, to be learned in preference to their forms. It would be better to teach the forms and the names together, just as we become acquainted with men. With regard to syllables, the above plan is more admissible. Ivory letters may be given to children to play with; also other things that please them, and which they handle, examine, and name. For the purpose of learning to write, it is very well to have the letters graven into the tablets, and to let the children trace the impression with the pencil; it will thus be unnecessary to resort to the practice of guiding their hand. It is very important that a good hand, and skill in rapid writing, be acquired, for even thinking depends on this; the more cultivated ought not, therefore, to neglect this acquisition as much as they do. While the boy is learning to read, he ought at once to be accustomed to look ahead, at his right hand, while he is pronouncing. The syllables must all be thoroughly practised, in the succession in which they follow, and should by no means be passed over hastily. He ought to receive instructive (profitable) sentences to write, and not common words, as is usual."

"Many are opposed to the public schools, for the reason that the children acquire bad habits there, and also because the teacher can bestow more attention upon one than on many. But these objections against the good old regulation are not insuperable; there are also many evils connected with private instruction. If the children were not early rendered effeminate, and otherwise spoiled, they would not be so easily corrupted in the schools. The public instruction is to be preferred, especially for the future orator, in order that he may accustom himself to the multitude, and be stimulated by competition."

"The teacher should immediately make himself acquainted with the disposition and the capacity (naturam et ingenium) of his pupils, and for this there are sure marks. The most will depend upon how the memory, the imitative impulse, and the attention are constituted. Precocious minds rarely attain to eminence. The teacher should then treat every one according to his natural disposition and capacity. The good pupil will aim at winning praise. The young should also have opportunity for play and recreation. Whipping is not to be recommended, although Chrysippus advocates this mode of punishment."

From these extracts the reader will be able to form some little acquaintance with Quintilian's pedagogic views.

Aulus Gellius has very briefly and superficially discussed the obedience of children. In comparison with what Plato, Aristotle, and others have taught on this subject, his remarks are exceedingly meager, while the great principles involved are scarcely brought into view at all.

We have thus gone over that most important part of the history of pedagogics, of which it seemed particularly desirable to present a somewhat extensive view. Of the time which intervenes between the period at which we have thus arrived, and the revival of education in modern times, we shall take only a cursory view, designing to give a rather more detailed account of education as developed and systematized within the last centuries.

We have seen that, after the time of Alexander the Great, Grecian culture, in as far as it was involved in political institutions, underwent an essential change, and developed itself more in forms purely scientific; and that this course of development was powerfully influenced, and in a great degree guided, by the great Stagyrite, who laid the foundation in Athens of the polyhistory and learned culture of modern times.

At the mouth of the Nile, Alexander built, 331 A.C., the city which bears his name. Under the Ptolemies, who were his successors in Egypt, and who governed that country during several centuries, the sciences flourished. From the very beginning, these sovereigns, who were liberal patrons of learning, founded libraries in Alexandria, which filled up rapidly, from the circumstance that the papyrus was obtained in the immediate vicinity of the city. The principal library is said to have contained twenty-thousand volumes when it was destroyed by fire in the time of Julius Cæsar. In the same quarter of the city with this library was the royal palace, of which one wing was called the *μουσεῖον*, museum. Here assembled the learned, to whom a life void of care was secured in Alexandria, and constituted a sodality of scholars from all nations, having for their president a priest.

In the suburbs Racotis, another library had been collected in the temple of Serapis. Including the books which Antony brought thither from Pergamus, it is said to have consisted of 120,000 volumes. Under the Emperor Theodosius, this library was destroyed by fire, about A.D. 400.

Athens continued to flourish as a seat of learning. Here also large and valuable libraries were collected; and in this city, besides other sciences, grammar or criticism, rhetoric or sophistic learning, and philosophy were chiefly taught in academic institutions.

And thus Athens and Alexandria contained, even for the Romans themselves, the principal educational institutions, until the emperors elevated Rome itself, and afterward Constantinople, to a similar rank, and established other, though not as distinguished, seats of learning throughout their vast empire.

In Athens the gymnasia, with their regulations, continued to subsist under the Roman emperors. But, as regards intellectual culture and scientific study, the influence of the sophists, as we have already, in part, shown, was highly unpropitious. In the absence of all fixed institutions controlled by the government, parties arose among the students, who sought only, by proceedings the most rude, tumultuary, and violent, to secure all new-comers, for whose arrival they watched in the port, to some favourite professor. Of this riotous state of affairs among the students of Athens, Eunapius, Gregory of Nazianzen, both in the 4th century P.C , and Libanius (about 230–250 P.C.), a celebrated sophist, and the teacher of Chrysostom, make loud complaint. It was also complained that, as very few students paid the demanded fee, the income of the professors was not only so utterly inadequate to their support as to compel them to beg of the magistrates, but that they were treated with base ingratitude, yea, with contempt and ridicule; so that they had neither motive nor opportunity to exert themselves for the good education of their pupils, who ran from one instructer to another, as the whim of the moment guided them. Of this disorderly state of things, which reached its climax about six or seven centuries after Aristotle, we may already trace the beginnings in his time.

The professors themselves were arrayed against each other; they arranged meetings, in which they publicly disputed on a variety of subjects: for example, the grammarians on rules of language.

The philosophers had their schools adjoining each other, and, at the same time, stated places of meeting, where they came together for the purpose of disputing. The lectures and exercises were held daily in an auditorium. The students frequently engaged in a sort of contest, especially on certain festivals; so that here also we trace the transition of the national customs and higher culture of Attica, into the excesses of a degenerate scholastic life.

In ancient times, the Ἀνθεστήρια (a festival in honour of Bacchus) had been observed also as a festival for youth, boys of three years of age being, on the first day of the festival, crowned with a garland of flowers: in later times it was customary on the second day to send to the public teachers, especially the sophists, their fee, besides presents; whereupon these instituted a convivial feast, on which occasion great feats of drinking were performed. The best drinker was rewarded with a cask of wine and a garland of leaves. The practice which had prevailed in the better days of Athens, of instituting scientific and literary contests in connexion with different public festivals, seemed now to have entirely degenerated into drinking-bouts and absurd disputation, so that Athens exhibits the caricature of all subsequent student-life.

Aulus Gellius, however, portrays scenes of a somewhat different character, at which he was himself present. Of one of these we present the following abstract: "We spent the Saturnalia at Athens joyously, in jovial, but not indecorous entertainments. We Romans, who happened to be there, and attended the lectures of the same professors, assembled in considerable numbers. One, whose turn it was, provided the meal, and at the same time offered some work of an ancient Latin or Greek author, and a laurel-wreath, as a prize for him who should solve some question to be proposed. A question was assigned by lot to each: if he solved it he received the prize; if not, the question passed on to the next: if all failed, the prize fell to the god of the festival. The problem consisted of some passage from an ancient poet or philosopher, or some point in history, or some captio sophistica, or some philological question: for example, respecting frustra, as used by Ennius, or also a passage from Plato's Republic, or some captious sophism: for example, What you have not lost you have; but horns you have not lost, therefore you have horns; or, When I lie and say that I lie, do I then lie or speak the truth? and other like things."

Thus a fixed student-life had developed itself in Athens, in which we recognise nearly all the peculiarities and arrangements of the modern German universities. Yet, notwithstanding the trifling and the solemn fooleries which prevailed in this ancient city of the Muses, there were many who devoted themselves seriously to study, especially that of eloquence. When the Romans became masters of Greece, they took Athens under their special protection, from their partiality to Grecian literature: it became their favourite city, as we learn from Cicero, and more particularly from his friend Atticus.

The Romans now began to emulate the conquered Greeks. Julius Cæsar was the first who procured for Grecian scholars an honourable reception at Rome, by conferring the right of citizenship on grammarians and other teachers, as well as physicians, who occur, from this time forward, in the same category with the professors.

Augustus and his minister Mecænas were still more active in this cause, and they are justly regarded as eminent patrons of the sciences. The latter admitted to his intercourse the most distinguished scholars and men of talent, and encouraged them by honourable distinctions and rewards. Augustus sought to bring the schools into better repute by exonerating the teachers from public offices and other occupations, in consequence of which measure their number greatly increased. Sometimes the grammarians and rhetores were also philosophers, whose lectures were attended by such young Romans as set up pretensions to culture. These teachers, therefore, repaired to Rome in great numbers. But those who aimed at the highest degree of scholarship, visited Athens, or the celebrated school of the rhetoricians at Rhodes: many went to Mytilene, or even to Massilia in Gaul, and to Corduba in Spain. There were also many inferior grammatical schools throughout the Roman Empire.

But soon the decay of the Athenian institutions, as well as views of a political nature, excited a desire in the emperors to make Rome herself a prominent seat of learning. This purpose became more maturely developed in the mind of Vespasian (emperor from A.D. 69–79) by the circumstance that the so-called Magistri had private schools of learning in Rome, and more especially that the illustrious Quintilian was giving instruction as a rhetorician, with great acceptance, in the metropolis. Vespasian appointed him public professor of eloquence, assigning him a considerable salary from the public funds, and employed, at the same time, several other professors of rhetoric.

The idea which had originated with Vespasian was more fully carried out by Adrian, immediately upon his accession to the imperial throne. Adrian reigned from A.D. 117–138. He founded in the Capitol the so-called Athenæum, in which, besides the professors of rhetoric, he also appointed grammarians, with respectable salaries. The immunities which these teachers had enjoyed under his predecessors were now extended to freedom from all extraneous duties. From this time onward these public teachers were styled professors, or literati.

Antoninus Pius (emperor from A.D. 138–161) founded, in addition, a professorship of philosophy, and established in all the important cities of the Roman Empire institutions of learning, on the model of that in Rome.

After Constantine the Great had converted the ancient Byzantium, under its new name of Constantinople, into the imperial capital, he sought to establish there, in an improved form, whatever was excellent in the institutions of Rome, and particularly to elevate his new metropolis into the first seat of learning in the world. As the Athenæum in Rome had eclipsed the mother-institution in Athens, so was Constantinople to possess a similar, but far more illustrious institution of culture. He had here erected a Capitol, in which he now established an auditorium: and this he designed to be the highest institution of learning in the empire; the professors being strictly required to confine their labours to its halls, in order thus to prevent any from hawking about their learning, like the circumforanei, in the public streets and market-places. In the fifth century there were engaged in that (so-called) auditorium thirty-one professors, classified as follows: 1. *Eloquence*, eight; Latin language (oratores), three; Greek language (sophistæ), five: 2. *grammarians*, twenty; *i. e.*, ten in the Greek and ten in the Latin language: 3. one *philosophus:* and, 4. two *professores juris.* At the public library were employed four Greek and three Latin antiquarii, whose business it was to arrange, repair, and correct the ancient manuscripts.

Athens, Alexandria, Rome, and Constantinople were, until the fifth century, the principal seats of learning and of study in the Roman Empire: we should say in the world, had there not still existed in Eastern Asia a number of institutions of the old style. Under the patronage of the emperors, such resorts of the studious were gradually multiplied. Gaul had been, from early times, distinguished for the cultivation of the sciences and for eloquent men; first at Massilia, then in Lugdunum, and afterward at Augustodunum (Marseilles, Lyons and Autun); and thus there were necessarily erected similar institutions at Trier (Trèves), the capital since the time of Constantine, as also in other cities of that region.

From the writings of Suetonius, Gellius, Quintilian, and others, we learn that the course pursued by the professors was as follows: they expounded the writings of Cicero, the poems of Virgil, Horace, Statius, and others, in the Latin department; and, in like manner, the works of the Greek authors. The grammarians, also, had introduced the system of certifying, *i. e.*, of giving testimonials respecting the respective merits of their pupils. In giving instruction they scarcely ever laid aside the rod; and Quintilian is, as far as we know, the first who condemned the practice of whipping. The rhetores practised certifying still more extensively; but, though severe in their discipline, no longer used the rod, for they took up those pupils who had completed their studies under the grammaticus, and also instructed adults. The new methods of instruction rendered necessary a plan of classification, or system for arranging the pupils in classes: the origin of this system we therefore discover in the division into grammatica, the lowest class, into rhetorica and philosophia, the pupil advancing from one to the other until he reached the highest class. The arrangements were the same in the schools of the rhetoricians. Quintilian says of his teacher that he had retained the very useful plan of dividing his pupils (pueros) into classes and sub-classes, according to their capacities, which were determined according as each pupil solved the proposition given to him: to be at the head of the class was the highest honour. At the end of every thirty days the process of certification was renewed, so that then another might advance to the first place. This, he says, had operated far better, and effected more than all the admonitions of the teachers, all the vigilance of the pedagogues, and all the vows of the parents could have accomplished.

These glimpses of the academic life of that period are the more interesting to us, because of the resemblance between many of its arrangements to those of modern times. This appears also in the academic laws which the joint rulers Valentinian, Valens, and Gratian drew up, A.D. 370, more immediately for the institutions in Rome. These statutes were given to those imperial institutions at the time when they were at the height of their prosperity and fame. We have not space to recapitulate them here; but it is obvious that, when the Western Empire was approaching its dissolution, there existed in Rome a public institution of learning formally organized according to prescribed statutes. Here, then, we discover the basis of the later German universities: here already we find immatriculation, relegation, and the archetype of three faculties. Here assembled students from all provinces, and the institution continued in some degree to flourish even down to the reign of Athalaric the Goth. In presenting this sketch of Roman education, the difficulty has not been to find materials, but to select, from a vast amount of interesting and valuable matter, what might seem to be most important, and we hope that nothing that is essential has been omitted.

We are now to enter upon a new epoch in the his tory of human education, beginning with the intervention of a new power, a new cultivating energy: we speak of Christianity. But, before we proceed to draw a brief sketch of education as gradually affected by our divine religion, and finally developed in those forms which it has assumed since the Reformation, we shall, though it be at the expense of chronology, give an account of Arabian culture in this place, in order that the thread of history may not hereafter be broken by the introduction of this subject.

SECTION VII.

ARABIAN CULTURE.

Muhammed, the founder of Islamism, made, since A.D. 622, extensive conquests with his Arabians, and at the same time extended his religious creed. This impostor, but still more his successors, established, as is well known, new dynasties in Asia, Africa, and Europe. His sacred book, the Koran, has derived many things from the Jewish and Christian religions, while it contains maxims and imagery in the Arabian style; for, like other Oriental nations, the Arabians also had their poetic creations.

It could not be otherwise that the conquering hosts of Muhammed's successors would be hostile to the culture which was advancing in its development, through the influence of Christianity, in the Roman Empire. When, therefore, in the year of our Lord

641, they took possession of Alexandria, the Caliph Omar caused the libraries of that city to be destroyed, and countless volumes, repositories of the treasures of antiquity, were cast into the flames in order to furnish steam-baths to rude barbarians and voluptuaries. Yet it was not in the nature of the Arabians to be enemies of the sciences; on the contrary, they zealously promoted them in several countries where they had established their empire. And thus they favoured them in Egypt also; and although liberal studies had now entirely died out in Alexandria, they gradually revived again, and after the lapse of some time they were established anew in that city by the Arabians. The caliphs extended their conquests in North Africa, and with sweeping rapidity the current rolled its whelming flood from Arabia to the Atlantic, and, led on by Abd-el-Malek, across to Gibraltar, soon reaching the Pyrenees, and over and beyond them: and who can tell to what extent Europe would have been inundated, had not Charles Martel, A.D. 732, by his great victory on the banks of the Loire, arrested and driven back this tide of barbarian invaders, and thus saved to Christianity the ground which it had gained.

As well in the measures of individual sovereigns as in their whole mode of thinking, the Arabians manifested their intellectual capacity and activity, and their love of the sciences. It was not only by their fairy tales and other poetic creations, but through their cultivation of several of the severe sciences, that they became the instructers of the Middle Ages, after they had introduced some of the treasures of Grecian literature among themselves. They cultivated with zeal the natural sciences, mathematics, medicine, and philosophy; they translated, and commented upon, works of Greek authors; they had authors of their own, and made independent progress in the field of science and literature. They were thus the inventors of algebra, the name of which indicates its origin. Jews and Christians studied among them and with them, and though religious enemies, they often lived together as friends, in the common bonds of learning and scholarly intercourse. They left unmolested some of the earlier institutions of education, such as the law-school at Berytus, the seminaries of the Jews and the Christians at Nisibis, and those of the Christians at Antioch and at Edessa; but they also established several of their own, for the special benefit of Muhammedans, at Basra and Kufa in the ninth century, at Emesa and Samarcand in the twelfth, at Aleppo and Bokharin in the tenth, and in other cities.

Haroun al Raschid (A.D. 788–809), the illustrious contemporary of Charlemagne, is pre-eminently extolled by Arabian writers as the friend and promoter of the sciences.

Grammatical studies, poetry, philosophy, jurisprudence, medicine, astronomy, mathematics, natural science, and, sad to relate, magic also, flourished among the Arabians during the reign of this great prince; and to strangers also, his capital, Bagdad, was open as an emporium of learning. His successor Mamoun (from A.D. 813) also cherished this scientific and literary spirit; but he suffered it to stoop to small matters, and to stray into astrological and magical follies: his highest praise is, that he caused the great works of the Greeks to be translated into Arabic.

The first prince who distinguished himself as a lover of art in Spain was Hakem (796–822), who built stately structures at Cordova; and during the reign of his successor, Abd-er-Rhaman II., the great musician Zaryab came from Irak to Spain. The third caliph of that name enlarged and beautified the capital just mentioned (about A.D. 940), and founded the institutions of learning which flourished there, and of which there were seventeen, besides seventy libraries. Females were also instructed there, and the works of distinguished poetesses read and explained in the schools. This excellent sovereign maintained the most friendly relations with the other European monarchs, especially with the Greek emperor Leo, and the German emperor Otho I. Thus were liberal studies established among the Arabians in Spain, especially at Cordova, for the benefit, also, of Jews and Christians. Similar academic institutions existed at Toledo, Salamanca, and Seville ; and in Africa also they established high schools in Kairwan, Tunis, Fessan, and Algiers.

In Egypt, likewise, the Arabian princes were, at different times, patrons of learning, especially from 946 to 967. The same is true of their Asiatic empires, particularly the Persian. In this empire flourished, during the splendid reign of Mahmoud, among others, the celebrated naturalist and physician Avicenna; here, about A.D. 1030, were libraries, and schools of learning, of which Christians, Parses, Muhammedans, Jews, and perhaps also Brahmins, availed themselves in common. In Syria, Damascus became a seat of the sciences ; also Emesa, Aleppo, and other cities ; and when, in the eleventh century, the Jewish seminaries about the Euphrates were discontinued, the studies which had been cultivated in them were transferred to the West, and especially from the Arabian institutions to Spain. Cordova remained, during several centuries, one of the most important seats of culture.

Thus we observe, in all this, the influx, through various channels, into Europe, even to the Atlantic, of ancient Oriental science, and of the culture of those institutions which flourished, in hoar antiquity, in the remotest East.

There were yet recently found, even in Africa, higher schools of the above description : for example, one in connexion with the mosque at Cairo, and another at Bornou, connected with the principal mosque of that city; this institution possessed a library, and was frequented by many men of learning, and by pupils who were supported at the expense of the sultan. Besides the higher sciences, there was here also instruction given in reading, writing, and arithmetic. We have no knowledge of the present condition of this institution. But in all the Muhammedan cities there are schools for boys, usually close by the mosques; nor are the higher studies neglected. Political convulsions, which have shaken the Muhammedan empires, revolutions which may not be far distant, and the labours of Christian missionaries, will probably open new channels for the tide of learning and culture which once flowed over Europe from the East, to return, with tenfold volume and power, to that now benighted region.

THE CHRISTIAN WORLD.

We have endeavoured to set before the reader what was great, and good, and beautiful in the culture, in the education of the nations of antiquity, and truly we have found much to admire and to commend; much that is valuable in our own day, especially among those classic nations whose glorious literature still constitutes a principal means for the intellectual, and more particularly the æsthetic culture of the modern scholar, and whose eminence in the fine arts has not been attained by any subsequent age.

But while those nations of the East, among whom the institutions and arrangements of remote antiquity still continue unchanged, are in a state of bondage and torpor as respects the development of mind, the highest interests of society, and the noblest purposes of human life; while the Israelites, who became the channel through which was transmitted to us the earlier revelation of the living and true God, forfeited their highest privileges, through their devotion to lifeless forms and external temple-worship and Rabbinism, the educational institutions, the beautiful culture, the civil and social organizations of Greece and Rome have utterly passed away, intellectual degeneracy and moral corruption preceding and ushering in the decay and downfall of those once mighty and illustrious nations. The sweet breeze of morning has long since ceased to whisper in the palms of

Zion; many centuries have passed since Grecian sages wandered and meditated under their shady plane-trees; and from the forest of their laurels the power of the Romans has long since departed. A proof, all this, that the wisdom of the ancients, however effective for a season in regulating and adorning the life of separate nations, was not competent to benefit, essentially, the great family of man; to remedy corruptions, to arrest the progress of degeneracy, to establish virtue, to secure substantial happiness; that *their* culture could not, therefore, conduct either the individual or the race to the true end of human existence; that hence this wisdom, or this culture, having within itself the seeds of decay, could but last its little day, and then cease from among men as though it had not been; and that an element was wanting in the education, the general culture of man, which might, with pervasive energy, embrace the entire race, and adapt its influence to every age, and locality, and condition of the human family; satisfy every higher want of the soul, unlock the mysteries of the present, and the glories of the future life, and guide the free and immortal spirit in the paths of eternal truth, and by the unchanging principles of true virtue, to peace on earth, and to unfading happiness in the life to come. And this element, this divine energy, this "one thing needful," came among men in the religion of Christ.

Jesus, born as the promised Messiah among the Jewish people and in the time of the Emperor Augustus, lowly in his human relations, but declared by Divine glory to be the Saviour of the world, approves himself, by word and deed, highly exalted above all the wise teachers of antiquity. He himself proclaims that the time had come in which men should cease to regard this or that temple as exclusively sacred, and when all the world should learn to know that God is a Spirit, who must be worshipped in spirit and in truth; that he had come to reveal him as the Father in heaven, and to make those who believe in him "free indeed;" to redeem them, and to bestow on them, as the children of God, eternal life.

The history of his life is inseparably connected with his work of redemption. He dies on the cross, is buried, rises again on the third day, gives his disciples the commission to preach the Gospel of the kingdom to all nations, and ascends before their eyes to heaven. They obey his command after having received for this purpose a higher power, the Holy Spirit, and bear witness of Christ, as the Son of God, the Mediator, the Lord: they preach that whosoever believeth in him shall be saved, and exhibit in themselves that newness of life whereof they testify. They were, in a worldly point of view, unimportant men and unlearned Jews, with the exception of the apostle Paul, who, familiar with the culture of the Jews and the Greeks, joyfully proclaims his own experience of that new power which had appeared among men: "I am not ashamed of the Gospel of Christ, for it is the power of God unto salvation to every one that believeth."

What no priests on the Ganges, the Nile, the Euphrates could accomplish, with all their wisdom and their mysteries; what no teacher like Zerdusht, Confucius, Pythagoras, or Socrates had been able to achieve, that was done by poor fishermen from the obscure sea of Tiberias; what those far-famed sages never could even conceive of, was introduced among men by persons of humble rank, and through their instrumentality communicated not only to a few of their contemporaries, but extended, as the kingdom of light, over the whole earth: they proclaimed the salvation of mankind. This had been obscurely anticipated and eagerly desired by the purer and nobler minds of preceding ages.* This was not that human energy, habituated merely to self-government, but it was a Divine power, liberating from sensual bondage to the extent of entire self-denial, exalting to holiness of life, renewing the spirit of man; it was, and ever continues to be, a new creation. Such is the nature

* Witness the Eastern Magi, whom the star guided to the manger at Bethlehem. Dr. Harris, in his "Great Teacher," refers to the remarkable language which Socrates held on this subject to his pupil Plato, by whom his words are recorded.

I

of Christianity. It cultivates, it forms the individual to resemblance of God, and it develops the human race to the attainment of its destination. Thus, after the winter, in which perished the creations of antiquity, has appeared the spring, in which the Divine Spirit of love calls forth a new life. The kingdom of God, which was thus introduced, is an inward, a spiritual kingdom, yet manifesting itself also in an external form, inasmuch as it breaks forth gradually, amid the conflicts which it sustains against human corruption, into greater extent and power, leads on the victory of good over evil, and will ultimately glorify the earth. Here, then, is more than that harmony, nationality, calocagathia, and humanity of classic antiquity: a new life rises upon the world, in which the spirit of man is glorified, and the nations of the earth become united in the public spirit of humanity—a spirit of love, that embraces the whole great family of man. The one eternal, living God, who worketh everywhere, and, as our Father in heaven, carries out gloriously his holy will; the sinfulness of man, of which each individual must, for himself, obtain an experimental knowledge, in order that he may desire and obtain the pardon which the Saviour wrought out for him, and freely offers to him, and consecrate himself, through the grace that is given, entirely to God, for this life and that which is to come: these are the great and new doctrines which Christianity has introduced; not merely set up as a theory, but implanted as a living and operative power in the mind and heart of man They will extend farther and wider, and exalt and regenerate the human race. The faculties of the individual renewed into a child of God are thus to be developed for his own real good and the good of others: and thus shall nations, pervaded by its regenerating and sanctifying power, pursue their interests, and prosecute their benevolent efforts in peace with each other; the whole race shall be developed to a life of true wisdom and virtue, the earth become the abode of love to God and man, and the kingdom and glory of God be promoted in all things: and this, therefore, is also the great idea of Christian education.

As the light of Christianity first exhibited the idea of education in its full import and its entire compass, this distinctness will appear, also, in a complete account of the history of education as affected by Christianity. The historian will consider the operation of the new cultivating power or principle, and show, at the same time, how those elements, which had been retained from the systems and institutions of antiquity, have been changed, and thus point out the gradual development of the culture of modern times.

The history of education thus becomes, in one sense, more general; in another, more definite. It becomes more general because it considers less the peculiar education of particular nations, than the education of man in general, as it ought to exist among all nations It becomes more definite, because it has to portray the institutions, the instrumentalities, and the methods which have developed themselves in this age of the world. And as this development has taken place principally in Europe, it is to that quarter of the globe that the historian will be almost entirely confined.

In presenting such a history of Christian education, the author from whom our materials are derived goes very much into detail. He adopts, very naturally, two periods: in the first, the Christian culture effects a gradual entrance among the nations of Europe, contending with the opposition of enemies and the obstinacy of ancient custom, &c.; in the second, it shakes off the yoke, asserts its power, and begins to exhibit its effects in the life of nations; in domestic life, in the instruction of youth by the Church, in Britain, Germany, France, and elsewhere; in the scholastic arrangements and institutions of those countries, and in the pedagogic literature of this period.

We have already stated that on this earlier period we shall not dwell in detail; its history is more or less identical with that of the Church, from her first beginning in Judea, to her final extension over the length and breadth of Europe. We shall therefore be very brief until we reach the second period, with its extensive arrangements, its theories and methods, its pedagogic sects and literature.

SECTION I.

HIGHER INSTITUTIONS OF EDUCATION.

1. *School of the Catechists at Alexandria.*

THE first teachers of Christianity established no fixed institutions of education. They instructed men by preaching; and several of them, also, by those invaluable epistles found in the sacred volume of the New Testament.

In Alexandria, the Gospel is said to have been first preached by St. John, whence he is often, but erroneously, regarded as the founder of the school of catechists in that city. Instruction in the Christian religion was termed catechesis, but by this was usually meant popular instruction in Christianity; and with this, we are not to confound that learned instruction given, in the school of the catechists, to those who were designed for the work of the ministry. The founder of this higher institution for Christian teachers, was Pantænus, a Stoic philosopher who had become a convert to Christianity. His activity in Alexandria commenced A.D. 181, but how long he held his office there as president of the school is uncertain: his successor was Clement. The latter was succeeded by Origen, who was (from A.D. 213) the most distinguished teacher at this first Christian seminary. His lectures were much frequented, even by pagans, many of whom, for instance his successor Heraclas, became Christians. He instructed his theological pupils also in the profane sciences, mathematics, logic, rhetoric, natural philosophy, metaphysics, ethics, astronomy; and aimed, in general, at comprehensive encyclopædic culture. This school was under the authority and superintendence of the episcopus of Alexandria, by whom the teacher was appointed. We find no notice of any separate building appropriated to its purposes: the lectures were prob ably held in private houses, perhaps sometimes also in a church. It gradually declined, lingering after the Arian controversy through a precarious existence, till the beginning of the second quarter of the fourth century, when, after an attempt to revive it in the fifth century, every trace of it disappears.

About A.D. 600, Pope Gregory the Great seemed inclined to establish a seminary in Rome for the education of Christian teachers; but his taste led him to other pursuits, which prevented this idea, if ever he seriously entertained it, from being realized.

Individual clergymen, distinguished for learning and influence in the Church, frequently became the instructers of others, without establishing particular institutions; and many educated themselves, by means of the writings of such eminent men.

Thus, during several centuries, the Christian Church had no fixed method of communicating theological instruction.

2. *The Imperial Schools, and the Universities.*

We have already, on a former page, spoken of those public institutions of learning which the Roman emperors established in the principal cities of the Empire, and among which the Athenæum at Rome first attained a splendid reputation, and afterward the Auditorium at Constantinople. The Museum at Alexandria also enjoyed considerable patronage.

In the provinces, the schools of the rhetoricians, at which also the grammarians usually gave instruction, continued to flourish for a while longer. The schools of Berytus, Rhodes, and Mytilene were particularly frequented by those Romans who devoted themselves to the study of law.

It has been seen that Gaul was early distinguished for the cultivation of the sciences, and the imperial schools in that province enjoyed great consideration, even to the invasions of the Visigoths, Burgundians, and Franks (428). Several such schools had also been founded in Belgium and in Germany; and a number likewise, it is said, in Britain, among which those at Cantabrigium, Oxonia, and especially Eboracum, were most distinguished. These, however, became entirely extinct when the Romans, about A.D. 440, left Britain to its fate, and the Angles and Saxons, A.D. 449, commenced their irruptions.

Similar schools existed in other parts of the Empire, but with the fall of the Empire and the immigration of the Germanic tribes, towards the middle of the fifth century, they entirely disappeared.

But a new class of educational institutions now sprung up in Western Europe, whose organic principle it would be difficult to point out: and these are the universities. If they derived their organization in part from the imperial schools just spoken of, and partly also from the ancient medical schools, the student-life, wild and lawless, which characterized them, was copied from that which, as we have seen, existed at Athens in its later times.

The universities occur first in Italy, and among a great number that might be mentioned, that at Bononia (Bologna) was probably the first of all, being founded in A.D. 1158. Its professors first obtained their jurisdiction from the Emperor Frederic I., in 1158. Its constitution, as finally settled, was much the same as that of modern German universities.

The students, classified according to the nations whence they came, enjoyed great and singular privileges, and none more distinguished than the German nation.

The statutes, which imbodied the constitution of the university, might be altered every twenty years, but only by the students themselves, who elected for this purpose eight statuarii from their midst. In A.D. 1253 they were, for the first time, ratified by the pope.

Since the thirteenth and fourteenth centuries, there existed at this institution several distinct collegia, or, as they are termed in modern times, faculties: they were the following five: 1. The collegium of the canonical, or canon-law; 2. that of civil law; 3. the medical; 4. the philosophical; and, 5 the theological collegium. The first consisted of twelve, the second of sixteen regular members.

Besides the regular, there were also extraordinary lectures. The regular course comprehended one year, beginning on the nineteenth and twentieth of October, and ending with the seventh of September. With this day commenced the principal vacation; but there was a number of minor vacations during the year. The recitations and disputations were conducted according to fixed statutes; and even the clothing of the students, both as regards the material and the cut, was prescribed, in order to prevent extravagance. The colour was usually black.

Next in importance among the early universities is that of Paris, whose origin is entirely unknown. Our limits do not admit of a detailed account of its arrangements. It differed from the universities of Italy chiefly in that the doctores and magistri passed resolutions and enacted statutes themselves, and not, as in Italy, the students, who appear to have had no influence whatever in Paris.

Among the collegia of the Paris university, which were very important, and more numerous than in Italy, the Sorbonne, founded in 1520, was the first and most celebrated, equalling in fame the theological faculty, which appears to have gradually identified itself with it.

The theological faculty of Paris was pre-eminently distinguished. It was first in rank, and in influence the most important. Its decisions, as we often note in history, were in request throughout Christendom even as late as A.D. 1631.

The other French universities adopted for their organization either that of Paris or that of Bologna as a model.

Those of Spain have been mentioned in connexion with the Arabians.

The English universities were constituted in imitation of that of Paris, yet so that the power of the professors and the dependance of the students were still greater.

In Germany many universities were founded on the Parisian model. That of Prague, which was opened in A.D. 1348, was the first. Similar institutions soon sprang up in Sweden and in Denmark.

From the very beginning, the student-life at these institutions was characterized by great frivolity, loose morality, lawless and riotous conduct. In the thirteenth century this state of things had greatly increased, and only gradually did the influence of Christianity effect a partial reformation.

SECTION II.

CHRISTIAN EDUCATION AMONG THE NATIONS OF WESTERN EUROPE.

CHAPTER I.

Domestic Life, and Religious Instruction of the Church.

The power of Christianity to regenerate the human race has manifested itself in the life of individuals, of families, and of nations, through the transforming influence which it exerts on the inner man. It has thus effected, and continues to effect for mankind what we can discover nowhere else. The sacredness of the marriage-union, and of the personal rights of man, is recognised among Christians, not only in theory, but in practice. The emancipation of woman, the sanctity of family-life in its proper sense, of which the ancients had scarcely any conception, and the abolition of slavery, have been introduced by our divine religion, and the great Head of the Church will more and more extend and glorify its influence among the nations of the earth.

Domestic education thus belongs essentially to Christianity: it is not only expressly enjoined as a duty; but as parents are to regard their child as the child of God, as their love to God sanctifies and exalts to the utmost their affection for their offspring, this domestic education has fully asserted its influence over the whole of human life. The spirit of love became the spirit of education, and is the only spirit capable of promoting the true culture of man. Governing the father himself, it modified the severity of Jewish discipline and of the Roman patria potestas; but it inculcates the more strenuously that firmness and rigour, which are necessary not only to train the young to good habits, but to exercise them in self-denial, and to bring them to devote themselves to God. Through the influence of Christianity, the love of family, and kindred, and of country became more pure, and firm, and vigorous, and, extending its compass, became subservient to the love of the human race, to universal philanthropy. Who does not admire the heroism of the first Christians, which they so often exhibited amid the terrors of martyrdom; while they were ready to sacrifice everything for that country which is above, and whose citizens they were, they were educated in the simplicity and purity of true virtue, and in genuine benevolence.

The effect which Christianity produced on the social position of woman, claims our highest admiration and gratitude. A heathen sage once admiringly exclaimed, "What women the Christians have among them!" From the earliest times of the Church, bright examples of noble women, exemplary in every relation, as wives, as mothers, and as members of the community, abound.

With this fundamental and thorough reformation of man himself, the regeneration of education, in respect of the community at large, although gradual and always contending with obstacles, and for a time even interrupted by the corruptions of the Church, has been generally advancing down to our day.

In the beginning the children of Christians received their instruction partly in the existing schools and partly in the Church; the former being communicated by heathens, the latter both by the parents and the clergy. Religious instruction was mostly given by the clergy, sometimes also by laymen: the bishop adding that special instruction which preceded baptism. For the regulations respecting catechetical instruction and catechumens, the reader is referred to ecclesiastical history.

The monastic institutions which arose at an early period of the Christian Church in Egypt, we mention here merely on account of their subsequent connexion with education. In early times the monks were faithful and zealous missionaries of the Gospel, and became instrumental in converting many European nations to Christianity. In England, Scotland, and Ireland, and in various other countries, especially France and Germany, they preached the Gospel, instructed the young, established schools, founded extensive monastic institutions, which, by their libraries and other arrangements, sustained an important relation to the progress of Christianity, and the advancement of education and general culture. It would lead us entirely too far to give anything like a detailed account of the gradual Christianization of Europe. Of the agencies and institutions employed in this work; of the vicissitudes, and difficulties, and trials, and hardships, and triumphs of its agents; of its general and beneficial effects on family, social, and public national life, peculiarly, and certainly not healthfully, modified by the superstitions and corruptions of papal Rome, the reader can obtain ample information in any extensive work on the history of the Christian Church. We proceed to take a cursory view of the pedagogic literature and methods of this earlier period.

CHAPTER II.

Pedagogic Literature and Method.

The seven liberal arts had become the basis of such scholastic instruction as went beyond the elements of reading, writing, and vocal music. Before we offer a brief account of that encyclopedic instruction, we shall notice the principal authors who promoted it by their writings.

The most distinguished among these was Marcianus Mineus Felix Capella, a native of Madaura, in Africa, who, in his old age, published his schoolbook at Rome, A.D. 470. No book of this kind has ever en joyed a greater and more permanent celebrity than this: it remained about a thousand years the one great schoolbook of Western Europe. Its title is Satyricon, and it consists of nine books in prose and poetry: the first two compose the work, De Nuptiis Philologiæ et Mercurii; the following seven are, De Septem Artibus Liberalibus Libri Singulares, in the following order: Grammatica, Dialectica, Rhetorica, Geometria, Arithmetica, Astronomia, Musica. It is written in bad Latin.

Soon after him (about A.D. 500), Boëthius, a Roman vir consularis (of consular rank), wrote a far more valuable schoolbook on three of these arts, so-called: 1. De Arithmetica, in two books. 2. De Musica, in five books. 3. De Geometria, in two books. This work was, at the time, truly valuable in various respects.

Not long after, Magnus Aurelius Cassiodorius, also a Roman of consular rank, who afterward became a monk, published a work, De Septem Disciplinis. It was a popular schoolbook.

The celebrated Archbishop of Seville, in Spain, a zealous promoter of monachism (died A.D. 636), published a far more copious work, entitled Originum seu Etymologiarum Libri xx.: a sort of extended encyclopedia, treating of a great variety of subjects.

The venerable Bede also published in England, about A.D. 700, a sort of encyclopedia, containing, 1. Cunabula Grammatices, in questions and answers. 2. De Octo Partibus Orationis. 3. De Arte Metrica 4. De Orthographia. 5. Several books treating of particular parts of arithmetic; and a number of other productions.

And, lastly, the celebrated Rhabanus Maurus published a book, De Universo.

Latin Grammar was studied in the West of Europe with no little difficulty, from Priscianus, Diomedes, and Donatus, until Alexander, a Franciscan monk, published (about 1230) his metrical Latin Grammar, entitled Doctrinale, by which the study was considerably facilitated. Vocabularies were gradually constructed, chiefly from the Vulgata: for example, that of Rhabanus Maurus. The Greek language was but little studied during this period.

Dialectics were taught chiefly by collections of rules, until the study reached its culminating point at the University of Paris, under the scholastics.

In rhetoric, Quintilian was superseded by Capella, Bede, and Alcuin, until, about the middle of the tenth century, the schoolmen returned to the writings of the master in this department, Cicero.

In arithmetic, the operations were exceedingly im perfect and clumsy until the celebrated Gerbert (Sylvester II.) was led, by his love of learning, to leave his monastery, Fleury, and crossed the Pyrenees to Cordova, in order there to learn from the Arabians. He brought back with him the Arabian figures, and with them a new and far more easy method of calculation.

Geometry was very imperfectly taught from a wretchedly meager abridgment of Euclid, until the same Gerbert gave a new impulse to this study, as he had done to arithmetic In astronomy, nothing worth mentioning was accomplished, astrological superstitions being more in vogue than anything like scientific observation.

To Gregory the Great belongs the merit of having, on the basis of the ancient tunes, completely introduced sacred music among Christians, for the use of the ecclesiastical institutions and the schools, and for the purposes of public worship. Rome therefore became the principal seat of sacred music, especially vocal, but also instrumental; and this city was therefore much frequented by those who desired to learn thoroughly this valuable art. Charlemagne imported singers from Rome, and introduced the improved church music, with the institutions necessary for its cultivation, in Metz. In England, also, a Roman singing-school was established in the monastery of Weremouth.

Instrumental music was cultivated in monasteries, at the courts of princes, by knights, ladies, and itinerant harpers; and the instruments mostly in use were the harp, the guitar, and the lute.

The other sciences were not studied in the schools. Little progress was made in geography. History consisted of little more than legends and chronicles, although Bede, who had opened a broader path, found some followers. Notwithstanding the host of the most absurd superstitions, and the prevailing faith in magic and black arts, there was some advancement made in physics: witness John Scotus and Albertus Magnus. Medicine was chiefly practised by the ecclesiastics. It was more frequently studied with care by Jews, who often attained the station of court-physician. By the Arabians a new impulse was given to the study of this science.

At the University of Paris theology was treated in a scientific manner, the effect of which was not favourable to the religious culture of the people. More salutary was the influence of the practice, which began in the thirteenth century, of preaching in the vernacular language of Germany; and in the fourteenth century, the celebrated John Tauler laboured in Strasburg, with great acceptance and effect, as a powerful pulpit-orator, and some of his writings are still read with profit. The most important, perhaps we ought to say the only, pedagogic writer of the Middle Ages was Vincentius de Beauvais, who flourished about the middle of the thirteenth century, under Loius IX. and his daughter Margaret. He published a copious encyclopedia, entitled Speculum Majus. But more important in the history of pedagogics is his work on the education of the children of kings, dedicated to Margaret of France. This work has sterling value, and, bating the monkish principles of the age, deserves a place among the most recent productions on pedagogics.

SECTION III.

Education strives to become Free, and to liberate the Human Mind from the mediæval Thraldom. The Gospel emancipated from Papal Bondage. From A.D. 1350–1520.

The reader who is familiar with the period which is referred to at the head of this section, will be aware that any attempt to present a comprehensive view of its pedagogic history would lead us into extended discussions and almost endless details. Within its limits occur many and highly-honoured names: it embraces educational developments, and events in the Church and the state, of the utmost importance to the Christian culture of the human race. But, as it is our principal purpose here to give an account of Christian education in its more recent developments, in the more matured state in which it presents itself within the latest times, that is to say, since the labours of Lord Bacon, we shall offer no farther apology for the meager sketch which is here subjoined.

Not only had Christianity now been fully introduced among those European nations which had formed the Western Roman Empire, but the Gospel had been employed as the immediate means of civilizing others which had never bowed the neck under the Roman yoke, so that the Christian religion may be said to have, by this time, been the religion of Europe. But, although it was thus outwardly received, the nations of Europe were as yet far from having imbibed, or so much as adequately comprehended, its true spirit: its transforming power was yet far from having pervaded and completely renovated the public, the social, the domestic, and private life of those nations who called themselves Christian. This was, of course, in a high degree, owing to the inherent corruption and depravity of human nature, which did not and could not immediately be made to harmonize with that "perfect law of liberty." Other causes, political and moral, and especially, also, the character and methods of popular and (so-styled) learned education, combined to obstruct the progress of Christianity in the hearts of men, in the life of nations. But this was not all, nor the worst. Christianity itself had come to the nations of Europe enveloped in the superstitions, burdened with the corruptions, bedizzened with the sumptuous trappings of papal Rome; and the light of the Gospel was hid, if not under a bushel, under the triple crown of the pretended vicegerent of Christ. On this subject we need not expatiate; it is, in general, well understood. All the institutions that had sprung up — monasteries, universities, popular schools — were involved in a night of ignorance, superstition, and semi-barbarism; and those who set up for teachers and guides were little less blind than those whom they pretended to guide and instruct. Yet was the light of the Gospel not extinguished: it shone forth, here and there, in the words and lives of illustrious men, who glowed with a holy zeal for the glory of God, and the emancipation of men from the intellectual and spiritual bondage which bowed them to the earth. If the occasional labours and public avowals of such men of God furnished evidence that the light of truth was yet present in the Church, and betokened its bursting forth, in due time, from the midnight clouds which encompassed it, there was one circumstance which signally contributed to prepare men to hail with gratitude and joy that new and glorious day, by dispelling, in a great measure, the mists of ignorance; by liberating, to a great extent, from the bondage of superstition, numbers whose influence would be widely felt; and by introducing at the universities better things in the place of the dialectic games of the scholastics. We speak of the revival of classical studies which preceded the great revival of evangelical religion in the reformation of the sixteenth century.

First in order of time among those who powerfully contributed to this revival of classical learning is the celebrated Petrarch, born Aug. 1, 1304, at Arezzo, in Italy. He was himself a truly eminent poet; and profoundly intimate with the Roman classics, and averse to scholasticism, he strenuously recommended a prompt return to the healthful fountains of antiquity. He therefore gave the first impulse to those classical studies which are so inseparably connected with the higher culture of modern times.

Among the Italians, two other celebrated poets, Boccacio, the friend of Petrarch, and Dante, powerfully contributed to the revival of elegant literature. An important influence was exerted in the same direction by another Italian scholar of great learning and genius, Vittorino da Feltre, who was eminently distinguished as an educator of youth, whom he instructed in the sciences, and initiated in the spirit of classic antiquity. In this path he was followed by other distinguished men, especially Niccolo Niccoli, through whose exertions, and those of his pupils, Florence became the seat of classical learning under the splendid house of the Medici.

In the Netherlands, a similar revival of liberal learning, embracing theology and philosophy, was developed under the guidance of gifted men. The most celebrated among these, the one whose influence was most extensive, was Erasmus of Rotterdam. His connexion with classical learning, his ambiguous position in reference to the reformation, his friendly relations with some of the reformers, are matters of history, and well known.

Among the distinguished Germans who were prominently active in this great movement for the emancipation of human culture, none is more deservedly celebrated than John Reuchlin, born at Pforzheim, in Baden, Dec. 28, 1445. His exertions for promoting the study of the Greek language were specially important, and, to some extent, eminently successful.

Highly distinguished in this connexion were John Colet, an Englishman, and the intimate friend of Erasmus; and Luis Vives, a Spaniard. The school (St. Paul's School) which the former, as Dean of St. Paul's, founded in London, still flourishes, and enjoys a high reputation. The latter was the author of some important works on pedagogics and educational methods, and many of his rules have been placed to the credit of modern writers on these subjects.

The impulse which the labours of such men had given to the culture of Europe was very extensively felt, and productive of highly beneficial effects: it had commenced the emancipation of the human mind from the shackles of scholasticism, and the overthrow of monastic dungeons. But the restoration of classical studies could not remedy the evils under which society groaned, could not regenerate that public life which was thoroughly corrupt in all its institutions. The liberty of the mind is a gift of Heaven, and belongs to the destination of our race. But no classical studies could achieve that liberty which harmonizes with law, and practises self-government and self-denial. This could come only by restoring to the pure Gospel of Christ, that "power of God," its due influence on society, in all its classes and relations. "If the Son shall make you free, ye shall be free indeed." This truth was felt by many of those enlightened men, so that there arose an increased tendency to return to apostolical Christianity. There were many among the people, also, who felt this, and to whom the corruptions of the Church became daily more intolerable.

And that great change, for which there had thus been some preparation, now came, in all its power and glory, in the reformation of the sixteenth century.

On the labours of the reformers for the regeneration of human culture, we shall not dwell. They must be familiar to most of our readers. Through their influence, not only the Church, but the entire system of education, experienced a reformation. New schools were founded, old ones thoroughly remodelled, and real, efficient schoolmen, of sound principles and large views, took the lead, especially in Germany, in the business of education. The most distinguished among the schoolmen of the age immediately succeeding the reformation were Johannes Sturm and

Valentine Friedland, commonly called Trotzendorf, from the place of his nativity. Other great names might be mentioned, besides a long list of learned philologists, who contributed, in the capacity of professors and of authors, to the complete revival of liberal education. It must, however, be observed, that the labours of these men had reference, chiefly, to the higher seminaries of learning.

Thus, towards the end of the sixteenth century, the new culture had completely established itself in Germany, France, the Netherlands, and other countries of Western Europe. The classic literature was the cultivating principle, and with this the Reformation formed an intimate alliance. The Protestant teachers too well appreciated the high aim which the mind, imbued with the Grecian and Roman literature, attains, that they should not have made it the principal subject of the instruction of youth. Those schoolmen should not, therefore, be blamed, if they were too partially devoted to this one subject. Their labours hastened the coming of that day, in which profound reflection, and a comprehensive, experimental development of principles led to the adoption of an enlarged, and liberal, and sound method, embracing every department of the culture of man.

It is well known that this revival of education, produced by the reformation, aroused also the Catholic Church to adopt, in sheer self-defence, an enlarged and improved system, and that soon the Jesuits became the educators of the Roman Catholic world. The excellence of their educational system, and especially of their methods of instruction, even their enemies can scarcely call in question ; yet their pedagogics had great defects, and their general mischievous purposes were betrayed, to a great extent, in their labours as educators.

During the Middle Ages, for centuries before the Reformation, the student-life had been, as we have in some measure seen, one of wanton indulgence in erratic propensities, of confusion, and riot. The teachers of schools, both in city and country, were, for the most part, itinerant students, who, either having some other personal interest in view, or receiving a very scanty compensation for their labours, either neglected their business, or, rude in manners, tyrannized over their pupils, or disagreed, in one way or another, with their employers, so that little was effected, and things perpetually grew worse; or, if men of letters and principle undertook the office of teacher, they were often treated with ingratitude and contumely, so that those who were fit to teach had no inducements to devote themselves to so thankless a business. But since the emancipation of educational culture, down to the beginning of the seventeenth century, many improvements had been made, and a better order of things had supervened. There were public schools of different kinds, higher and lower, both in cities and in the country; and here and there, also, female seminaries. Besides these, a variety of other arrangements and institutions for the purposes of education grew into vogue, all which introduced a time of inquiry and reflection, in which men could select, from a multitude of methods, those which seemed best, form various combinations, and strike out new paths. The importance of the business of education was more and more understood and felt.

As regards the subjects of instruction, these had become more and more extended, and undergone various changes with the developments of the times. The following sketch follows the order of the ancient encyclopedia.

Grammar was taught in the old fashion; but, after the art of writing had been introduced in the city-schools, and especially after the press had more and more separated it from instruction in reading, this study was treated as a distinct branch, and now the children were taught to spell and to read by means of printed primers.

In teaching children to write, the ancient tricks of stenography and the like were abandoned, and due attention was paid to a good current hand. In arith metic a more suitable method was adopted, and, at the same time, its higher departments were more cultivated.

In geometry the instruction was wretched, as unmethodical as possible, so that very few acquired any knowledge of it. Geography and history were treated as distinct branches of study in the schools of the Jesuits: they were introduced elsewhere, for the first time, by a pupil of Trotzendorf, between 1530 and 1543, in the school at Sorau. Astronomy had been abandoned by the schools; but astrology and alchymy continued to be, even in the sixteenth century, the favourite study of deep thinkers.

Mnemonics was very generally cultivated at this period in Italy, and secretly, also, in the monasteries.

A new and highly important addition had been made in religious instruction. With a view to this, the reformers, or, rather, the great reformer himself, had drawn up and introduced the catechism; and, lastly, the progress of culture to greater freedom became manifest in the reference which school-instruction had to the common affairs of life. Since the appearance of Reynard the Fox, the Germans had cultivated the department of literature to which this admirable poem belongs, and been eminently successful in the production of instructive fables; and the young were now made acquainted with the well-known collection of Æsopian fables. If these productions were not actually used in the schools, they were collected in books, and extensively circulated among the young.

SECTION IV.

Methodic Pedagogists and their Labours.

This new spring which had arisen on the culture of Christendom was broken in upon by dark and portentous clouds; peace and war alternated in various parts, but especially in the centre of Europe, until the fearful storm of the Thirty Years' War devastated the states of Germany. The effects of this convulsion on the culture and the educational institutions of central Euurope are easily imagined: yet these evil consequences were not as extensive as might have been expected. Something still continued to be done for education; and some sections of Germany, which had almost entirely escaped the general devastation, had not ceased to offer asylums to the sciences. The interest which had been excited for the culture of man had not expired; and when, in 1648, the peace of Westphalia restored repose to Germany, and security to the Protestant Church, the business of educa tion was resumed with unabated zeal and energy.

Since then, the culture of man, which had itself been emancipated from oppressive bondage, tended to the complete liberation of the human mind from all extraneous fetters. It first exhibited this tendency in its opposition to ancient usages in education; against practices which had nothing but their age to recommend them; for, soon after the culture of Christian nations had been thus emancipated from thraldom, education became the subject of enlightened and profound reflection, and the judgment of men respecting it shook off the prejudices, the bias of ages. The energies of the learned and wise were directed to the detection of errors and defects, to the rejection of much that was timeworn and superannuated, and to attempts at improvement. New methods were devised, and systems of education constructed; but there was, in general, more of criticism, more subversion of individual practices that were deemed objectionable, than of judicious effort at organization and construction. Yet men were now coming to these better efforts. The first part of the period now before us is therefore characterized by inquiries and experiments, and by critical reflection on the idea of education; to the second part will belong the complete development, and introduction into theory, instruction, and life, of this idea. We can scarcely be said to have advanced beyond the threshold of this second division of the period under consideration, and we have therefore reached the last epoch of our pedagogic history, in which we have three sections: the first, as stated above, treating of experiments in new methods; the second exhibiting new views on education; and the third presenting efforts at combining education and instruction, and thus, also, at reforming public schools.

Innovations as respects method consisted, in the first place, in alterations made in the ancient encyclopedism, and in general, in the mode of treating the sciences. And the first who distinguished himself in this path was the celebrated Lord Bacon, lord privy seal and chancellor of England, who was born A.D. 1560, and died in 1626. He was one of the most learned among men, and his acute mind clearly discerned the defects which burdened the learned culture of his, and of past times. He complained that too much attention was devoted to languages, and that, meanwhile, practical matters, important to human life, were entirely neglected; that philosophy, instead of seeking after truth, had fallen into the mischievous nonsense of scholasticism; that teachers followed undeviatingly the old and beaten path, while pupils bowed in slavish submission to the authority of their teachers; that, nevertheless, it was common to form hasty opinions and rash judgments; that the scholar did not sufficiently confine himself to some particular branch of science, and usually had not the proper aim in view, inasmuch as either vanity, or self-interest, or, at best, a love of amusement, was generally the motive. These and other like complaints were loudly raised by Bacon; and in opposition to all this, he propounded his own positive idea of improvement, of a thorough reform. This he did especially in his Novum Organum Scientiarum, which sets out with the principle that man is to be only the servant of nature, both in knowledge and action. In this great work he presented a new division of the sciences, arranged under the three principal intellectual faculties, memory, imagination, and reason. Although in his encyclopedic view there was yet much left to be desired, it yet created, as it were, new sciences; and, what is more, it roused a new spirit, which brought forth new thought, and which, while it produced a complete revolution in academic lectures, and in all matters of science as treated in the schools, yet tended too much to empty abstractions. As it was his fundamental idea that in a perfect system nature itself would appear, and that, therefore, the classification of the sciences, and the process of their acquisition, would coincide, he yet also considered adaptation to nature as involving the necessity of paying due attention to the progressive development of the child, and to the principles of psychology: and thus he decidedly distinguished a twofold course of instruction, the scientific and the pedagogic; and from this he developed his principles of education, which coincided, in general, with those of the Jesuits. The work in which these principles are exhibited is entitled, "De Dignitate et Augmentis Scientiarum," and is one of the most important in the history and progress of pedagogics.

In Germany there soon arose men who ardently desired the introduction of a complete pedagogic method, and who were zealous advocates of the cultivation and improvement of the language of their country, which had so long been supplanted, in matters of science and literature, by the Latin. The first among these men was Wolfgang Ratich, born 1570, at Wilster, in Holstein. The universal complaints about the great defects of the school-instruction of his day stimulated him to the attempt to introduce a better method: and with a view to prepare himself for this undertaking, he visited Holland, and England, and other countries, spending thirteen years in these travels. He commenced his operations in his thirty-second year, found favour in various high quarters, and excited a great deal of attention wherever he appeared. He had, undoubtedly, many correct views, and manifested a good deal of skill in the application of his principles; but a great mistake was made, in that his method was employed only in instructing adults. He was not entirely free from charlatanry; and being, withal, of a quarrelsome disposition, and totally destitute of judgment and tact in managing his assistants, he soon fell into disgrace, met with opposition everywhere, and died, abandoned by nearly all his former friends, in 1635, as a pedagogic adventurer. He was soon so utterly forgotten, that his age has, and no doubt justly, been accused of having been rather ungrateful towards him; for, a century and a half later, other pedagogists met with far better success, with methods much like his; and he may be regarded as the founder of the modern didactics, or art of instruction, as appears from his numerous writings.

The next pedagogist of importance was Christopher Helwig, born 1581, near Frankfort on the Mayne, and professor at Giessen. He was a man from whom much was to be expected for education, but, in consequence of excessive exertion, he died at an early age, and before his views and plans could be fairly tested.

After him, Amos Comenius, of Comna, in Moravia, born 1592, was highly distinguished in the business of education, on which he entered in early life. After encountering various vicissitudes and severe trials, he went to Lissa, in Poland, where he soon after became president of the school in that place, and bishop of the Moravian brethren, in the early history of whose peculiar pedagogic system he shines as a star of the first magnitude. He now wrote his great work, one of the most important in the history of pedagogics, which, as the title indicates, was to unlock the door for the acquisition of all languages: "Janua Reserata Linguarum," &c.

Comenius was about thirty-five years of age when he came to Lissa. His work soon carried his fame to foreign lands, and everywhere the necessity of a reform in education began to be more deeply felt, and first of all in England. By an act of Parliament, this worthy man was, in 1631, invited to England, and received with every mark of respect in London. His ideas would probably have been realized in that country, had not disturbances in Ireland interrupted, and eventually altogether suspended the meditated reform; and even to this day England has not organized a public system of school-education.

Comenius now laboured in Sweden, where he was again interrupted by war, which induced him to return to Lissa. From here the Prince of Transylvania called him to Patak, in order to organize the college which was established there; and during four years he here prosecuted his efforts in behalf of education with considerable success, and wrote, among other works, his celebrated Orbis Pictus, which has passed through a great many editions, and survived a multitude of imitations. He now returned to Lissa, where he enjoyed a few years of repose in his episcopal office. But the disturbances which broke out in 1656, between the Moravian Protestants and the Polish Catholics, brought upon him various misfortunes: his house, his library, and, worst of all, his manuscripts, the labour of ten years, were consumed by fire. Having found an asylum in Amsterdam, he reproduced his pedagogic works, which from 1657 appeared in print. But he suffered many persecutions on account of his faith; for he was a man of deep piety, although his luxuriant imagination led him to the adoption of some extravagant notions. He died at Amsterdam in 1671, at the age of eighty, after an eventful life. The great idea by which this life was animated was the promotion of the happiness of the whole human race by education, and the adoption of methodical instruction from earliest childhood. This idea was expressed in his writings with all the clearness and completeness that could be expected in that age, and all his efforts were directed against the indolent trifling of existing methods, and the realization of his better views; and the influence of his writings and labours is more or less visible in the educational arrangements of our day. The labours of Comenius may be called the clear and distinct expression of a state of public sentiment, which was a necessary phenomenon in the development of European education. It is only when brought into connexion with Bacon's psychological views on the one hand, and the modern pedagogic views on the other, that they are duly appreciated. The triad comprises the whole of what the age of new and improved methods brought forth respecting the idea of education. Subsequent efforts consist only in controversy, in farther improvements, and in finishing touches.

This combination appears first in the educational views and principles of Montaigne and of Locke.

1. Michel E. de Montaigne was born 1533, at Perigord, and died 1592. His father, who had peculiar and sound views on education, and was deeply sensible of the great defects of the prevailing methods of instruction, gave his son, in early childhood, a German tutor, who educated his pupil in a manner very different from that generally in vogue. Montaigne wrote a book of essays, abounding in moral and religious reflections, and which, though altogether deficient in respect of the religious element, contain many valuable thoughts on pedagogics. But we cannot present even an abstract of his views on education, as our limits admonish us to hasten to a more important writer. The writings of Montaigne were productive of fruit out of his own country. His principles were first made use of in England, for the development of a system of education that has become the most important, by one of the most eminent philosophers and most cultivated men of his age.

2. This man was John Locke, who was born in 1632. He was sent to the Westminster school, under whose vigorous discipline he remained till his nineteenth year. After he had spent some time on the Continent, and afterward continued his studies at Oxford, he experienced various reverses of fortune, which grew out of his connexion with Lord Shaftesbury, who was his warm friend and benefactor. Having returned, in 1689, to England, which he had been more than once obliged to leave, he declined the public employments that were offered him, and took up his abode in a family of noble friends in Essex. Here he wrote several political treatises, and also his im-

portant pedagogic work, which appeared in 1693, in the form of letters to his friend Clarke, and under the title, Thoughts Concerning the Education of Children. In the following year appeared his celebrated Essay on the Human Understanding, which work also imbodies the spirit of his views on education. His peculiar views made Locke a welcome teacher to the new pedagogic spirit, which desired to confine its attention to the sphere of common life, and to reject as fanaticism all elevation to ideals. Yet in this respect his pedagogic principles have been very much misapprehended. Locke died as a true Christian, in the midst of the study of the Bible, A.D. 1704, and at the age of seventy-two years. His book on education begins with the principle, Sana mens in corpore sano: a healthy soul (mind) in a healthy body. Thus this principle of the ancients, which especially the legislation of Lycurgus had so distinctly avowed, was again expressly recommended by Locke to modern educators. Of his pedagogic views we present the following summary:

I. Physical education. He recommends rather too decidedly that children should be made hardy.

II. In cultivating the mind, habit, in respect of the desires or appetites, is of paramount importance.

III. He protests against the abuse of corporeal punishments and of rewards, and inculcates liberal, but not lax principles. He warns against the influence of domestics.

IV. Children should have but few rules given them, but the observance of these should be insisted on and enforced. It is best if their own habits lead them to the discovery of rules and laws. The child should be kindly treated, and in accordance with its individuality. All affectation is to be guarded against, and a natural and beautiful development of the inner man to be promoted.

V. For the acquisition of good manners he recommends the dancing-master and the example of good society, but protests against children being required to conform to conventional forms.

VI. He strongly urges the advantages of domestic education. In schools, good manners are too much sacrificed to Latin and Greek. He disapproves of boarding-schools, both on account of the numbers that frequent them, and for other reasons.

VII. In respect of pardonable and punishable faults of the young, and their general treatment, his views are liberal, and generally sound; but some are decidedly erroneous, and have been productive of mischief. Towards children who are too lazy to learn, he is rather too liberal of blows.

VIII. A governor or private tutor should possess knowledge of the world and refined manners. If he be a man of talent, his instructions will soon enable the boy to help himself.

IX. Confidence between parents and children, in their mutual intercourse, is strongly recommended.

X. The love of ruling, and selfishness, should be suppressed in children: covetousness should not be encouraged: their real wants should be provided for: they should be habituated to modesty, and their complaints against others not always listened to: conscientious honesty, and, at the same time, liberality in giving, should be encouraged in them.

XI. The screaming and crying of children should be prevented.

XII. Both fear and courage are good; but effeminacy and extremes must be guarded against.

XIII. Children should not be suffered to be cruel towards animals, and kindness towards servants should be inculcated.

XIV. As respects the desire of knowledge and indolent inattention, his observations are less profound than those of later writers.

XV. Children should not receive too many toys, and, in general, be induced to make them themselves.

XVI. Children must learn to regard lying as unnatural and detestable.

XVII. Religion and virtue should be promoted by simple views, which may be occasionally communicated. At the same time, the child should be taught to pray, to speak the truth, and to exercise love towards all. They should never hear a word about ghosts.

XVIII. The child should be taught to be prudent, but not cunning.

XIX. The outward deportment of children should be equally remote from impudence or presumption, and awkwardness.

XX. As respects the method of instruction, his views are, in general, very correct, and many of his rules exceedingly judicious and valuable. Some of them have been much misapprehended and misapplied. He considers the desire of applause and praise as the strongest motive to urge the young to strive after perfection. If it be the strongest, it would be a monstrous pedagogic error to regard it as the best.

At the close, Locke acknowledges the defects of his work, and admits that much remains to be determined according to the individual peculiarities of children. Would that the German pedagogists of his school had always borne in mind this modest and candid admission of their great master!

SECTION V.

Modern Development of the Idea of Education.

We have seen that earnest inquiry and diligent search after improvements in the culture of youth, and especially with respect to the method of instruction, had been awakened, and the efforts that were made promised great results: but these promises were not fulfilled. Had the classics been studied in the right spirit, and the Gospel appreciated and improved as it ought to be, the result would have been different: but this was not done. The fundamental principle of human culture had not even been, as yet, clearly apprehended, to say nothing of its being brought into connexion with the increase of knowledge. If there had not been an actual retrograde movement, it is yet certain that the root of culture, religion, and the sweet odour of its developed blossom, taste, had, notwithstanding the evident increase of knowledge, rather retrograded than advanced. The evidence of this is found in the controversies of the theologians and of the philologists in the seventeenth century, and even later.

The malady of vanity and self-conceit, the most pernicious to men of learning, appeared in a new, at one time offensive, at another, ridiculous form—namely, pedantry. Schoolmen, principals of seminaries, became the laughing-stock of the public, and pedagogues and pedants were held up to ridicule on the stage; and thus even men of genuine scholarship and sterling worth were involved in the common contempt. Such men strove earnestly to call forth a better state of things, and to promote a spirited and tasteful study of the classics. But such a change requires time, and the proper study of the classics did not make much progress. In France and elsewhere it even met with opponents, among whom Perrault was the most prominent. His opinions were controverted by Boileau.

In England, as witnessed by Swift's "Battle of Books," and in Germany, these controversies respecting the comparative merits of the ancients and moderns were also prosecuted.

If the good cause always does triumph in the end, it is often long enough persecuted and desecrated by the mob, the profanum vulgus. And thus classical studies were indeed extolled in France, England, Germany, and elsewhere, as the fountain of taste, and even better taught in the schools; yet by many they were still viewed in a false light, or clumsily treated by pedants, and abused, even down to the latest times, by impure worshippers, to the still greater perversion of inflated boys.

In France, the false taste went hand in hand with irreligion, with infidelity, and brought forth idols to suit the popular spirit. A principle of disruption pervaded the culture of Europe, and purged away, as men fondly believed, a great deal of dross, and only about the end of the eighteenth century the loss of the good was felt: but this principle contained also a stimulating power to excite reaction. Men, highly and thoroughly cultivated by the classic spirit, soon stood forth, prominent and illustrious, in England, although in the colleges the ancient pedantry still practised its antics. In other countries, also, sound philologists arose. Germany especially now became the great arena for the enactment of all sorts of literary and pedagogic manœuvres. German industry, combined with great susceptibility of culture and depth of feeling, did indeed possess itself of all the treasures of foreign culture; but it strayed also too far into the stern asperities of controversy respecting matters unworthy of serious consideration, and neglected too much that Socratic irony, which should always distinguish the more eminent scholars.

In the past arrangements of the Church and the scholastic system, the mind had gained too little in true piety, although efforts had not been wanting in this respect, also, to improve the schools. While the theologians were addicted to controversy, religious instruction was, for the most part, left to unlettered schoolmasters, or treated by clergymen in a lifeless or even controversial manner. It was high time that something should be done on all hands for education in this most important concern. And now, in the providence of God, two men appeared, the one a Protestant, the other a Catholic, in whom the spirit of the Gospel was alive and operative, and whose names are illustrious in the history of education.

The first was Philip J. Spener, born at Rappoltsweiler, in the Alsace, in 1635. He was distinguished from his early youth, not only for his ardent love of knowledge, but for his fervent piety. Having finished his academic studies, and spent some time in travel, he became preacher and doctor of theology at Strasburg, and soon after, in 1666, he accepted a call as Senior, to Frankfurt on the Mayne, where his kindly but vigorous activity produced great effects. He contended against the prevailing spirit of controversy, and by his mild but energetic labours effected an extensive revival of evangelical religion in Germany. Denounced as a mystic, he persevered in his course, and became the founder, by his example and through his writings, of the German system of catechetical instruction. His influence for good was great and deep. He died in the triumphs of Christian faith, in 1705, at Berlin.

The other benefactor of his race was the celebrated Francois Salignac de la Motte Fenelon, born 1651, at Perigord. He was a man whose extraordinary excellence of character extorted admiration even from the infidel Voltaire. His little pedagogic work, De l'Education des Filles, induced Louis XIV. to appoint him tutor to his three princes. For their benefit he wrote the universally known work entitled Telemaque. Though this eventually brought him into disgrace at court, and exiled him to his diocese, he was in no wise disturbed, but pursued, through good and through evil report, the even tenour of his benevolent, his truly Christian life, and died at the age of sixty-three years. His two pedagogic works still continue to exert a healthful influence.

But the most important attempt to supply a want universally felt, by the establishment of a truly Christian school, was now at hand, and two men arose whose efforts in behalf of Christian education deserve our most grateful acknowledgments.

1. Augustus Hermann Franke, born 1663, at Lubec, was distinguished at an early age for deep piety and a vigorous spirit of enterprise. By his zealous efforts to promote vital piety, he accomplished much good in various places as a preacher of the Gospel, made many friends, and raised up troops of enemies.

After preaching some time at Erfurt, he accepted an invitation to the newly-founded university of Halle as preacher, and professor of the Greek and Oriental languages, and afterward of theology.

The religious influence which he exerted in this place was productive of deep and abiding results. But the great work which he accomplished here was the establishment of the far-famed asylum and school for orphans, which he succeeded in erecting, amid innumerable difficulties. Yet, notwithstanding he often lacked means, which were as often providentially supplied, the work went forward rapidly: the foundations were laid in 1698, and as early as 1700 the large building was already occupied. The establishment consisted of a number of connected institutions, not only for orphan boys and girls, but for poor students: the pædagogium regium; a seminary for teachers and educators; a collegium orientale; one of the most extensive book and printing establishments, an apothecary's office, and other benevolent and highly useful institutions, all founded, sustained, and more and more perfected by this one man. The institution soon numbered among its beneficiaries two hundred orphans: sometimes nearly two thousand pupils received instruction here at a time: in the higher schools alone there were sometimes five hundred students and one hundred teachers, who here trained themselves for the business of instruction. Franke died in 1727, aged sixty-four, and his institution continued, after his death, to flourish amid frequent storms. But the spirit which had directed its affairs at the beginning, departed with subsequent developments of the age. However great and beneficial had been the influence of Franke and of his institution, which was the first orphan asylum in Germany, and in which education was treated *on a truly Christian plan*, though in a manner too contracted and one-sided, neither the culture of youth nor the cultivation of piety continued to advance and prosper to the extent desired by the wise and good; and a desire universally prevailed that good schools might be established, *that education might be brought into fit connexion with instruction, and that thus religious culture might be brought into closer union with the scientific and classic culture of youth.* If this was the object which Franke had aimed at, it was, to a far greater extent, attained by the distinguished personage of whom we are now to speak.

2. The idea of a culture of man proceeding from a

religious centre, or of education on a Christian basis, was first distinctly seized upon by a man of Franke's school, who, with a profound apprehension of the distinctive peculiarities of Christianity, sought to develop and realize this idea with greater consistency. This man was Count Nicholas L. de Zinzendorf, who had received his school-education in Franke's pædagogium regium at Halle, and whose mind was so deeply affected and penetrated by the Christian spirit that prevailed there, that he conceived, with striking clearness, his great idea, and, through the energy of his character, and the wealth which he possessed, succeeded to admiration in giving it a real and tangible existence. He founded at Herrnhuth, in Saxony, the religious society known as the Church of the United, or Moravian Brethren, which soon sent out branches, not only throughout Germany, but to the remotest parts of the world. And thus the spirit of vital piety was once again revived, and various edifying developments were witnessed in different places. Zinzendorf's idea was, a sodality, or association of like-minded Christians, which, even in their external organization and arrangements, should fully express the spirit of their faith; a Protestant-Christian Pythagoræism, far more elevated and pure than the monastic institutions of earlier times, and exhibiting, in every respect, its great superiority to the institutions of the Jesuits; for the Brethren's Church tended more to the inward life, to the repose of the soul, and to external tranquillity, and thus came but little into collision with the state; while the Jesuits aimed at an external life of their religious society, which brought even states into peril. Education in the Brethren's Church was more complete, because it took up and treated the child from its earliest existence, and embraced also the family relation: the culture of the Jesuits, *so far as it was good*, was purely scholastic; in other respects, political, moral, and religious, their influence was evil, and tended to evil.

The institutions of education at Barby, Neuwied, Niesky, Hennersdorf, Montmirail, &c., manifest this spirit to the present day, and a number of the most distinguished men in Germany, among whom are some celebrated philosophers, owe to these institutions their earlier culture.* The pedagogic principles and arrangements, notwithstanding their general excellence, could not deny their one-sidedness, and have, through the influence of the later pedagogics, undergone various improvements. The great principle of this system is, to make Christianity, in its most definite and positive form, that of true inward piety, the principle of education, as well as of the whole life. Both the negative and positive arrangements adopted for the attainment of this object, and the general discipline of these institutions, have, in the main, been well adapted to the end in view; and although the general character of these institutions has doubtless undergone considerable changes with the alterations in the spirit of the times, they must still be ranked among the best and most efficient, both as regards scholastic instruction and general education, that modern times have produced.

These, then, were the attempts at improving education from a decidedly religious point of influence and operation. But the spirit of the age pressed forward more strenuously in a different direction, and thus arose the new pedagogics.

SECTION VI.

THE NEW PEDAGOGICS.

Thus men sought and hoped for improvements, and had dim and remote views of what was wanting; various good things were brought to light, but still the right thing was not yet found. The school of Halle and the Moravian Church had opened up a new path for the culture of youth; but here also there were de-

* The Moravians have similar institutions in this country: a boarding-school for boys at Nazareth, and female boarding-schools at Bethlehem and at Litiz, in Pennsylvania, and another at Salem, in North Carolina. The first two were established about the middle of the last century. These schools have a deservedly high reputation, and are in a flourishing condition.

vious movements, and the great goal was yet far from being distinctly in sight. But the demands of the age were pressing, not only for improvements in the narrow circle of existing schools, but for efficient institutions for the education and culture of the people at large. The defects in the prevailing state of things were many and great, and were, by many, deeply felt. Religion especially was too much a matter of mere doctrinal belief and of lifeless forms, as though Christianity were not designed to influence and mould the whole life of man, and to manifest its divine power to sanctify, in all his relations and circumstances. Theological controversies were the order of the day; and so deficient were the great majority of schools, whether high or low; so little, in general, were the instruction and example of teachers in accordance with the precepts, the spirit, the great design of the Gospel, that the earnest complaints of wise and good men were growing louder and louder. Among these was that eminent man of God, Spener. From among his many bitter lamentations we select only the following passage: "Must we not be surprised that nearly all the industry of the schools is bestowed upon Latium, so that little is left for Hellas, and scarcely any at all for Judea? I will not farther speak of the other defects of the schools, which they have in common with the other modes of life, inasmuch as the vicious desires, which gain strength with age, break forth more and more in impudence and other unseemly manifestations, and yet are not restrained with becoming zeal and with pious wisdom; for the more there are in the schools, all being creatures depraved by nature, the more prosperously, or, rather, unprosperously does wickedness thrive and increase, the profligacy of the one supplying what is lacking to the impudence of the other; if not by great wisdom, which, indeed, is more than human, and must be sought of God, the tender, and, therefore, yet docile minds are led from this corruption of the age to real virtue and piety. But since, for this purpose, the holy example of the teachers is necessary, it is obvious to every judicious person what mischief must accrue to the public good from the circumstance, that among those who teach in the schools numbers are found who do not at all know what it is to be a Christian, and who are, therefore, still less Christians themselves, and hence totally unfit for the wholesome performance of the duties of their office ; and, lastly, whereas, in domestic education, the boys are chiefly urged to do what is required of them by stimulating their desire of praise and distinction, whereby they are, at the same time, filled with the unhappy seeds of ambition, it grieves me that the same procedure is continued in the schools. Such being the case, it is but too true that young men often leave the schools quite unlearned, inasmuch as God withholds his blessing from the industry of those who prefer all other things to him: intimate indeed, to a considerable extent, with other departments of knowledge, yet not with those which they will always need, but without knowing God, while, on the other hand, they are immersed in the love of the world and in the desire to please it ; wise in their own conceits, but, alas! the more unfit for the divine wisdom. What, then, do the efforts of the professors benefit their hearers, except that they fill their brains with what I am fain to call a theological philosophy, or a human expertness in holy things, while their hearts are empty of all true heavenly knowledge! And it is a fact that, at this present time, the youth bring away from the majority of schools more that is heathenish than of what is Christian, so that the fears of the far-seeing Erasmus are but in too high a degree fulfilled, inasmuch as he somewhere declares that his pleasure at witnessing the progress of certain studies in his day was considerably diminished by the apprehension that gradually much heathenism would insinuate itself in the minds," &c.

By many other voices complaints had been raised respecting the corruption of the clergy, the schools, and the universities. A reform was needed, and this want was deeply felt. The mind, liberated from its bondage, had in education, as well as in other matters, adopted partial views, and employed itself with one-sided developments. Men began to perceive that it was necessary to bring the schools into due connexion with the concerns of life; but the right way had not yet been found of carrying out the culture of youth from this only true starting-point. From this point proceeded two divergent courses of education: the one advocating the farther development, on improved methods, of the principle of culture hitherto recognised; the other aiming at the complete adoption of the new principle, which had, for some time past, been brought into action. Both these directions soon became still more divergent; the former, indeed, dividing into two distinct branches, which, however, at no time diverged as much from each other as the latter did from both these; and thus there soon arose, one after another, three principal systems in respect of schools and education. The first proceeded from piety, which had been extensively revived through the restoration to the Gospel of its influence upon mankind; the second proceeded, in like manner, from the revived study of the classics; the third adopted the new encyclopedism as its basis. It has been usual to denominate the first the Pietistic, the second the Humanistic system of pedagogics; by analogy, and without intending any severe reflection, the third will be here styled the Egotistic system. A fourth might yet be adopted, namely, the Eclectic; but this is not, in reality, a system: it is rather the mode of thinking of those teachers who do not approve of the sharply-drawn distinctions of one-sidedness, but reserve to themselves an unbiased judgment, and, while they connect themselves with no particular party, recognise that which is good in each. But such Eclectics, so-called, who indiscriminately adopt whatsoever, upon a superficial view, appears valuable, do not at all deserve a place here.

A new epoch usually derives its form and character from the circumstance that a number, be it greater or less, of energetic men hold to one and the same views or opinions, and are brought, more or less, into contact in life. Such friends generally impress, in a certain sense, their character upon the new generation. And thus it was here, when, at the beginning of the eighteenth century, the business of education assumed a new form at Halle, and the existing generation proceeded in carrying out the principles of this school. The succeeding generation inclined more to the second system; and with the third generation, the third pedagogic system acquired a sort of predominance. Thus the three systems succeeded each other: first, the Frankean, usually called the Pietistic, from about 1700 till after 1730; then came the Humanistic system of the philologists, continuing until about 1770; and, lastly, the Egotistic system, or the pedagogics of the philanthropists, originating with Rousseau, and extending into the nineteenth century. It must, however, be observed, that these systems are not to be too sharply distinguished from each other, either as regards time or the mode of their manifestation. They existed, for a long time, side by side, in decided opposition to each other in respect of a few prominent doctrines, and scarcely has any one of them yet reached its utmost point of development. We proceed now to consider them separately in their chronological succession.

1. *The Pedagogics of Piety.*

The founder of this system is Augustas Hermann Franke, although we must not overlook the influence of his teacher and friend, Spener, in the same direction. Franke's principles are most clearly exhibited in his own useful life; but he has also, here and there, expressed them in his writings. They may be summed up as follows. Christian piety is the foundation and aim of education; without it, all knowledge is more detrimental than useful. In every child there is evil, and we are therefore to begin by watching against it and counteracting it, especially in view of certain prominent defects that are peculiar to this age of human life; but, in so doing, it is necessary to have regard to the natural disposition of each child, and not to combat minor defects in such a manner as to give rise to greater ones.

External points of culture must also be attended to. Whatsoever may be the future destination of the child, he is to be habituated, from an early age, to prayer, to self-examination, to self-knowledge, and to piety. Religious instruction is therefore, at all times, the chief concern; but it must be practical, and therefore accompanied with devotional exercises. The young should be left, as little as possible, without supervision; but far from all educational institutions be monastic discipline: the whole course of education must be paternal: love must reign, yet combined with due rigour; the rod should be used as little as possible, but kept in view, in terrorem. Those who are intended for the ordinary pursuits of life should be instructed in the practical matters connected with them, but those who are designed for some learned profession should only incidentally practise them, for to them the Latin and the Greek languages are the chief concern. In the higher classes they should also study logic and rhetoric.

The Latin language must be studied with grammatical accuracy, but practised also in conversation. A selection should be made from the classics, that nothing immoral may be presented to the pupil. For the study of the Greek language, the New Testament is chiefly to be used, as every student ought to read it in the original. The teachers are to exercise strict supervision over every pupil, and to prepare, previously to each examination, *i. e.*, every three months, judicia respecting pietatem, studia, affectus, mores et constitutionem corporis, which are afterward to be entered in a book, in order that each pupil may be treated according as his case may require.

In order to give efficiency to this system, a variety of well-adapted arrangements were adopted, which our limits will not allow us to recapitulate. Among other important improvements, Franke made excellent provisions for the external accommodation of the pupils, for an adequate supply of books, and for the other apparatuses of schools, which had before been scarcely thought of.

In this plan of education, we still find the two first-named systems, to a considerable extent, united; but the point where they separate is also clearly discernible. Even the third and later principal educational direction was, in some measure, founded in this system. But Franke's spirit and practical genius still embraced the whole; and, though he treated the element of piety as paramount, he accorded to the others their due weight. His disciples and successors became more and more deficient in this spirit, however excellent they were in character and zealous to do good. The best things among men are subject to perversion and abuse; and thus the good cause of piety suffered from the one-sidedness, and the injudicious methods and contracted views of its friends. The neglect of classical culture, particularly of the Grecian literature, and thus, also, of taste; an assumed appearance of sanctity, excessively multiplied devotional exercises, which, in the absence of true piety, produced either hypocrisy or disgust, and Phariseeism, even among the better pupils; secret vices, and intellectual shallowness—these constituted the morass into which this course of education led; whereas, seeing that it proceeded from the right principle, it might, if it had been judiciously organized and wisely carried out, have led to the happiest results. None of the teachers of this school can be altogether exonerated from mistaken management, though it would be doing injustice to each of them if we refused to acknowledge the peculiar excellences which characterized the labours of each in the development of this system.

Among the many and deservedly distinguished authors who proceeded from this school, and who produced a great number of valuable schoolbooks, embracing new editions of the classics, Latin and Greek grammars, &c., Joachim Lange is particularly celebrated. We have not space to mention more of these men, of whom but few were, to any extent, affected by the errors of the system, and whose labours in behalf of education are deserving of grateful acknowledgment.

2. The Pedagogics of the Humanists.

The Italian and Flemish school of pedagogics, as we have seen on previous pages, looked upon the study of the classics as the principal source of culture, and since then the literature of the Greeks and Romans has been studied as constituting the humaniora (the humanities), *i. e.*, the principal means for the true culture of man. Even the Frankean school at Halle laid great stress on this *so-called* humanistic pedagogics. So long, however, as this school cultivated classical studies only in connexion with what is called the pietistic education, the pedagogics of the humanists did not urge its pretensions in all their rigour. The professors of philology at the universities of Wittenberg and Leipsic, from Melanchthon down to Mosellanus, had given great prominence to this study; and in Franke's time, a professorship and a seminary of the humaniora (the humanities) was also established at the University of Halle. Of this institution, the first teacher and superintendent was the celebrated pedagogist, C. Cellarius (born 1638, died 1707), who has particularly distinguished himself by his schoolbooks. He founded at Halle the Seminarium Doctrinæ Elegantioris.

A still more distinguished promoter of classical studies was J. M. Gesner: born 1691, died 1761. From the rectorship of the Thomas-school at Leipsic, he was, in 1734, called to the new university at Gottingen as the first professor of ancient literature. Here he immediately established the philological seminary, which soon became very flourishing, and was instrumental, under Gesner's great successor, Heyne (born 1729, died 1812), in educating a number of highly distinguished philologists: it continues to flourish under the direction of eminent scholars. Gesner, who rather inclined to the encyclopedism, and desired to see the study of the ancients brought into connexion with the acquisition of the useful knowledge of later times, is not to be ranked among those who are, in the strictest sense, called humanists. To this school belonged, more decidedly, J. A. Ernesti, born 1707, died 1781; who taught at Leipsic, and distinguished himself as a Ciceronian Latinist, as his schoolbooks still show. In 1759 he became professor of theology, but remained faithful to his humanistic views. In 1784, a philological seminary was also founded in Leipsic by Chr. D. Beck, which continues to flourish under the direction of Hermann.

We have remarked the establishment of the Seminarium Doctrinæ Elegantioris at Halle by Cellarius; but another seminary of the latter kind was now established in that city by G. G. Schütz, born 1747, who, although a humanist, inclined to the so-called philanthropism. When he removed from Halle to Jena, Trapp succeeded him as first professor of pedagogics; but soon after, Fr. A. Wolf, born 1750, died 1825, became his successor at the philological seminary. This profoundly learned humanist united in himself the multiform culture of his age, educated many distinguished philologists, and contributed greatly to deliver the humanistic pedagogics from its one-sidedness. And since then the new epoch has commenced.

3. *The Pedagogics of the Philanthropists.*

In proportion as education was more diffused among the mass of the people, the more was it drawn into the service of common life, and the more was it aimed at to educate children for its affairs. This tendency soon became the prevailing spirit of the age, which developed the egotistic system of education. The polymathy, which had, since the restoration of the sciences, been the hobby of the learned, was now about to appear as a rage for much knowledge, among all classes of society; the past simplicity was lost in a multiplicity of pedagogic subjects; the ties which bound man to society, as a whole, were regarded as oppressive chains; and while society was, as it were, resolving itself into atoms, the individual claimed to be independent as such; and this chemical tendency of the spirit of the age was too agreeable to egotism, that it should not have welcomed the regard which was manifested for the pupil's self. Those who saw only what was good in this development, found in it, from want of penetrating sagacity, the true enlightenment, and regarded the prevailing zeal to educate the young in accordance with it as that true philanthropy, which, as they weened, had long been a stranger on earth. Thus it was this spirit of the age which procured for the eighteenth century, in its latter half, the name of the philosophical, and in respect of education, the philanthropic. If the strict sense of these terms be not insisted upon, we may, in our turn, safely venture to designate this period as the egotistic.

This period began to develop itself with the efforts to devise new methods, of which we have spoken, and with the commencement of the new encyclopedism. Bacon, Ratich, Comenius, and Locke introduced the better aspects of this period. So far from indulging in lamentations at this tendency, we must recognise in it a necessary and profitable point of transition in the progress of pedagogic science towards the right culture of man. But the more to be lamented is that degeneracy of the Protestant clergy in Europe, respecting which, as we have seen, good men bitterly complained; for it was in this emergency that the Gospel ought to have been set forth in all its power, in order to counteract the invading egotism: then would the school and the Church have truly gained, and that directly through that public enlightenment which such men as Thomasius had sought to promote, with respect to important relations of human life. But now the clergy had to suffer for having neglected the true culture of the mind and heart, and it was, in a great degree, their own fault that men looked with suspicious eyes on ecclesiastical organizations; but the people, also, and the rising generation, were, to a great extent, defrauded of that better culture, which, under more favourable auspices, would have appear ed, and what might have been gain turned out to be loss.

The schoolmen had been no less culpable in giving themselves up to pedantry, for vanity has at all times been more pernicious in its influence on the learned class than is generally supposed; and this we learn from the history of the men who belonged to it, and from the very confessions of the wiser among them. As long as the so-called spirit of caste was cherished by this class of society, pride prevailed among its members; but when the higher studies more and more became common property, everybody began to set up claims to polymathy; and from this union of vanity and pride proceeded the pedants, first in the humanistic department, then in the useful sciences, and so on to the newest airs of pedagogues and college-students. It is obvious that such a spirit could not give to youth the culture that was so much needed, and that it necessarily spoiled much of the good that had been gained. The pedagogic systems which belong to this category originated more immediately in the principles of Montaigne and Locke. The first who developed from these a system was Rousseau; next followed that of Basedow; and lastly, occupying higher ground, that of Pestalozzi.

A.

Jean Jacques Rousseau, born 1712 at Geneva, expressed with much genius, and in an elegant form, those principles of the modern pedagogics. We shall not follow him through his erratic and eventful life. With some few points which we may admire, it presents, on the whole, a vile and often disgusting spectacle. His writings produced an astonishing effect on the public mind, and had, perhaps, no inconsiderable influence in bringing about the French Revolution. In 1762 appeared his celebrated pedagogic work, with which we are here more particularly concerned, entitled "Emile, ou de l'Education." This work bears a deep impress of its author's character, which the uninformed reader will find depicted in Musset-Pathay's

"Histoire de la Vie et des Ouvrages de Jean Jacques Rousseau."

We deem it unnecessary to exhibit Rousseau's pedagogic views in detail; the more so, because his general principles were more completely reduced to system by men of whom we shall hereafter speak, and who were guided by other, and higher, and purer principles than this unhappy man. Many of his rules that are truly valuable are imbodied in the forenamed work. His rules for the physical treatment of children correspond, on the whole, with those of Locke. He regards man from a false, a low, worldly, utilitarian point of view; and while he gives many excellent rules for the physical and intellectual education, and the general worldly culture of man, he abounds in glaring absurdities; and to him are chiefly to be traced the grovelling tendencies which have manifested themselves in modern pedagogics. He utterly repudiates religious instruction for the young as absurd. But, as he had not himself any knowledge of the great God of the Bible, and would none of the religion of the New Testament, of whose character he had, certainly, not the remotest conception, he is not entitled to a judgment in the premises, and his assertions are worth nothing, for he knew not whereof he testified. In announcing these views, he seems to have been, in some measure, actuated by a spirit of hostility against Locke, between whose educational opinions and his own there are strong points of resemblance, but no less obvious ones of difference, especially on the subject of religious education.*

* In farther confirmation of the views expressed above, we append the following note from p. 50 of "The School and the Schoolmaster," a work which we most cordially recommend to all who take an interest in the progress of education in our country. "This," the Emile, "may be regarded, says a late writer, as the principal work of Rousseau. It is a moral romance, which appeared in 1762, and treats chiefly of education. The plan of instruction which it inculcates is to allow the youthful mind to unfold itself without restraint, and rather to protect it against bad impressions than to attempt to load it with positive instruction. The objects of nature are to be gradually presented to it. Necessity alone is to regulate and restrain it, till reason, unfettered by prejudice and previous habits, is able to weave the drapery in which it is afterward to be swathed. The child of reason, thus thrown into a mass of human beings, actuated by different motives,

Even before 1770, the doctrines of these two men had been completely domesticated in Germany, where, however, the new spirit of culture had already manifested its activity under a somewhat different aspect. New institutions, of various descriptions, had been everywhere established, and domestic education had experienced considerable changes. It was constantly the subject of thought and inquiry how the young might be educated to be well-informed, enlightened, and good men and women; but the mode of procedure was still too one-sided. It was agreed that classical studies ought to be pursued according to a better method, but that method was not so easily found; that these studies constituted the principal element of higher culture was asserted by a numerous party, but this was denied by many who made the highest pretensions to taste. Disputes arose, and the schools underwent many metamorphoses.

B.

And now it was that a celebrated man, John Bernhard Basedow, born in 1723 at Hamburg, took his seat on the oracular tripod. Having experienced various reverses, and even persecutions on account of his theological opinions, he devoted himself more and more to pedagogics; and the enthusiasm with which he contended against the defects of the prevailing methods, as well as the universal and deeply-seated desire of a reform in the schools, procured him the favour and patronage of noble and actively benevolent men. He published in 1768 a remon-

guided by different principles, and pursuing different objects from itself, like a skilfully-constructed bark without its rudder, and stripped of its canvass and cordage, can have no other fate than that of being dashed against the cliffs, or sunk beneath the waves. In discussing the subject of religious education, he exhibited the same inconsistency and absurd views. The French savants were displeased with his glowing sentiments of piety, with his impassioned admiration of the morality of the Gospel, and of the character of its Founder; while the friends of religion and social order were shocked with his attacks upon miracles and prophecy, with his insidious and open objections to Christianity, and with the application of human reason to subjects beyond its sphere and above its power. The French Parliament not only condemned the Emile, but compelled Rousseau to retire precipitately from France, by commencing a criminal prosecution against him."

strance addressed to philanthropists, in which he earnestly sought to direct attention to the neglected claims of education. Soon after appeared his celebrated elementary work, and lastly, his book of Methods for the fathers and mothers of families and nations. In 1771, the venerable Duke of Dessau furnished him both buildings and money for the establishment of a new institution, which Basedow opened in 1774, under the high-sounding title of Philanthropinum. But had not his prince had sounder and clearer views than himself, and watched, with parental care, over the institution, which at the very beginning suffered a severe blow through Basedow's listlessness and want of skill, it never would have achieved the good which in the end it did accomplish, chiefly through the wise exertions of the excellent duke. The eyes of all were anxiously directed towards this new institution, and the first public examination produced an exceedingly favourable impression.

But Basedow was in no respect the man to continue, with success, the experiment which had thus far succeeded, notwithstanding the striking defects of his character. His assistant, Wolke, contributed most to the establishment of the new institution; he was aided by a number of young men, who afterward ranked among the most eminent pedagogists of Germany: among these, Campe and Salzmann are the most celebrated. Basedow soon left his institution, which had no reason to mourn his loss. He died, 1790, in poverty, more to be pitied than blamed, for he had good intentions and benevolent purposes, and showed great activity in reducing them to practice; but his temper was violent, his own education defective, and his abilities were inadequate to the work which he had undertaken. His pedagogic idea is expressed in the following sentences:

"The culture of the understanding is the chief thing, for even the way to the heart is through the head. The cultivation of the memory is apt to induce stupidity. Religion is communicated by means of enlightened instruction, and moral character is produced by simple instruction in morals. Languages are to be studied only in subserviency to practical studies ; and things serviceable to culture are not supersensuous, but consist in the commonest concerns of daily life. These useful matters are the chief subjects of instruction. The process of learning must always proceed from the observation of sensuous objects : it should be made as easy as possible, and children should learn only when they please, and in an entertaining manner. Attention must be paid to physical health and strength. In accordance with these principles, all schools should be regulated; and they ought, in general, to be, more than they are, institutions of education. Such an institution will rather educate man, as such, than the citizen or scholar; for the general interests of man are more important than those of particular callings. Until the fifteenth year the boy should be educated only as a citizen of the world. Man is by nature good! and God, as the father of all, loves all. Children naturally love men, and must, therefore, be educated to be philanthropists and cosmopolites. Such an institution deserves the name of Philanthropinum : with its encyclopedism of instruction, it will bring on the Golden Age."

According to these principles, absurd and mischievous as the most of them are, Basedow had drawn up his elementary work for schools, and laid down the rules for instruction in his book of Methods. Those who are acquainted with the writings of Montaigne, Bacon, Comenius, Locke, and Rousseau, can find little or nothing that is instructive in these works. Basedow stood, indeed, on the shoulders of these men, and the views to which they had given currency he knew well how to beat out into tinsel; but he possessed neither their genius, nor a profound acquaintance with their works.

C.

Far more successful, and deservedly so, than Basedow, was Christopher G. Salzmann, born 1744 at Sömmerda, near Erfurt : a man of great learning, sound judgment, correct feeling, pure taste, and deep piety, and one of the best teachers of his age. He laboured for some time at the Philanthropinum at Dessau (Basedow's), to which he had been invited in 1781, and where his labours for the religious education of the pupils were greatly blessed. But the institution of Basedow did not please him: he wished for a sphere in which he might carry out, independently, his own idea of education, and desired, therefore, to found an institution of his own. An opportunity soon presented itself. A friend made him a present of a small estate in the neighbourhood of Gotha, and the reigning duke, Ernest, advanced him a considerable sum of money for the erection of new buildings. Salzmann trusted in God, and the work which he had undertaken advanced and flourished more and more from day to day. "I had commenced it," he writes, "in order to be able here to give children a good education, and, as yet, no father has had sufficient confidence in me to intrust to me his child." But soon pupils flocked in from every part of Germany, from Switzerland, England, Portugal, and the northern kingdoms of Europe; and he soon presided over the largest and most respectable real *institution of education* among all that had yet been undertaken. Six of his assistants became his sons-in-law: his whole patriarchal family were entirely devoted to the interests of the institution; and though it suffered severely through the catastrophe which Napoleon's wars brought upon Germany, it still flourishes, since the father's death, under the direction of his children, or, perhaps, children's children.

Such permanency proves that the fundamental idea was good and sound. Simplicity, order, a healthy mode of life; gymnastics, useful studies, culture of the understanding; cultivation of a healthful state of the feelings, of a true love of nature, and of sincere piety; vigilance against any unchaste manifestations; the regular division of the day between bodily and intellectual activity: all this operated together, under the influence of parental kindness and care, in so happy a manner that the idea of an extended family-education has never been more fully realized. This, indeed, was not yet the idea of a complete education for boys and young men: it was still burdened by the one-sidedness of philanthropism.

Educational institutions now increased in number, and there was no end of the new arrangements that were tried. The imitations of the Philanthropinum were the least successful; for these attempts were now made either with a view to profit alone, or from a mad zeal for improvements; adventurers and young enthusiasts embarked in the business of education. It had become a matter of fashion. One of the better developments was the institution of M. de Rochow, born 1734 at Berlin, died 1800. This worthy nobleman exerted himself practically for the improvement of the village-schools on his estates, so that from every part of Germany young teachers were sent there, in order to study the model of a good country-school, and of the method of instruction best adapted to them. He also published a schoolbook suited to his plan. All this concurred with the universal tendency to disseminate every species of knowledge among all classes of society.

D.

J. Heinrich Pestalozzi, born at Zurich 1746, died 1827; of a patrician family, was, from his sixth year, left, by the death of his father, to the care of his mother and of some kind relatives, who gave him a plain education. He visited the schools at Zurich, distinguished himself, among other things, in the study of the Greek language, but forfeited the good-will of his teacher by translating better than he, a portion of the Philippica of Demosthenes. This induced him to discontinue his studies, and to retire to one of his estates, of which he possessed several. He is, no doubt, to be regarded as having been, in a great measure, self-educated. In the country he became acquainted with the wretchedness that prevailed among the people, and undertook to provide for more than fifty poor children (mendicants), whom he undertook to instruct in agriculture and in various manufactures. At great cost, and amid contempt and ridicule, he persevered in his enterprise, which a total want of funds at length compelled him to abandon; yet he had the satisfaction of knowing that he had brought up more than one hundred poor, vagrant children to be useful members of society. In 1776 he returned to Zurich. About this time Iselin was publishing at Bâsle his periodical, entitled "Ephemeriden der Menschheit," and Pestalozzi became a frequent contributor. In 1786 he published his popular romance, Lienhard und Gertrud, which gained him great celebrity. He now travelled in Germany, where he acquired the friendship of many distinguished men, but brought back a very unfavourable opinion of the schools which he had visited. Soon after his return he wrote his "Inquiries respecting the Course of Nature in the Culture of the Human Race," on which work he spent three years.

His desire to engage personally in the work of education soon revived, and he resolved to "become a schoolmaster." After an unsuccessful attempt at Stanz, he opened, in 1799, his elementary school at Burgdorf, in which, though at first only a day-school, he soon received a number of boarders. It was the period of the Swiss Revolution, and, amid many annoyances and difficulties, this excellent man persevered in his arduous labours until 1806, when he was compelled to remove to Hofwyl, where the government of Berne assigned him a commodious building for his school. Here he associated with himself the celebrated De Fellenberg: but the connexion did not long continue; and already, in 1807 (other authorities state these dates differently), he transferred his institution to the roomy schloss (castle) at Yverdun. He had, ere this, again published several books, to wit: "How Gertrude instructs her Children," in 1801; Elementary Books, in four volumes, 1803–4; some years later he also edited a periodical. His institution became very flourishing, numbering frequently as many as one hundred and fifty pupils, and, besides, fifty young persons, who came, often at the expense of their governments, from almost every country of Europe, in order to study Pestalozzi's method with a view to introduce it at home. At first his assistants were animated by a common spirit, and vigorously co-operated with their venerable principal; but gradually this good understanding disappeared, discussions arose, and the institution declined more and more, while others grew out of it, as from a common root. Pestalozzi had spent upon it nearly his whole fortune, and now saw himself, in his old age, abandoned by those assistants to whom he had ever been, and still desired to be, a father. At eighty years of age he still comforted himself with the idea of his youth, to establish a school for poor children; but even this plan was frustrated; and having yet experienced the mortification of reading a lampoon directed against himself, he died.

In order to become acquainted with his pedagogic idea, we must recur to some of the earliest statements respecting it, which he made in the Ephemeriden der Menschheit, to which we referred above. In this periodical he says, in 1779: "Childlike docility and obedience are not the result and invariable consequence of a complete education: they must be early, nay, the first foundations of human culture." And again: "Faith in God is the source of a peaceful life; a peaceful life is the source of inward order; inward order is the source of a well-directed (unverwirrten) application of our powers; order in the employment of our faculties is again the source of their expansion and of their culture for wisdom; and wisdom is the source of all that is good in man and in human life; and thus faith in God is the source of all wisdom and of all blessings, and the path of nature to the proper culture of mankind." The idea here expressed developed itself farther in his own mind, yet the spirit of the age exerted upon it, in various ways, its modifying influence; and Pestalozzi himself, with whatever clearness he announced his views in "Lienhard und Gertrud," seems never to have mastered it completely. While he attached the highest importance to the influence of Christianity on education, he was yet too strongly tinctured with the egotistic views of his age, in aiming at the elevation of the individual to independence through an energy unconnected with the interests of society.

The one-sidedness was soon discovered, but the good that was involved in his idea was not sufficiently appreciated.

When Pestalozzi made the true culture of man dependant on his being developed entirely from within, his meaning was, that the child and the youth should, in accordance with his natural development, be excited to purely independent activity, and strengthened for an unbroken progress. This is his method. It achieves, in the first instance, the strengthening of the mental faculties, in order to their developing themselves progressively from within; and thus the culture of the intellectual powers for the successful performance of their appropriate functions is made the chief concern of education. And as this development ought to commence in early childhood, Pestalozzi has assigned to the mother the first instruction of the child; and, in order to aid in the discharge of this duty, he wrote his "Book for Mothers."

Elementary instruction is, in general, of great importance. It cultivates the power of observation* and of thinking by means of the three elements, figure, number, and word. Hence, the doctrines of form and magnitude belong to the earliest subjects of instruction, and the square is at the foundation, not only of intellectual, but even of moral culture, so that the educator has only to pronounce the (imperative) word "measure!" For he that observes* angles and lines correctly, will also learn to discern clearly and without confusion what is truth and what is error; to distinguish, with the greatest accuracy, between right and wrong, and desire only what is true, and right,

* In the second part of this work, this peculiar use of "observe" and "observation" will be found explained.

and good. In the elementary books, teaching the relations of numbers and of magnitudes, the mode of procedure in the application of this method was fully described. Religion also was to be developed out of the child's filial feelings, which manifest themselves in confidence, gratitude, and obedience towards the parents; and here also the mother was to be the first agent, as in her the Deity was, as it were, to appear to the child.

Here, then, we have a complete, compact whole. But that, in this system of education, in the so-called method, the only true culture of man should have been regarded as discovered, proves how extremely one-sided was the spirit of the age. The sacred truth that salvation has come into the world, and that its power needs only be properly introduced in the hearts of the young, was too much lost sight of by the inventor of this method, however full of love and of piety he may himself have been.

Pestalozzi carried the egotistic mode of education to its utmost height, so that in him it found its culminating point. He was deeply sensible of the egotism of the age; he desired to educate the individual for society, and we can discover in his labours various tendencies to this end. In him we find the point of transition to the newest educational developments, and he belongs, in a measure, to that period, which had already commenced in his day. Ratich wished to lead the world of thoughts and of language, Comenius that of the senses, *into* the pupil; Rousseau desired to conduct him to an ideal world, and Pestalozzi to create one out of him.

And here our history of education, as pertaining to the past, is, in fact, at an end; for the labours of Fellenberg, who has been mentioned in connexion with Pestalozzi, belong rather to the educational developments of a later day. This very excellent man, Philip E. de Fellenberg, born 1771 at Bern, after his connexion with Pestalozzi had been dissolved, in consequence of their totally different characters, exerted himself in different ways for the improvement of agriculture in his native land. At the same time he accomplished, what Pestalozzi had attempted without permanent success, the establishment of an institution of entirely forsaken and destitute children. He opened, also, an "Œkonomisches Lehrinstitut" for instruction in practical matters of life ; in connexion with which, he established, in 1808, a seminary for children from the higher classes. As this soon became very extensive and flourishing, he resolved to devote to it his chief attention, and therefore gave up, in 1818, the Œkonomisches Lehrinstitut, or agricultural manual-labour school.

We must not omit to notice here the celebrated philosopher J. G. Fichte, born 1762, who, in his "Reden an die Deutsche Nation," 1808, says many important things concerning education, but contends that children should all be taken away from their parents to be educated in a manner entirely different from that to which the corrupt generation of that day was competent: of course an utterly impracticable idea, unless educators could have been obtained from some other world.

The development and growth of this spirit of the age appears from its extensive pedagogic literature. The number of writers on education, of authors of instructive books, and every variety of schoolbooks, was very great in Germany and in France, but especially in the former country. Besides the works of authors already spoken of, we may here mention the Conversations of Madame de Beaumont, and in Germany, the numerous writings of Campe, as books very popular and useful in their day, and important, on account of the countless imitations to which they have given rise.

Intellectual activity received a new impulse through the vast multiplication of books, which exerted, also, an important, in many respects very unfavourable, influence on the culture of youth. There was much written and much read, and this produced a fondness for writing and a rage for reading; and both these effects were prejudicial to that careful industry which produces classical works, and weakened the attention of the reader, and thus prevented profitable reading. Thus writers and readers mutually spoiled each other: instead of graver studies, ephemeral entertainment was sought after, and literature became the servant of amusement and shallowness. The many journals and so-called literary periodicals which now sprung up, catered liberally for this depraved taste. And now came the flood of modern novels and romances, the great majority of which tend only to produce, in the young, a morbid sensibility, to fill them with false notions of life, its affairs and duties; to give loose reins to the imagination; to weaken the power of attention and of observation, and to produce that general enervation of mind, through much and hasty reading, of which there has been so much complaint.

Since about 1780, the number of schoolbooks and of pedagogic works increased to such an extent, that a separate work of the history of literature would be required by this branch alone. Systems mutually supplanted, absorbed, or flattered each other, and true Christian education was more and more lost sight of: to this the spirit of the age did not tend. In respect of classical studies, though here also there were clashings and wanderings from one extreme to another, some better things came to light.

The mass of cloud had refracted the light of the rising sun into colours, and one had called forth the other. The one-sided culture of the heart led on its opposite, the one-sided culture of the head: and this proceeded to such extremes, that the colour, which had seemed the harbinger of enlightenment, only receded from the light; for this has shone forth, and will forever shine forth only from the Gospel: and the union of the refracted rays, through a truly Christian education, had not yet been found. The presumption of that egotism, which was thoroughly cultivated in the school of mere reason and worldly prudence, constituted a very remarkable point of transition in the history of the human race. It appeared in three different metamorphoses, until, like the night-moth, it burned its wings in the light. It first came forth in Rousseau's admonition, "For God's sake, let the rising generation not hear a word about God!" and, next, in the self-worship of the philosophy of nature, exhorting man himself to become God: and, lastly, in the thinking faculty, rent loose entirely from the Eternal, and claiming kindred with the Titans, and saying, "Bring forth everything out of the idea, out of thyself: the world, the commonwealth, even the Deity, &c.!" That all this involved the subversion of everything sacred, and of the whole order of nature, appears from the latest history, civil and pedagogic, of Europe; yet not without comfort, for the present state of the schools and the whole system of education exhibit decided tendencies towards the only right aim.

To this, then, it had to come, when the Christian cultivating principle was departed from. To this led the age of Louis XIV. in France, and of Frederic the Great in Germany; but in France burst forth that fearful storm, which was averted from Germany by its remaining piety and the better elements in the German national character.

And thus it also appeared that modern culture, déstitute of the power of Christianity, was afflicted with even greater poverty than that of the ancients, who, in their common public institutions, trained the young to order and good habits of life.

CONCLUSION.

Prospects for the Complete Realization of the Idea of Education.

The inquiries and attempts of the emancipated mind of man must, in the end, lead to the recognition, in the fulness of its truth, of that cultivating principle to which the mind is indebted for its liberty, and to the unqualified elevation of this principle to the supreme control of all the great concerns of human life. We trust that we have seen the beginnings of this important period even in the preceding; in the labours of some men who belong both to the former and to the latter. It remains for us to consider what has already been accomplished towards the attainment of the desired end, and what are the prospects before us. In contradistinction from the past period, with its great errors, its one-sided and mischievous developments, its separation between the school and active life, or, more distinctly, of school-instruction and of education, it will be characteristic of the present period, which is to achieve the true freedom of man, that it will effect a perfect union between instruction and education, proceeding from the innermost centre of life.

In Germany, the renovated public life, the beautiful dreams and hopes which succeeded the seven years' war (1762), were broken in upon by the whirlwinds of the French wars, which harassed Europe during twenty-five years. This awakening from delusion, even from the much-admired dreams of the philanthropists, however dreadful, was necessary. The restless doings of this philanthropism, in institutions and in writings which only deserve to be forgotten, led to nothing; nay, it is doing it too much honour to ascribe to it all the educational developments of its age. Vulgarity was called culture, sentimentalism was regarded as excellence of character, unruly insubordination was mistaken for energy, unbelief for enlightenment, revolutionizing states for liberation from slavery, the dissolution of family-life for refinement and enjoyment of life.*

Thus everything had become unsettled and loose, and there was no longer, in education, a counterpoise to egotism. From it proceeded the principles of education, and the means employed were in its service. Thus impudence had become natural to the young, and it was even sometimes regarded as a virtue, and exalted above that of Sparta, or that of any other people or age. It was heightened by the prevailing

* For illustrations of all this, we would refer the reader to Professor Felton's elegant translation of W. Menzel's German Literature.

polymathy, and among students by the philosophical systems; and, of course, licentiousness increased.

But now influences of a better character, tending more or less towards the improvement of the theory and practice of pedagogics, and some of which had been in operation for some time, began to make themselves more distinctly and extensively felt. The classic writers of Germany, beginning with Gellert, but more especially since the days of Lessing, rebuked, by precept and example, the prevailing pedantry, and gave rise to clearer and profounder views respecting the culture of youth, than all those one-sided teachers and polyhistors. And as the necessity of improvement became more and more deeply felt, the desire to minister to it grew daily stronger. Even from the writings of J. P. Miller, born 1725, whose "Principles of a Wise and Christian art of Education" is one of the earliest instructive works on pedagogics, we learn that, during that state of pedagogic anarchy, men were earnestly striving, throughout Protestant Germany, to bring about an improved plan of school-education. More important and directly to the purpose were the writings of J. M. Ehlers, whose work, entitled "Thoughts concerning the Requisites necessary to the Improvement of the Schools," appeared as early as 1766. Thilo's "Thoughts concerning Education" contained many wise and well-timed hints. And from this time more and more was written respecting the relations between the school, the church, and the state, between public and domestic education, &c., all which writing, if it accomplished nothing more, kept alive and stimulated the spirit of inquiry. Many existing errors, in theory and practice, were exposed and protested against, and sounder views and better methods gradually fought their way into public esteem. Among the most important measures must be ranked the establishment of seminaries for the education of good teachers. In Catholic countries, also, the interest of the clergy and of princes in behalf of education was revived, and various effectual steps were taken, and institutions established for its improvement.

Thus, since about the last quarter of the eighteenth century, the *business of education* has been vigorously prosecuted in Germany ; the *idea of education* is gradually pervading it, and has already brought forth in it divers encouraging developments. The higher institutions of learning and the popular schools, both in city and in country, give evidence that great progress has been made.

The European nations of Germanic descent more immediately participate in this culture ; and among them Denmark, for a considerable time past, and more recently Holland, which has almost outstripped Germany in its course of improvement as respects common schools. It is only of late years that the business of popular education has experienced a revival in England, and the measures of government, as well as the influence of public-spirited men, have already effected great and extensive improvements. The methods of Bell and Lancaster are of importance only in communities where nothing has as yet been done for popular education, and where no well-organized and suitable plan for common-school education is in successful operation.

Sabbath-schools, which existed as early as 1754 in the Grand-duchy of Baden, first became general in England through the exertions of Robert Raikes, and have since proved, both in other countries of Europe and in our own land, one of the greatest blessings to society. Since the middle of the eighteenth century, the attention of men has thus not only been occupied with the improvement of schools, but diverted more and more to the true culture of man and the public education of nations. Among the writers who have, in quite recent times, done most for the diffusion of sound principles and the development of good methods, are Niemeyer, the author of a noble work, entitled "Principles of Education;" Schwarz, the author to whom we are mainly indebted for the materials of this history, and numerous extracts introduced in the following system ; Harnisch, and Graser.

Institutions of education, of every name and description, are open to the young in the different countries of Europe, and especially in Germany. One of the best features of the age is the provision that is made in some countries for the education of poor children. There are yet, indeed, many errors to be corrected in every department of education; many inconsistencies to be removed; many absurdities, and follies, and littlenesses, and vagaries to be rebuked, and driven from the schools and the firesides; many prejudices to be conquered; and there remains much to be developed in theory, and to be rendered efficient in practice.

And, above all, when we consider the progress of demoralization and irreligion throughout the civilized world, let us take heed that we boast not of advancement where there is retrogression, and remember that "pride cometh before destruction, and a haughty spirit before a fall;" and let all who labour for the improvement of human education take for their motto that word of unchanging truth, "*the fear of the Lord is the beginning of wisdom.*"

In our historic sketch of modern education, our own country has not been brought into consideration, for the simple reason that its pedagogic activity and institutions belong, in reality, entirely to the present period of that history, and because no peculiar systems have been here promulgated. If we belong to any school, we must be Eclectics. Our culture is essentially European, modified, of course, by our political institutions, our peculiar civil and social organization; and, while we are prompt to appropriate what we consider as good in the pedagogic arrangements, and institutions, and systems of Europe, we have fallen into many of the errors which, as we have seen, prevailed, or still prevail, in the Old World. These errors we have not here space particularly to discuss; they are referred to, sometimes directly, but generally by implication, in the second part of this work.

Yet we must add that our young country deserves great praise for much that she has independently accomplished in education, and for various good features in the character of her schools. The practical character of our people is prominently exhibited in our educational affairs; and improvements in the arrangement and management of schools, in the methods of instruction, in schoolbooks, are the order of the day. We have scholars among us of whom we need nowhere be ashamed, and who deserve the highest praise for their efforts to promote an intelligent and spirited study of the classics in our higher seminaries of learning. In the cultivation of the exact and the natural sciences, our professors are competing with those of learned Europe. England seems to be aware of the increasing excellence of our schoolbooks, if we are to judge from the eager but disingenuous manner in which she makes them her own.

But there is too much mere book-learning and too little education on all hands.

Since these sheets have gone to press, we have received a copy of a new work, entitled "The School and the Schoolmaster," by Alonzo Potter, D.D., and George B. Emerson, A.M., about to be published by Messrs. Harper and Brothers. We hail the appearance of this work with sincere joy, and cannot but hope that it will be productive of much good, both in instructing the public mind relative to the ends which ought to be aimed at in the education of the young, and in guiding and counselling educators in the appropriate and successful prosecution of their efforts for the attainment of those ends. The work, differing materially from the present in its character and design, is decidedly one of the most valuable contributions which our country has yet made to pedagogic literature. Its chief design seems to be to exhibit the principles, and to present, in ample detail, a judicious and well-digested method, according to which our common schools should be conducted. The authors have long been known as men of distinguished talent and learning; and as their work is the result of mature thought, and long experience in the business of education, it comes before the public with the strongest claims to their attention. In the first part there is much able and acute discussion of general principles; and we regret that the work did not appear early enough to admit of our extracting some of the beautiful and impressive passages in which it abounds. The second part, while it contains a great amount of sage counsel and direction for the teacher, will also, we trust, serve to enlighten trustees and inspectors, as respects the location, the arrangements, the ventilation, the warming, &c., of schoolhouses, and enable them to proceed with increased intelligence and prudence in employing instructers. The entire work is of great practical value, and the public are greatly indebted to its gifted authors for the time and labour which they have devoted to its preparation. Other valuable pedagogic treatises by American writers, referred to in the work above spoken of, are the following: "The Teacher," by Jacob Abbott: "Hall's Lectures:" "Hall's Lectures to Female Teachers:" "The Teacher Taught," by Emerson Davis: "The Teacher's Manual," by Thomas H. Palmer: "Suggestions on Education," by Catharine E. Beecher.

We have reason to rejoice at the zeal and energy with which the Protestant churches of our country have engaged in the establishment and improvement of Sabbath-schools. As an omen for good we would regard the extent to which Christianity is allowed to influence our institutions of education: they are, indeed, for the most part, monuments of Christian effort for the improvement of mankind. The presidents of the great majority of our colleges, and many of their professors, are Christian ministers, who make their influence as Christians felt; and the number of American authors who have written in the purest Christian spirit, and in a popular and attractive style, on matters of education, or furnished instructive books for the young, is cheeringly great, and constantly increasing. The superior discipline of our colleges to that of similar institutions of Europe is doubtless, in a great measure, to be ascribed to the Christian principles on which these institutions have been established. And we merely add, that the future true, healthy, and beneficial development of our system of public education, which is yet in its infancy, the permanent existence of our free institutions, and the true greatness, and progressive culture, and abiding glory of this rising nation, all depend on this one thing: the religion of Christ must preside over, direct, and pervade the entire education of the free people of this mighty realm, otherwise we can but add another to the list of republics in which public corruption achieved national ruin.

O

PART II

A PLAN OF CULTURE AND INSTRUCTION.

BASED ON CHRISTIAN PRINCIPRES, AND DESIGNED TO AID IN THE RIGHT EDUCATION OF YOUTH, PHYSICALLY, INTELLECTUALLY, AND MORALLY

"A sound mind in a healthy body."

PART II.

A PLAN OF YOUTHFUL CULTURE AND INSTRUCTION.

Outline of the Work.

PEDAGOGICS is the science which treats of the principles on which man should be educated. And here the great question presents itself on the threshold, For what purpose does man live? or, In what does the value of life consist?

We shall not enter into an ethical or theological discussion of this great question, but answer it by simply asserting that the object of human life is the enjoyment of happiness; and we shall consider human happiness as dependant on the two following conditions:

I. On the culture of the understanding and the sensibilities. This division will embrace the affections, as being, indeed, spontaneous in their motions, yet susceptible of development and training in a particular direction: and we shall here consider man as a being possessed of mental faculties and instincts, which are necessarily called into action by the relations and circumstances in which he is placed, and which require education in order to their becoming the means of promoting his own happiness and that of others.

II. On the culture of the moral powers, which comprehends religious instruction. Under this head we shall consider man as a responsible agent, and treat of the duties which his various relations impose upon him.

Under our first division, then, we are to present a plan for the education of the understanding and the sensibilities. Here we are to consider man from two different points of view: and, first, Man as an Individual. In this respect, his education in the graces of the mind will be considered. This will involve, from obvious reasons,

1. Physical education, having in view the proper development of the body, by negative provision for health, by bodily exercise, and by regular education for the true enjoyment of life. Under this head belong, 2. Intellectual culture, which aims at developing the understanding for the perception of truth: 3. Æsthetic education, which aims at the cultivation of the feelings for the perception and enjoyment of what is pure and beautiful in the relations of life; and, 4. Practical education, which is designed to develop the character in general, for the public and active affairs of life.

Under the last division we shall treat of practical education in general, or education in business-habits and in the proprieties of life, and of practical education in view of some particular calling. The nature of these is such as obviously to require a theory of didactics; and this will be presented under two heads: first, didactics for the learned professions, or instruction in the sciences; second, didactics for the popular or common occupations of life. Our second division regards man as a social being, and treats of his education in the social affections. This will be considered under three aspects, as, 1. Education in the sentiments of private friendship, love, and benevolence in general: 2. As education aiming at the right development of the sentiment of love in its narrowest sense, *i. e.*, the love of family and kindred: 3. As education in public spirit, having in view a development of the affections in harmony with, and promotive of, the interests of the community. And here we shall consider man, 1. As a member of the Christian community: 2. As a member of the civil community, or a citizen of the state. In connexion with the first point, we shall treat of his intellectual, æsthetic, and practical education in view of his Christian relations; and under the second, his education in pure and enlightened patriotism.

Under our second general division we shall present a plan for moral education. And here, again, we shall consider man, 1. As an individual, under which aspect we shall treat of his education in what is ordinarily designated as a sense of honour, or the cultivation of a proper self-respect: 2. As a social being, which aspect comprehends the cultivation of a sense of justice; a due consideration of the rights of others; or moral culture, in its narrowest sense: and, 3. As a being subject to Divine government and responsible to God. This involves the religious education of man, or the cultivation of the religious sense, under its three necessary aspects.

General Principles.

By pedagogics we mean a theory of education; a system of principles for the culture of the understanding, the sensibilities, and the moral powers of the young. The former department comprehends all that is denominated learning, or the scientific culture of the mind: the culture of the moral powers embraces virtue and piety.

The difference between the theorist in pedagogics and the practical pedagogue is not to be lost sight of.

The system of pedagogics must embrace every variety of education, and make provision for all its departments, however widely the subjects to be educated and the objects to be attained may differ. As the theory cannot provide for every possible case, its principles must necessarily be subject to many and various modifications. These are, of course, left to the judgment and sagacity of the educator.* Highly as we estimate the value of a theory of education, and of a systematic digest of its most judicious methods, we must yet regard both as subordinate to this highest principle, that the judgment and skill of the educator are superior to all prescribed methods.

* This word, which is not actually in use, is frequently employed in this work in preference to teacher, because the latter word is, in its ordinary acceptation, of very limited meaning; and because a general term, embracing all engaged in the work of education, is here wanted.

The value of a theory of pedagogics arises, not so much from its actually forming future pedagogues, as from its directing their attention to the various and difficult duties of the teacher, which are so often sacrificed to self-interest, to the love of ease, and to other improper motives. The educator of youth should be animated in his employment by pure love to his race, and by nothing else. He that devotes himself to the business of education from any other motive than that of developing his pupil's understanding for the apprehension and appreciation of all that is excellent and desirable within the compass of human knowledge, and of cultivating his heart for the love of virtue, the love of God and man, is destitute of the spirit that ought to actuate all who would educate the young: an office second to none that can be intrusted to the faithfulness of man.

And, in this connexion, we cannot refrain from observing that, though the world may have men of disinterested liberality and benevolence to boast of, it is vain to expect that any should possess the right spirit for the duties of education but those who are under the influence of the high motives and the holy principles of the Christian religion. It is of supreme importance that the teacher should himself eminently exhibit, in his character and conduct, those attainments and excellences to which he aspires to conduct his pupils; for education can be successful only when the educator's love of mankind is sustained in its efforts by the force of his example: and hence the immense difficulty, we may safely say impossibility, of a *perfect education* is apparent. Want of success is more frequently owing to the incompetency or the unfaithfulness of the educator than to the perverseness of the pupil.

Education has reaped much contempt from the mistakes and failures of those who have professed to be her servants: but while men are ready to heap censure on public or professed teachers, they are but too apt to forget that *parents* are educators no less than certain individuals who make education their fixed employment; and that it is the former who, by their all-powerful example, as often, if not in most instances, train up their tender pupils for happiness or misery.

From all this, the great responsibility that rests upon teachers, and the importance of their being thoroughly prepared for their high office, are abundantly obvious. This preparation consists in *perfect self-education.* This, indeed, is an ideal, but it is one whose closest approximation should always be aimed at. But we repeat, that among all the qualifications required in one who aspires to be an educator of youth, pure love to man is the sine quâ non.

Education, when it is what it ought to be, embraces the interests of man, not only in the present, but still more in the eternal world. It is, hence, the most important of all occupations, and it demands to be recognised as such. However extensively this demand may be responded to in theory, it is beyond expression deplorable to witness the extent to which the practice of society is at variance with its professions. And this is utterly inexcusable; for it is obvious, that if education were universally what it ought to be what the doctrines of Scripture require it to be, all men would become what their Creator has designed them to be, as far as this destination is attainable in this world. How little is education understood, and its importance appreciated! How mistaken is the notion that education consists in what is usually called a school-education! This is but one department of the great system, and a limited one indeed. The world is one vast schoolhouse, in which education, such as it is, never ceases for a moment. Oh! that the mighty power of Christianity might control it exclusively, through the influence, not only of the instructions, but of the character and example of its teachers!

Admonitions and counsel are by no means to be despised; but in education, example is omnipotent, and its importance is therefore paramount.

DIVISION I.

PHYSICAL AND INTELLECTUAL EDUCATION

SECTION I.

I. THE CULTURE OF THE UNDERSTANDING AND THE SENSIBILITIES.

CHAPTER I.

Man, in his Individual Capacity, educated in the Graces of the Mind.

a. WE begin with physical education, or the proper development of the body: and here we are first to consider that negative provision for health can be made in various ways. This subject is one of the utmost importance to parents, and to others intrusted with the education of children, and a great deal of attention has been given to it by writers on pedagogics. We would refer particularly to the admirable work of Schwarz. Apart from its own distinct value, the body is highly important as the substratum of the mind. Hence the duty of parents and others to provide negatively for the health of the body, on which the health of the mind depends.

The unimpaired health of parents is, in general, a guarantee of healthy offspring. It cannot be too seriously urged upon the attention of mothers, that the mode of life which they observe, and the tempers and feelings which they cultivate previous to the birth of their children, and during their early infancy, has a great influence, not only on the physical health, but on the disposition of their offspring.

Great progress can be made during the infancy of children in the due development of their senses, especially those of sight and hearing. Let the child look as long as it pleases at every object that attracts its attention, not passing from one to another before it has examined one to its satisfaction. Let it be entertained with agreeable sounds of the human voice, by talking to it pleasantly, not seriously, but as much nonsense as you please ; and especially by singing, not loudly and harshly, but softly and sweetly. Similar rules for the development of the other senses will suggest themselves to every intelligent mind. This subject will be discussed at large on a subsequent page.

Infants should be permitted to spend a good deal of time at the window ; and whenever the weather is suitable, they should be carried about in gardens, or wherever nature's green abounds.

For the development of gentle and amiable dispositions in the infant, nothing can be more influential than its being surrounded by cheerful, pleasant faces ; faces not wrinkled and clouded with care, but beaming with joyous love towards the new citizen of the world. It is important that it should very often see the father's face lighted up with the smiles of affection, and hear his voice expressive of joyful emotions ; for if, in its earliest intercourse with human beings, it be too much confined to the mother or to other females, an influence on its character will be wanting which can be supplied only by the manly features and tones of the father.

In respect to the physical education of the child, we observe farther, that its food requires the utmost attention. As regards the *quality* of the food, care should be taken that it be neither too strong, nor contain too little nourishment, but that, in all cases, it be adapted to the age and constitution of the child. On this point we refer to medical authorities, merely adding, that the practice, which prevails so extensively in this country, of giving children a large proportion of animal food, deserves to be condemned as mischievous.

Parents, and others intrusted with the education of children, should pay special attention to the *quantity* of food which they receive. This point is of the utmost importance, because children are not led by reason, as grown persons often are, nor, like animals, by instinct, to observe moderation in eating and drinking, whence they frequently indulge themselves to excess.

It is no less important that they be not suffered to eat too rapidly. They should be taught, with care, to masticate their food properly. And it is, in like manner, necessary to guard against their making use, at one time, of articles that accord ill together, such as fat food and cold water. As regards the *time* of eating, regularity should be observed. Children may require food more frequently than grown persons, but it is always best to limit them to certain stated times; to give them moderate meals in the evening, and not too shortly before their going to bed; and, in general, to indulge them but very little in cakes and confections. Plain, nourishing food is best for all stomachs, especially for young ones.

With respect to the natural discharges, we here merely observe, that some children are affected with peculiar infirmities, which require the most careful and judicious treatment, as these early weaknesses often become confirmed habits, and induce general, habitual filthiness. It will be obvious to most of our readers what infirmity is here more particularly referred to. The manner in which children subject to this weakness, or, for want of early and suitable management, addicted to a vile but stubborn habit, are generally treated, is highly injudicious. The habit may arise from sheer laziness; and, when this is ascertained to be the case, let correction be administered. But it is often a real infirmity, whatever may be its origin. For such cases, Dr. Graves, professor of the institutes of medicine in the school of physic, Trinity College, Dublin, recommends the following treatment. We quote his language: "A boy, perfectly healthy, but of a nervous temperament, studious, and extremely anxious about his lessons, is subject from his infancy to pass his water under him in bed. He is, suppose, arrived at the age of six or seven years, and has no disease; but still this habit sticks to him, and cannot be removed. The irritability of his disposition has been increased by injudicious correction; he has been taken up at night and whipped; he has been ridiculed during the day; his infirmity has been made known to his companions, who call him nicknames; and in this way the habit has been rather confirmed than removed. . . . . . Now what are you to do? In the first place, you must remove the boy entirely from all companions of his own age who are acquainted with his bodily infirmity. In the next place, you must not allow him to be corrected or reproached, and you must adopt every moral means to diminish general irritability. The boy should not be too much confined; he should not be allowed to apply too closely to his lessons; and he should have generous diet, good air, and sea-bathing. On these general principles I have cured several very obstinate cases, with the use of infusion of buchu, with tincture of cantharides, in small doses."—GRAVES's *Clinical Lectures*, 2d Am. edit., p. 235.

We merely add, that the above-prescribed medicines should not be meddled with without consulting a physician.

Cleanliness in every respect can never be too strongly inculcated, by precept, example, and discipline. Nothing is more important to a healthy state of the body. Some children seem to have no notion whatever of cleanliness—no capacity for it. But we know that in such cases vigilance and unremitted attention can accomplish a great deal, though it may be necessary, for a long time, daily to direct such children to brush their teeth, to comb their hair, and to attend to other points connected with a due cleanliness of person.

Bathing is highly to be recommended. Even in the case of those who are really cleanly in their habits, the accumulation of dust during the winter, to the obstruction of the pores, renders bathing decidedly necessary for the preservation and promotion of health. If practice in swimming can be combined with it, the acquisition of a valuable art will furnish additional inducements to frequent bathing. It is considered most conducive to health not to prolong ba thing beyond half an hour at a time..

Another point of the utmost importance is the ventilation of rooms. Children should never be suffered to inhabit ill-ventilated rooms, much less to sleep in them. In boarding-schools, where many children often live and sleep in one room, this matter should be carefully, conscientiously attended to. A foul atmosphere is pestiferous to the human system, but especially so to the tender organs of the young. The artificial impregnation of the air with foreign ingredients, by fumigation or otherwise, should be avoided. It is not only an unnecessary, but a pernicious practice. It is, under all circumstances, best to keep up a moderate temperature in inhabited rooms. Much that is valuable on the ventilation of rooms may be found in the writings of George Combe.

A great deal may be done for the preservation, the development, and the strengthening of the bodily organs. And here it is of primary importance that perspiration be not in any way, *e. g.*, by too much or too little clothing, either too much excited or too much repressed. But the promotion of this necessary excretion by the pores, by means of suitable bodily exercise, is much to be recommended. Tight clothes obstruct the development and prevent the free exercise of the bodily organs. It is painful to see how often children are thus cramped, and screwed up in stays and buckram, in order to gratify the bad taste of their fashionable parents. Children delight in their natural freedom, in the use of their limbs, and to make fools of fashion of them requires much and laborious effort in training them to habits which are unnatural. They cannot be taught to prefer fashionable clothing to such as nature prescribes, except at the expense of their health and comfort.

The preservation of the teeth, the eyes, and of the sense of hearing, is a point which calls for the most vigilant care on the part of parents and teachers, because children are notoriously careless of it them selves. As regards the preservation of the teeth, children ought not to be suffered to eat or drink anything either too hot or too cold. Hot food or drink is exceedingly pernicious. The greatest harm, however, is done by rapid transitions from one extreme to the other.

Children are very apt to injure their eyesight by having their books at either too great or too small a distance from the eyes, and by often poring over them in the gloom of twilight, or when seated too far away from the candle. On these points they require to be advised by the experienced. So they will often injure or destroy the sense of hearing by thrusting pins and other pointed articles into their ears, which practices parents and others should peremptorily prohibit, and if repeated, punish, instead of setting the evil example, which they often do.

In general, we may here remark, that it will be well to make children hardy in their whole mode of life; for, by so doing, they will be saved a host of ailments and of imaginary wants in after life. Only avoid extremes; for, while many parents train their children to effeminacy, others kill them by ill-advised methods of making them hardy.

Care should be taken that children get an adequate amount of sleep, and no more. Assuming seven hours of sleep as sufficient, on an average, for a grown person, we may safely set down nine hours as quite enough for children. Too much sleep interferes with and obstructs the circulation of the blood, produces enervation and indolence, relaxes the fibres, and thus occasions many diseases. Infants, on the other hand, should be suffered to sleep as much as they please.

Of the utmost importance to the healthy development of the body is the prevention of all unchaste habits of thought and conduct, and the most assiduous cultivation of the strictest purity. The writer had originally discussed the physical aspects of this subject at considerable length, and dwelt extensively on the prevention and cure of certain vicious and pernicious habits, into which the young are so often, and in various ways, seduced; but sundry weighty reasons subsequently induced him, after his work was entirely ready for the press, to suppress this discussion. He feels bound, however, to urge, in this connexion, upon parents, and others charged with the education of the young, the necessity of guarding their tender offspring or pupils, with the most solicitous vigilance, against the pollution of unchaste language and conduct; of protecting them from all temptations to fall into practices and habits which would necessarily degrade and demoralize their minds, and sap the energies of their physical constitution: in short, of adopting every possible means of preserving uncontaminated their purity of soul, and of exciting, whenever the necessity arises, their utmost abhorrence of all obscene allusions, all impure and lewd language—of all unchastity, in whatever form it may be exhibited.

Another point which deserves special attention in our negative provision for the health of the young, is to check and prevent all ebullitions of passion, and use every means for promoting their uninterrupted cheerfulness. In this connexion we may repeat, that the games of boys, which furnish incitements to active exertion, and the best means of recreation, not only deserve, but require superintendence and wise direction.

Violent affections of the mind, such as fear and anger, jealousy and envy, desire of revenge, as well as effeminate sensibility, are very prejudicial to health; while, on the other hand, the influence of the gentler and more agreeable emotions is decidedly beneficial.

With respect to the proper treatment of the sick, we only observe, that children should be accustomed to bear pain with fortitude, and to bear up under indisposition as long as possible. Many parents do all they can to make children commiserate themselves whenever an accident befalls them or they are unwell. This absurd practice should be studiously avoided. It is best to make light of falls and other accidents; turn them into a joke, and the child will laugh at them instead of crying. If the accident be more serious, it is still better to cheer up the little sufferer than to magnify the evil by lachrymose speeches of wo-begone condolence. The practice of teaching children to beat the floor on which they have fallen, to strike the table against which they have run their heads, is to be utterly reprobated, as systematic training to the indulgence of vindictive passion.

Boarding-schools must, of necessity, provide a suitable sick-department, and it is a very important concern of their superintendents to obtain the services of a sensible and faithful matron to take care of the sick. One who has herself been a mother should always be preferred. The matron should possess sagacity to detect, and firmness to resist all needless intrusion into the sick-chamber; for while the really ill should be treated with due tenderness and care, those who are subject to the camp-fever, *i. e.*, feign sickness in order to get rid of school, should find no encouragement to resort to the sick-department. From this department all luxurious indulgences should be carefully banished. Make every provision for the wants and the comfort of the sick, but furnish no temptations to those who are well to pretend or imagine that they are sick. To those who are in health, the sick-department should present no attractions, lest, by their frequent visits and lounging about, they waste their own time, and become burdensome to the sick, while they are themselves beyond the restraints of supervision.

The following additional remarks on the physical treatment and education of infants, were communicated, at our request, by an esteemed friend and highly intelligent and successful physician, expressly for the present work. They give little more than hints on a subject to which a separate volume might be profitably devoted. We hope they may awaken attention, and prove effectual in correcting mischievous practices, and induce many to adopt a more judicious mode of treating their children.

"The present age is pre-eminently distinguished

for the attention which is bestowed upon the moral and physical training of the young. It is pleasing to the philanthropist to observe the wise and good of the civilized world devoting their energies to these important subjects. The laws governing the moral and physical constitution of infantile existence are thus brought, more and more fully, to light, and rules of treatment, in harmony with those laws, are adopted and practised.

"Our purpose in furnishing the present communication is to treat of a few of the more prominent *errors* in the physical management of infants. It is unquestionably true, that from one fourth to one third of the children, born in the most favoured communities upon earth, are carried off by death before they reach the period of childhood, or the age of two years, and from one third to one half before the age of five years is attained. The bills of mortality, published annually in Europe as well as in this country, most fully establish these melancholy facts. Does not a strong presumption, then, arise from developments of this nature, that great errors are committed by those upon whom devolves the care of infantile life? We discover no similar fatality among the young of the brute creation, whose structure most nearly resembles that of man, and which are guided, in the treatment of their offspring, by an unerring instinct. Man is left to his boasted prerogative, *reason*, to guide him in this momentous business. In order, then, that he may perform his duty appropriately and successfully, it is self-evident that he should make himself acquainted with the elementary principles of that nature, of which the young being intrusted to his care is a specimen. We do not mean to assert that a thorough knowledge of anatomy, physiology, and medicine is necessary to parents, in order to stay this widespread desolation of human life; but prejudice and erroneous customs, having nothing but antiquity to recommend them, should give place to reason and observation, guided by experience and the advice of medical men. The several popular works on these subjects, now accessible to every one, and accommodated to the most moderate capacity, should also be consulted.

" Contemplate, for a moment, the condition of the infant, previous to its being ushered into a state of independent existence. It enjoys a tranquil state of growth and nutrition, wholly dependant upon a portion of its mother's organism. Those organs which connect us with the external world are then in a state of inactivity and repose. The function of respiration is not yet needed, other organs being provided for effecting the necessary changes in the blood. The digestive organs have not yet been called upon to receive aliment, and to fit it for the uses of the system, all sustenance being, as yet, elaborated by the parent; the muscular system has not yet been excited into action, there being no feeling, no intellect, no will to need or control it.

" But the connexion is severed: how great the change! what a revolution in the infant's mode of existence! In a moment it passes from a state of unconscious repose to life, and light, and action; from mere vegetative to independent animal existence. A multitude of new and important relations are established between its tender and delicate organism and the countless objects of external nature. The current of the circulation finds new channels, and abandons those heretofore the conduits of the vital fluid The digestive, assimilative, and respiratory functions hitherto dormant, must now originate their primary movements. Animal heat, until now furnished by the parent, must hereafter be elaborated by its own organs. Until this moment guarded by the mother's sensations, its own nerves must now warn it of impressions made by external objects. How important, then, that the treatment of the infant should be in harmony with the feeble demands of its constitution, and adapted to the incipiency of its delicate organism. How absurd and preposterous to abandon the plain indications of nature, and to expose the infant to a regime better suited to adolescence, with a view to render *hardy*, to *invigorate*, and *nourish*. No wonder that the garner of death is filled by so large a proportion of infants not a month old, while many of those that survive this period eke out a miserable existence of but a few months longer: the vital principle being reduced so low, that teething, or any of the milder diseases common to infancy, furnish a ready avenue out of this world, to them peculiarly one of suffering and distress, short as their career in it may have been.

"We are persuaded, from extensive opportunities of observation, and very special attention to this subject, that deficient clothing, inappropriate food, and improper domestic medical treatment, constitute the three principal errors in the physical training of infants. We shall, therefore, briefly notice these three causes of disease and death among children, our limits not admitting of our entering more extensively into the subject.

"1. *Inadequate protection from cold.* The sudden transition from a long-continued and uniform temperature of 98° to one of 60°, or even lower, we should suppose, would severely try the vital resistance to morbid action of the adult; how much more that of the infant! It is reasonable to infer that infants are capable of generating a much smaller amount of heat proportionally than adults, because all their bodily functions are yet in a state of incipiency. Physiology teaches that animal heat is generated principally by the functions of respiration, circulation, and innervation. These are, in infants, necessarily feeble and imperfect, and hence exposure to cold is met by a very imperfect resistance. Respiration and the nervous influence commence their first movements at birth, while the circulation finds new channels; having been hitherto confined in a great measure to the skin, which is extremely vascular, it is now directed towards the internal viscera, which have not yet been excited fully to the performance of their appropriate functions. We can have no difficulty, then, in deciding, à priori, that the exposure of infants to a low temperature, whether from deficient or improper clothing, will prove injurious to them. In accordance with this are the experiments of Doctors Edwards and Villermé, of France, made upon young, warm-blooded animals, by which it was incontestably proven that their temperature decreases very rapidly at an atmospheric temperature which had no effect upon adults; for example, when new-born dogs and cats were taken away from the parent, and exposed even to a moderate degree, they were chilled even to the very point of death.

"The researches of Doctors Fontanelle and Trevisano, of Italy, also sustain these views: from them we draw the following conclusions: 1. That out of one hundred children born during the winter months, sixty-six die in the first month of life. 2. Out of one hundred born in summer, only seventeen die during the first month. 3. Out of one hundred born in spring and in autumn, only about one half die during the *first year;* and, 4. That the mortality is greater among children born in northern than among those born in southern climates.

"From these physiological principles and facts, so clearly ascertained, it is evident that infants should be furnished with a greater amount of clothing than adults. Agreeably, however, to the present mode of attiring infants, especially in fashionable life, not only are they more thinly clad than the parent, but large portions of the surface are wholly uncovered. Nothing is more common than to see children with their arms, necks, and upper portions of the chest bare, thus exposing these parts to the continued sedative influence of a low temperature.

"When we reflect on the close sympathy that exists between the skin and the internal organs of the body, we have, under such circumstances, no difficulty in deciding upon the probable cause of disease in the liver, lungs, stomach, bowels, and brain; and hence croup, catarrh, fever, diarrhœa, cholera, and convulsions are frequent consequences, but constitute parts only of that wide outlet to infant life which deficient clothing creates. Some endeavour to justify their practice by maintaining that such exposure is calculated to inure their children to the impressions of cold, and to render them hardy. This *may* be the result with those who have stamina sufficient to survive the experiment, but, before the system is thus invigorated, the child may be carried off by some inflammatory affections produced by such exposure. I have often had occasion to admire the ruddy health which characterizes the children of the plain people of the country, who, in matters of this kind, follow the indications of nature and the dictates of common sense. These cover, from the commencement, the entire surface of their children in winter with warm flannel, and in summer with cotton; they rarely have any diseases among their children except such as are natural, and these, in a majority of instances, are so mild as not to require medical treatment. I do not remember, during a practice of fourteen years, to have been called to a case of croup, catarrh, or cholera in such a family; and I have frequently met with such families, who had raised from ten to fourteen children without having at any time had occasion to call in a physician. The pure air of the country, I am aware, also exerts a healthful influence; but we have *there* also seen undue exposure producing disease; while *in town* we have known many instances of ameliorated health, by the adoption of more suitable clothing, in families whose children had previously suffered in consequence of improper clothing.

"2. *Inappropriate food.* The digestive organs of the newborn babe have not, as yet, been exercised, having been in a quiescent and passive state during the whole period of gestation. The stomach has not yet been distended, and participates in the universal delicacy of the whole organism. The question now presents itself very forcibly, what substance can be found in nature, sufficiently bland and nutritious, and suitable for so delicate an organ? The benevolent Author of all being has made the most appropriate provision in the milk of the mother, the proper and only food for the infant; art cannot supply, nor does nature af lord, any adequate substitute for this fluid. When the child is applied to the mother, at from six to eight hours after birth, it receives a watery fluid which possesses laxative properties. This excites the stomach and bowels to action, and frees them from the tenacious, dark-green substance, the expulsion of which is necessary to prepare them for the exercise of their proper functions. In due time, more nutritious milk is furnished, in sufficiently large quantities to nourish the infant until the first teething. Should the secretion of milk not be fully established even before the third day, it is unnecessary to substitute as food any extraneous substances. The idea entertained by some that the child has been fasting all the while, is erroneous, for to the last moment of its connexion with the mother it has been supplied with a rich and nutritious blood, prepared expressly for its support; so that, in fact, instead of fasting, it has just finished a continuous meal of nine months.

" But, notwithstanding the admirable provision so bountifully made, and so benevolently adjusted to the peculiar wants and condition of the helpless being intrusted to our care, it is scarcely ushered into existence, and invested in its disease-inviting habiliments, when a system of drenching and stuffing is commenced. A mixture of molasses and water, of salt and water, manna tea, or even some of the common purgatives, is first given, to purge off the meconium or green matter already mentioned. This is usually the first offence. We have already made it appear that this is unnecessary;* but positive injury is also inflicted by creating irritation on the tender surface of the alimentary canal, not only producing pain, but unfitting it for the digestive process which is subsequently to take place. The pain thus induced robs the child of repose and sleep, and causes wakefulness and fretting; the latter is looked upon as a symptom of hunger; it is forthwith decided that 'the child must be

* " It will be borne in mind that the writer here assumes that the mother is in a healthy state, actually furnishing her infant with what its Maker has intended for it."

fed after having fasted so long,' and straightway an ample bowl of panada, thick pap, grated cracker and tea, or some other equally improper article of diet is prepared, and the stuffing commences, which is repeated at regular intervals; increased, however, so soon as colic, which is one of the invariable results of such treatment, sets in. When the proper time arrives for the milk to be secreted, the child has already been *broken to the spoon*, and, in a great measure, lost its instinctive knowledge of sucking, as also its desire for food, for by this time it is racked with colic-pains, flatulency, vomiting, and diarrhœa. The consequence is, that the spoon is, at least in part, continued; the mother's breasts are not drawn; they swell and become painful by distension; disturbed rest, and exposure to the chilly night-air in consequence of attentions to the suffering infant, bring on chills, fever, and inflammation, followed by abscess in the breasts, loss of milk causing much suffering and distress to both mother and child. In the mean time, the infant, which was plump and full of vigour when born, becomes pale and emaciated; diseases of various kinds, in addition to those already mentioned, invade the enfeebled frame, under the influence of one or the other of which it pines away and dies. Many, however, have a sufficiency of stamina to enable them to survive these severe trials; but we have most abundant reason to believe that, in such cases, the foundations of disease in after life are thus early laid. It is erroneously supposed that the nourishment afforded by the mother is, after a few months, insufficient to sustain the health and life of the infant. We would lay it down as a general rule, that when the mother is healthy, the infant needs no additional food before the commencement of the first teething, which usually takes place about the seventh month. The first food given should differ in its properties as little as possible from that which the infinitely wise Creator has himself supplied for the first stage of human life.

"To remedy the hurtful effects of insufficient clothing and improper diet, recourse is had to carminatives and opiates, and this leads us to consider the last error above mentioned.

"3. *Improper domestic medical treatment.* Were proper attention paid to infants in their diet and clothing, *medical* treatment would rarely become necessary. So soon, however, as the train of symptoms already detailed begins to manifest itself, the mother, or more officious nurse, without instituting any inquiry as to the cause, and the possibility of its removal to the immediate relief of the little sufferer, forthwith administers some portion of active medicine, to be repeated as occasion may require, until they become alarmed, and send for their medical adviser, who is gravely informed 'that the child took slightly ill, and that, notwithstanding full and repeated doses of calomel, magnesia, rhubarb, or laudanum were given, it continued getting worse and worse!' But, not content with giving drugs when disease is supposed to be present, many mothers are in the habit of constantly keeping and administering one or more of the many opiate nostrums and cordials, merely in order to quiet the child or to procure it sleep. The basis of all these preparations consists of opium. The almost invariable effect of these is to impair the powers of the stomach, to retard the development and growth of the body, to injure the nervous system, and to induce a state of the entire system adverse to the health and life of the child. But the evil of indulging in the use of opiates does not stop in merely producing disease, for death is very frequently the result. Agreeably to a report printed by order of the House of Commons in England, it appears that, of all inquests held in England and Wales in 1837 and 1838 in cases of death from poison, one seventh of the whole number resulted from the carelessness of mothers and nurses in administering opiates, with the properties of which they were unacquainted. Mr. Brown, the coroner of Nottingham, England, also reports that great numbers of children are annually destroyed in that borough by the use of 'Godfrey's Cordial.' There are, doubtless, many such cases which never become subjects of official notice, and the cause of death is reported as unknown. The majority of cases of this kind are the result of errors as regards the particular article intended to be administered, or in the amount of the dose. Cases of this kind frequently come under the observation of the physician: we will mention the following two out of many which we might adduce:

"Mrs. C., of N., had been in the habit of administering laudanum to her infant son; the dose was gradually increased until she gave eleven drops at a time. The opiate was then discontinued for several months, during which period the *acquired* capacity to receive so large a portion with apparent impunity was lost; the laudanum, also, being in a vial closed with a paper stopper, became much stronger in consequence of the evaporation which had taken place. The mother, however, ignorant of this, supposing a dose of laudanum necessary, gave the child twenty drops, because he was several months older than when she was in the habit of giving him eleven drops. The effect was a state of narcotism, which would certainly have proved fatal had not active measures been adopted soon after the laudanum had been given.

"The other case was also in N. Mrs. M. was in the habit of administering 'Godfrey's Cordial' to her infant. Her vial being empty, she gave it to her brother, and requested him to have it filled. When he arrived at the apothecary's, he could not remember the name of the article; but he 'knew that laudanum would make babies sleep:' he accordingly procured it. His sister gave the dose she was wont to give, a teaspoonful (holding sixty drops), to her infant, aged three months and two days, and laid it upon the bed. Having other family matters to attend to, she did not look at her child until more than an hour after she had given the opiate, when, to her inexpressible surprise and alarm, she found it in convulsions. We were sent for, and found her, with her babe in her arms, frantic with grief; for she had already discovered the error. The case appeared hopeless; but the almost immediate introduction of the stomach-tube, by means of which the stomach was entirely freed from the poison remaining in it, and by other appropriate means, with a view to counteract the poisonous effects of the portion which had found its way into the circulation prior to the evacuation of the stomach, proved successful in saving the child. It cost us the labour of a night, but there was a joy in the morning in that mother's breast which repaid us amply for all our watching and labour. We might state cases of this kind which terminated in death, but we forbear.

"Although we designed, in the commencement, to confine ourselves to a few hints on these three principal errors, which obtain in the physical education of infancy, we cannot, under this last head, refrain from adverting to the moral effect of opiates, when regularly administered to infants. The effect of this narcotic is to obtund the sensibilities of the nervous system; to becloud that sprightly vivacity, which gives an irresistible charm to the speaking countenance of the infant; to induce stupor—narcotism. We may easily conceive that permanence may be given to these effects by a frequent and long-continued use of this poison, just at a time when the brain and the nervous system, the organs of the soul, are being called into exercise, and manifest their earliest developments. We have met with several cases in which the children of sprightly and intelligent parents were dull, inactive, and stupid at adult age, notwithstanding they had had good opportunities of education; and, on making inquiry, our suspicions were verified by the information that during infancy those persons had, daily and regularly, portions of quieting medicines administered to them; and that, when an extraordinary engagement on the part of the mother, whether at home or abroad, had required it, a double portion had been given. But the moral malady thus induced extends still farther. In the majority of the male members of those families, there seemed to exist a natural propensity to *intemperance*.

"Never can I forget the heart-rending self-reproaches of an intelligent Christian mother, who is now, we trust, in heaven. In speaking to me of the case of her son, she exclaimed, 'Alas! my poor, wandering, forlorn, lost, firstborn son! He was intemperate from his boyhood; and O! mine is the guilt, for I made him a drunkard. He was a cross and fretful child; I gave him stimulating cordials and opiates; he continued to crave them when several years old; and ever after, when he could obtain spirits of any kind, he would have them. Thus I made him what he is. O! that I had withheld from him the pernicious drugs! My poor, lost boy!'"

b. *Bodily Exercise. Gymnastics.*

The exercise and development of the body is of obvious importance, not only in a mechanical point of view, with reference to profitable employment, nor in a physical or medical sense alone, *i. e.*, in respect of health, but also in an æsthetic sense, *i. e.*, with regard to gracefulness of carriage and motion. From these three considerations it is evident that gymnastics deserves the special attention of those to whom the education of youth is intrusted.

It may be divided into mechanical, common, or natural, and into æsthetic, elegant, or artistical gymnastics.

Mechanical gymnastics includes everything pertaining to the exercise of the body by manual labour. It may be said, however, to begin with walking and running. To this division belong all mechanical employments which are calculated duly to develop the physical organs. Here must also be mentioned riding on horseback and swimming, considered as useful arts. This division of gymnastics may be termed natural, because children will acquire skill adequate to the purposes of exercise in all the varieties embraced by it, if they be not subjected to unnatural coercion and oppression in a matter that ought to be made as agreeable as possible, which, unhappily, is very often the case.

The province of elegant or æsthetic gymnastics is to develop those physical organs which, apart from all actual, tangible profit, give strength to man, invest him with agility and grace, and enhance the beauty peculiar to the human frame.

In every system of gymnastics, dancing holds a prominent place, and is, undeniably, highly promotive of elegance of carriage and motion; yet its connexion with fashionable dissipation and its moral influence are of such a character, that, while we lament that no suitable substitute for it can be found, we can in no wise recommend it.

To proceed, therefore, to other gymnastic exercises, we mention, first, running, in which the degree of speed acquired will furnish a good test of the development of muscular strength, as well as the flexibility of the joints and the capability of the limbs to endure protracted exertion.

Wrestling, when under proper control, is favourable to the development of the sinews and joints of the upper part of the body, while running is more advantageous to the lower extremities.

Jumping, in which the arms also are often much exercised, is an important branch of gymnastics. We distinguish two varieties, the upward and the forward jump. The former consists either in jumping up and immediately coming down again, or in jumping upward to a more elevated position. The latter is performed either without extraneous aids, or with the assistance of the pole. All these exercises, if controlled with care and judgment, will have a very favourable influence in developing the bodily organs for agility, energy, and elegance of motion.

All the various games of ball, and the like, in which boys are fond of engaging, constitute an important branch of gymnastics: and to what has been said of these, we would add a few general observations.

The tendency of the present age is entirely too bookish. Compends in every department of science abound, and children study philosophy, mental and moral, and natural science in its various branches, before they are capable of understanding anything of the subjects presented. Pedantry and affectation come into the place of the artlessness and the unassuming docility of childhood. We rejoice to see the higher departments of knowledge made more generally accessible than in times past. In our country especially, liberal education must become general. But "there is a time for all things," says the wise man; and all things have their necessary limits. In connexion with the rage for book-learning, the impression seems to have gone abroad that children and youth should be no longer suffered to play, but, in order to keep up with "the march of mind," they should be early confined to their lessons, and learn to look grave and knowing when their elders discuss matters of science, and even to prate learnedly and wisely in literary circles. We are running into extremes, which many wise and good men have long deplored; and we, for one, desire to plead for the rights and interests of childhood and youth. Give your children ample time to play; encourage them to play; help them to play. They will then learn, not only more willingly and cheerfully, but more successfully, during the time necessarily devoted to books. The course so generally pursued at present results, after all, in the attainment of only a very superficial knowledge, which is never digested. By sound physical health and a flow of animal spirits, the healthy tone and activity of their minds, in maturer years, are much more effectually secured than by early confinement to the many textbooks of the day; and when they reach those years in which the sciences may be studied understandingly, and therefore profitably, they will possess a mental vigour which modern methods of education are calculated, in a great measure, to destroy. These games, or other varieties of gymnastic exercise, should be continued during the whole course of education. One of the greatest evils prevailing at our colleges—one that fills their halls with sallow faces and languid bodies, is a deficiency, or entire absence in many instances, of suitable exercise

Every boarding-school should possess several suitable play-grounds, one for each section of pupils.

In the years of childhood and early youth, all these gymnastic exercises ought to be engaged in systematically, *i. e.*, according to a regular plan. But they may be diminished in proportion as the physical and intellectual energies of the youth increase. As the young approach the age of manhood, the necessity of stated hours for gymnastic exercises should be superseded by the voice of nature and common sense, which will loudly forbid every student who has a regard for his health, physical and intellectual, to neglect exercises which are so essential to both.

c. *Education for the True Enjoyment of Life.*

Love of a simple and moderate enjoyment of the things of this life is essential to the healthy life of the soul. The blessings of Providence are bestowed for our happiness—to cheer our progress through this earthly existence. This design is frustrated, as well when we make the good things of life the objects of covetous and anxious care and burning desire, as when we indulge in the excessive enjoyment of them. Cheerfulness and moderation! This cheerful disposition ought to be cultivated in children: nor will this be a difficult task, as morose and unsociable minds are an exception to the general rule.

Those who multiply artificial wants are mistaken if they imagine that they contribute to the real enjoyment of life. A strong desire for a variety of enjoyments is a mental disease, which we should not seek to heighten, but to cure.

Everything will depend upon a wise combination of the ideals of comfort and discomfort, and hence on a just estimate of what must be termed luxury.

Luxury, *i. e.*, the influence of refinement upon the multiplication of wants, presents itself to our consideration under three aspects. First, that of ease or comfort; second, of fashion; third, of mental culture, *i. e.*, such culture as will qualify for the enjoyment of a luxurious mode of living.

Love of ease and fashion are the guides that conduct to effeminacy, to worldly folly and frivolity; they are in themselves worthless, and have no claim on our attention. But the mental culture above referred to demands farther notice, and requires that we should attend to its proper direction. With regard to a wise mode of living, we should endeavour to give children clear ideas, and more particularly exert a healthy influence upon them, by setting them a good example. The examples of the wise and good of every age should be held up to those who have reached the age of youth. It requires much prudence and judgment to manage suitably the treatment of children, in view of their general mode of living. In fitting them for the true enjoyment of life, all the various methods connected with the different departments of education must, in their due measure, co-operate. The reader will himself trace the bearings of subsequent discussions on the subject here considered.

CHAPTER II.

Intellectual Culture, aiming at the Development of the Understanding for the Perception of Truth.

The course of development taken by the human mind in the culture of the intellect proceeds from the *external sense* to *language;* from the *impressions* received from the outward objects through the medium of the senses, to the *expression* of these impressions in words. Next follows the exertion of the memory, often connected with the imagination; then, and but gradually, comes attention; and lastly, through the exercise of attention, and by the active employment of the internal sense, the power of thought is developed and brought into action. Many remain strangers to that effort of the mind which is called thinking, even to the later years of youth.

Education must here adapt its methods to the course of nature, and aim only at guidance and direction. Much injury is done by urging the youthful mind to premature efforts; by seeking preternaturally to develope its active but still slumbering powers. We need scarcely observe, that all the faculties above named must, at a certain age, be simultaneously exercised and cultivated.

Young children live entirely in the external world, and therefore this age should be carefully improved for the development and cultivation of their outward senses, especially those of sight, hearing, and smell. As this branch of education is much neglected, we would direct attention to it through the following observations, which are taken substantially from the excellent work of Schwarz.

Properly cultivated and well-trained senses constitute an important mark of difference between man and the lower animals. They are the avenues through which stores of raw material are conveyed into the workshop of the mind. If you suffer but little to pass through them, and confine the attention of children to a small number of objects, and to a particular view of them, you limit the free development of the capacity of the senses, and condemn it to poverty. If you leave all to nature, no readiness or distinctness of observation is acquired; the impressions, vague and confused, would confuse the mind itself, and surrender it to mere sensual excitement. And then man becomes more beastly than the beast, which is indemnified by its instinct for the want of what we possess in the power of attention.

In cultivating and training the senses, our object should be,

1. That each sense may perceive acutely and correctly, and by attaining vigour and firmness of capacity, make easy and copious acquisitions.

2. Æsthetic observation, leading the senses to a sense of the beautiful, and developing particularly those of sight and hearing for the exercise of taste.

3. The strengthening of the power of observation by means of the senses.

1. *The Sense of Sight.*

This is the first that is developed, and it is particularly susceptible of cultivation.

The eyes of children will always be turned towards the brightest object near them; but they should not, in early infancy, be permitted to look at any very brilliant light, for this is injurious to the eyes. On the other hand, by introducing them gradually from an artificial twilight to the full brightness of day, the sense of sight is strengthened. This may be done during the first weeks of life. Now let them distinguish different objects, according to the various degrees of light, and they will soon begin to notice different forms and colours. Then accustom them so to fix their regards on single objects as to recognise them when they see them again. Show them, as frequently as possible, natural objects, such as birds, flowers, trees, &c., and teach them to distinguish colours. They may thus learn, at two years of age, to distinguish several varieties of the same colour. Even before they speak, repeat to them often the names of many objects; after this, frequently pronounce certain names in a tone of inquiry, while pointing to the things mentioned; and soon, when they begin to speak, they will, even when not called upon to do so, frequently point out such objects, and mention their names.

Then take them out, also, into the moonlight, and let them recognise various objects: carry them out in dark nights.

Thus they will early learn to find their way in the dark without mistaking the stems of trees for men. Let them not closely examine minute objects in the twilight, for this injures the eyes; but direct their attention early to the starry heavens, pointing out to them stars of peculiar brightness, as well as particular groups. This will produce a strong impression, and a singular interest in young minds, and sometimes even elicit poetic sparks.

Accustom them also to discern and distinguish objects at a distance, as well as to observe accurately objects in rapid motion, and to discover a given object among a number of moving ones. Take them to elevated positions, such as high towers or steeples, and let them look down: this will preserve them from the infirmity of giddiness, to which so many are subject for want of proper training. Such treatment will give children, at seven years of age, acute and accurate habits of vision.

But it will now be necessary to continue the proper cultivation of this sense by regular exercises. 1. In observing: let the children recognise near and distant objects in different degrees of light, and name every object within sight Begin with single objects, then proceed to several, and finally to groups. Let them recognise objects, and even read at distances gradually increased. Then let the forms of lines and figures be noted, named, and drawn, *e. g.*, perpendicular, oblique, circular, &c. Continue to practise them in distinguishing colours. Finally, accustom them to make accurate estimates of the dimensions of objects, and of their relative distances.

2. In an æsthetic point of view: the previous training will teach them accurately to distinguish the outlines of a leaf, a tree, &c., and this, with suitable instruction, will enable them to draw such objects correctly; and as, in so doing, their attention is directed to the real form and dimensions of the objects as they appear within the sphere of vision, *i. e.*, to perspective, they will thus learn to draw masses or groups, without having their sense of the picturesque disturbed by the thought of the reality. In this practice great advantage will be derived from showing them painted landscapes, and letting them compare these with the appearance of the real landscape before them. With such training, they may learn, at fourteen years of age, to discern picturesque landscapes, or particularly picturesque features of them, and to collect these in their portfolios. A sense for the symbolical character of natural objects is best excited by poetry.

3. With regard to the strengthening of the power of observation by means of sight, we have nothing to add to the preceding. Various exercises might be recommended; but we shall only remark, that the

great object to be kept in view is to teach the young to discern and distinguish, with increasing acuteness and accuracy, both near and distant objects, and especially to describe them in words. Let them begin with isolated, small objects, such as a leaf; then proceed to a small plant; next to a tree; then take groups of trees, and finally an entire landscape, or whatever may lie within the sphere of vision. This describing in words should be first performed while the object is viewed, then with averted face, and lastly at home, after the lapse of some time, or after a walk. With these exercises, drawing from memory may be combined. It is astonishing what progress young persons will thus make, not only in acuteness, distinctness, and accuracy of vision, but in habits of order, in clearness of language, and in attention, besides enriching the memory with valuable treasures, and acquiring a keen sense of the picturesque.

The advantage attained by a methodical training of the sense of sight is twofold. First, it leads to an extensive and accurate acquaintance with created objects. A multitude of the most important observations and impressions are thus appropriated, in such a manner that they remain in the mind with truthfulness, freshness, and clearness. The understanding thus acquires a fund of necessary material; an abundance of seed is deposited in the memory; a fruitful soil is presented to the fancy; and to the feelings, the wide field of the beautiful and the significant is thrown open. Thus, by means of the sense which is earliest active, the mind is endowed with the riches of external creation, and thus enabled to prosecute its internal creations.

But this advantage consists, in the second place, in the sharpening of the sense itself, in the training of the eye for enlarged and sagacious action, and is, in this sense, perhaps still more important. If the child is left to its natural observation, its eye will generally become indolent, and its soul sensual. The attention is not practised except by the animal instinct which calls for food; excited only by objects that are otherwise serviceable, or such as awaken fear; and thus the most valuable sense is in early life subjected and habituated to the service of the lower propensities, and the child becomes a slave of sensuality. If the child looks at objects only with a view to ascertain whether they may be eaten, we need not wonder if the countenance of the adult betrays nothing but animal appetite and greediness. When the sense of sight is not early cultivated, it cannot be otherwise than that a sensual disposition must become dominant; and this will, in a great measure, account for the grovelling dispositions which characterize the uneducated classes, and for the more elevated and generous qualities which distinguish those who have received a good education. Cicero seems to have perceived the necessity of such an education as is here contended for, when he wrote the following words: "Nos ne nunc quidem cernimus ea, quæ videmus; viæ quasi quædam sunt ad oculos, ad aures, ad nares a sede animi perforatæ," &c.—Cic., T. Q., i., 20

2. *The Sense of Hearing.*

This sense is to be cultivated in a manner similar to the foregoing. Here, also, the objects to be aimed at are,

1. Acuteness and accuracy of observation. Sounds are to be recognised and distinguished, their direction and distance to be estimated, &c. The attention is to be directed particularly to language.

2. The æsthetic training of the ear. To this are conducive musical exercises, harmonious combinations of sounds, &c.

3. The sharpening or strengthening of the mental faculty of observing by means of the ear. To this, practice in discerning very low sounds, distinguishing certain sounds amid loud and confused clamour, and the like, are subservient.

It will be observed, in the first weeks of an infant's life, that its sense of hearing is sensibly excited. After the lapse of a few more weeks it will notice particular sounds, and it will now be well if it be frequently addressed in a kindly tone of voice. Thus it will soon recognise the voice of its mother, and not be long in distinguishing that of other persons. There will be no harm done if there be various noises about infants, so they be not of a violent nature, for this keeps the sense of hearing in a state of activity, without causing it strong exertion. Besides the human voice, young children should be made to notice the sounds uttered by various domestic animals.

When they begin to walk, call to them frequently at a distance, at one time with a loud voice, at another more softly; and thus, at two years of age, they will be accustomed to listen sharply. Now teach them to know different animals by their voices; permit them occasionally to hear more violent noises, *e. g.*, that of a mill; and sometimes speak to them in a very soft, scarcely audible tone. They may be taught, at the age of three years, to distinguish several varieties of birds by their voices; they will recognise with joyous feelings, among the voices of a number of persons engaged in loud conversation, that of an acquaintance; and not fail, in the midst of the clamour of play, to observe what their parents may say to them. If a piano-forte be played upon in the room which they frequent, they will soon be seen to note its tones attentively. The ear should be accustomed from early infancy to hear the tones of sweet song. In their fourth year, children may be taken to the piano-forte, and made to listen to different series of tones; first, the diatonic or natural scale, and the octaves; then the fifths, and thirds, and other intervals; and if their sense of hearing be not very obtuse, the ear will soon distinguish those tones correctly when they are sounded in their proper order of succession. By frequently repeating easy tunes for them, they will soon be led to endeavour to repeat them with the voice. Let this be their primary instruction in music without subjecting them to constraint. In the course of a year, the ear will generally be sufficiently practised to distinguish more complex musical combinations; and at five years of age, formal instruction in music, especially in singing, may commence. The ear should be habituated to distinguish tones on different, both wind and stringed, instruments; but no stunning noise, like that of the explosion of a gun or the sound of a drum, should be brought very near them, until the sense of hearing has, by gradual exercise, become strong enough to bear it; and even then it will be advisable to remove from them such sounds whose tendency it is to blunt the sense of hearing. With such training, children will, at six years of age, have a well-practised ear. Continue to practise them in distinguishing with increased accuracy, not only musical tones, but every variety of sounds, by which means they will acquire great readiness in distinguishing very soft sounds, and to point out the direction from which they come. It will be well, also, to give them something particular to listen to, while, at the same time, a loud noise is made. This cultivation of the sense of hearing may be continued by the following exercises.

Blindfold the eyes of the child under training, and let him name those whose voices he hears. After some time, let a number of other children be stationed at different distances from him, and let him, still blindfolded, specify whose voice he hears, and from what direction it comes. Again, let him state, with his eyes closed, what he hears another person do; describe the direction from which the voices of different persons who are speaking reach him; or specify the particular body from which some peculiar sound is elicited. Again, let something be read, or names pronounced, and let the child repeat what he hears. Let a key be sounded on the piano-forte without his seeing it, and call upon him to find out what key has been struck; or let him, blindfolded specify the particular tones that have been struck, with a variation in the succession of the intervals; and when his voice has been sufficiently practised, let him repeat the tones. Subsequent exercises will consist in hearing narratives, and then repeating them; in frequently hearing poetry read, and in acquiring a readiness at memorizing by hearing only, and in attending to oral commissions, of which many may be sometimes given at once.

The first advantage accruing from the exercise of this sense consists partly in its acquaintance with a vast number and variety of sounds, and partly in the firm retention of observations and ideas, acquired through the other senses, which this sense secures to us by means of the words which designate them. The ear is the organ which, by means of spoken words, directly excites the understanding to form for itself clear ideas of objects; it enriches and enlightens the memory; it excites the fancy by the pictures which it retains, and it unlocks the innermost sanctuary for the reception of intellectual and spiritual truth; for it is in the sense of hearing, and by means of the multitude of words familiar to it, that reason is particularly developed. But again, he that hears well has his mind fitted for an exact and thorough performance of its different peculiar functions; he becomes more susceptible of the beautiful, in its higher manifestations, as well as for the supernatural, and thus his taste is liberated from sensual trammels; the most sacred feelings are excited within him by words in which the sincerity of an affectionate heart addresses him. It is this sense, by whose agency the earliest transition is made from attention to recollection, to reflection, and to a respectful regard for the will of others: acute hearing awakes attention to the smallest word, however gently spoken, and this leads to obedience. If the ear, through the medium of sound, conducts us to a profound acquaintance with nature, it is, at the same time, the organ through which we hold communion with the spiritual world As the inhabitants of the East heard the voice of God in the sound of thunder, the child hears it in the communications of its parents, and every pious heart in the word of wisdom. He that has become accustomed to mark attentively the words of others, possesses an additional antidote against egotism. Pythagoras regarded attentive listening as such a means of culture, and discovered in sounds a depth which might lead the soul to the enjoyment of the music of the spheres. It is undeniable that the sense of hearing is, in a high degree, subservient to the cultivation of harmony of soul, of purity of heart, of holy love, and of spiritual life; in which respect its importance is far from being adequately recognised.

3. *The Sense of Smell.*

On this sense, which is intermediate between the two higher and the two lower senses, we shall be brief. It has doubtless been given to man for higher purposes than to the brute. Through its instrumentality children are, 1. To learn to discover the near or more remote presence of things, such as smoke and fire, injurious or beneficial exhalations: 2. To enjoy purely agreeable odours, and to be invited and led to a certain secret sympathy with the life of nature: 3. To acquire the power of enduring, in cases of necessity, disagreeable smells, without prejudice to the acuteness of the sense.

This sense is not likely to betray much activity before children have reached their third year, and your first care should be to guard it against everything calculated to exert a blunting influence upon it. Suffer them not to frequent places where the air is impregnated with disagreeable odours; but, at the same time, forbear the application of strong odours of an agreeable nature. Let them, in the open and pure air, inhale the balsamic fragrance of the vegetable world. This will make them sensitive against all disagreeable smells, and careful to avoid what may be injurious to them, as well as teach them to distinguish objects at a distance by their exhalations. Avoid stimulating the sense too highly by strong perfumes; but, on the other hand, accustom it early to relish the sweet odour of flowers.

For a variety of exercises designed to develop and cultivate this sense, and for many other interesting observations in relation to it, we refer to Schwarz, vol. iii., p. 102, seqq.

4. *The Sense of Taste.*

That this sense, also, is of importance to the understanding, appears clearly from the multiplicity of words in different languages by which its sensations are designated, particularly in chemical science. This sense becomes negatively subservient to the higher feelings just in proportion as it is secured against gluttony, and habituated to the relish of simple, healthy diet; and in this respect it may serve to illustrate what is called taste in a higher sense. The acquisition of such habits necessarily involves the proper cultivation, not only of the acuteness of the sense itself, but of the sagacity of the mind in employing it; and its proper development is betokened as well by a keen and accurate distinction of different tastes, as by the elevation of the soul above the mere animal pleasure or disgust excited by them.

An infant will, in the first months of its life, begin to distinguish between sweet, bitter, and sour; and beyond this the cultivation of taste should not, at this early age, be attempted, in order that it may not lose its susceptibility of the teachings of nature; for these are especially important to the sense of taste, because it is this sense which must guide us in the choice of food, without seducing the stomach into bad habits, contracted in consequence of the lustfulness of the appetite. Let, then, the early cultivation of this sense begin with your administering simple food; and put off acquainting the tongue with salt and spices, that its energies be not blunted, and become prematurely susceptible of the stronger stimulants, and therefore lustful. An early fondness for sugar should also be guarded against. Children thus judiciously treated will so much the longer relish farinaceous food and milk, and they will find their chief luxury in what nature alone presents perfectly prepared to every one, namely, fruit. This treatment will preserve the organ of taste healthy and uncorrupted, so as to enable it to distinguish the different varieties of fruit with the utmost acuteness.

Various exercises may be employed. Children may learn to distinguish different sorts of water by their taste ; and when chemical experiments are made, they may be taught, in the same way, to distinguish the different salts, and to discover the constituent parts of various mixtures, &c.

As there are many things that can be detected only by the taste, the cultivation of this sense has also its twofold use, in the same manner as the senses already spoken of. It may be that in this way the purity of intellectual taste is soonest and best provided for; but certain it is that young persons gain, in a moral point of view, when the palate is the servant of the stomach only, while the latter is in the service of health, if the demands of the palate do not interfere with the exercise of the higher senses; and the palate itself is capable of being extensively employed in the examination of various things.

5. *The Sense of Touch.*

However subordinate this twofold sense may be, belonging, seemingly, altogether to animal life, its cultivation is nevertheless of great importance to the culture of man. It is, in the first place, instrumental in the acquisition of many facts which are useful to man in determining accurately respecting the surface of objects, the surrounding atmosphere, &c. But, in the second place, it stands in the immediate service of æsthetic feeling, both negatively, by preservation from the slavery of animal gratification, and positively, a ready tact in discerning well-formed surfaces, by the expressive touch of musical strings or keys, and by the lively enjoyment of nature's pure air. Its cultivation tends, thirdly, to exercise the energies of the mind, by its being habituated to the endurance of heat and cold, and by being steeled, yet not unnaturally, against bodily pain.

If children be not spoiled in their infancy by treatment which must render them effeminate; this sense will not become the instrument of subjecting them to their animal nature. By accustoming them gradually to the endurance of heat and cold, and more especially to the utmost cleanliness, their animal feeling will be in accordance with nature, invigorating to their physical organism, and promotive of the free activity of the mind. But great care should be taken to sharpen this sense; to practise it in observing, in its own peculiar organ, the hand. Children may thus, before they are eight years old, acquire a multitude of ideas by means of an intelligent manipulation of bodies. These exercises may be continued by letting them examine surfaces by the touch. At the same time they should be more and more habituated to bear every degree of temperature, yet without exposing the nerves to the blunting influence of extremes.

This sense may be suitably exercised by blindfolding children, and letting them recognise different coins by examining them between their fingers; they should begin with the coarsest coins, and gradually proceed to the finer ones. In the same manner, let them estimate the number of leaves in a book; recognise and describe plants by the touch; and subsequently teach them to become conscious of the presence of a hand or other object held at some distance before the face. They may also be accustomed to recognise persons by examining their faces with the fingers, or other objects submitted to their touch. At the same time, they may be made to perform various operations with their fingers while their eyes are bound up; for example, guide the hand, and let them specify what they write: or let them write, and perform various other manual operations in the dark.

Of special importance are musical exercises, in which the greater or less degree of force with which the key or string is struck deserves particular attention. In order that accuracy in stating the degree of heat and cold may be acquired, let water be taken at various temperatures, and estimated according to the thermometer. In a similar manner, the hand may be practised in estimating different weights.

The young will thus acquire a large amount of knowledge. which is necessary to render their acquaintance with the external world complete. Another advantage they derive from such training is, that they become accustomed to distinguish between appearances and realities, attested by the evidence of the senses ; and that the sense under consideration is developed for the discernment of plastic beauty, for greater expression in musical performances, and for greater acuteness and correctness in general. There is reason to expect that a child habituated to external cleanliness will be likely to manifest a tender susceptibility for purity of soul, and that such exercises will be particularly useful for young females ; the more so, from their immediate connexion with various female employments. It cannot be denied that this methodical treatment of this lower sense is calculated to preserve the freedom of the soul in the development and use of the higher senses.

The author from whom this discussion of the best mode of developing the senses is derived, proceeds to expatiate on the treatment required in cases where, one or more of the senses are wanting ; but, as this subject does not fall within the scope of our plan, we shall only add a few general observations. With regard to those who are in the possession of all the senses, it is important to observe that no one sense ought to be developed at the expense of the others.

It has already been observed that the uneducated are generally governed by the sense of taste, and that, consequently, the higher senses are generally employed in the service of gross sensuality. If either of the higher senses be disproportionately cultivated to the neglect of the others, the effect on the mind must be to produce one-sidedness, and other evils which are to be deprecated. Not one of the senses, then, should be trained in preference to, or at the expense of, the others, but all should be fully developed, and judiciously cultivated in just equilibrium and pure harmony. And this is essential to the true culture of man.

We resume, now, the thread which was broken by

this long treatise on the cultivation of the outward senses, by proceeding to observe that language is the instrument which first unlocks to children the world of ideas; and it is this process by which they are invested with the peculiar characteristics of humanity. How important is it, then, that children should, from the very beginning, learn to speak correctly! Hence they must, at an early age, be carefully habituated to the use of correct language. Of course this practice ought to be natural, easy, and unconstrained; not formal, made up of rules, which could only serve to make them young pedants. The most appropriate practice in speaking correctly will always consist in their hearing no other than correct language from those who address them, or converse with each other in their presence.

Our readers will need nothing more to convince them of the necessity of such a course, than the recollection of the fact that children will imitate all they see and hear; therefore, let them have no other than pure and correct language to imitate. The foolish and childish dialect of the nursery is consequently not only useless, but injurious. The next step in the culture of the intellect consists in the exercise of the memory. Although some modern writers on pedagogics have treated the memory with indifference, we are persuaded that, in our day and country, the importance of carefully cultivating it is duly appreciated, and that, therefore, the following observations on the subject, derived substantially from Schwarz, will not be unwelcome to the reader.

Cultivation of the Memory.

We are then to observe, in cultivating the memory of children, that the retention of any subject involves the following three elements: 1. A clear and distinct impression; 2. Firm preservation; 3. Ready recollection. The design, therefore, of cultivating the memory is, that it may receive impressions easily, and thus accumulate stores of wealth, and acquire prompt and energetic freedom in the use of them. A faithful memory is one that retains impressions in their purity; one that retains many is a strong memory, and one that easily recalls them a happy one; a good memory must possess all these qualities. We have seen that the memory is exercised by practising the eye to see correctly, and the ear to hear acutely, and by requiring children to repeat what they have seen and heard. Thus they become acquainted with things. The predominating principle here is constant repetition. Children should be made to repeat very often what they have learned, for it is thus that they learn things perfectly by impressing them indelibly. "Repetitio mater studiorum." "Mnemosyne, the mother of the Muses." "Tantum scimus, quantum memoriâ tenemus." Among all the faculties of the mind, the memory is considered to be most in need of practice in order to its becoming good. Not to strengthen it is synonymous with weakening it. This practice is rendered efficacious by the psychological laws of associations, according to which, similar, synchronous successive, externally or internally connected impressions or ideas are so interwoven with each other that one will call up the other.

A principal requisite in practising the memory is, that the impressions be received in a manner lively, truthful, and distinct, and that the words by which they are conveyed have invariably a direct reference to correct observation; otherwise either something else than what is intended will be retained, or the impression will be untrue, wavering, and confused. The usual practice of memorizing has regard only to the forms of language; to names, words, and the like. But children should, above all things, be made to employ their sight and hearing in observing for themselves, and to revolve in their minds what is intended to be fixed in the memory; and this they should do with the clearest consciousness, and not be allowed, while professedly employed with one thing, to direct their attention to anything else. Even the locality where they thus learn is not unimportant. At first a secluded and quiet spot should be selected, but after a while they may be accustomed to commit to memory in the midst of bustle, and circumstances which demand an effort in fixing the attention. Thus they will learn to remember what is observed merely in passing.

The second requisite in this process of training is firmness of retention. As all modes of storing up like the arranging of books and other articles on their shelves, are here, of course, out of the question; and as, on the other hand, a living, intellectual activity which reproduces and vividly presents the same impression that has been made, and in the manner in which it was made, is required, retentiveness can consist only in a capacity to perform these operations and can hence be acquired only by practice, *i. e.*, by repetition.

The third requisite consists in easy and prompt freedom of recollection. This cannot be otherwise attained than by firmly connecting the impressions or ideas retained with one or more others, which are every moment at our command, and by which, therefore, those impressions or ideas can at any time be again called forth. When, therefore, children are learning words, they should be made to think of the objects which they designate, and to pronounce the word in the language which they are learning at the time, with its signification in their mother-tongue. It is well to explain the words, and to make them intelligible and interesting to them, and not often to let them learn, except after they have ascertained the signification of the words, in the connexion in which they occur; yet they should sometimes be made to learn by the sound only, in order that the memory, considered purely as such, may be suitably practised. In the same manner you may proceed with events, dates, sentences, maxims, and the like, at the proper time. Let these things be thought over separately, and presented in connexion with what is already known; let them be separately impressed and repeated, and that at different times, as, for example, in the morning and evening; and under different circumstances, in different states of the mind, in the house or the open air, in private or in company.

Not to continue this subject any farther, we conclude by repeating the rule of Quintilian: "Quotidie adjiciantur singuli versus;" and the well-known maxim, "Nulla dies sine linea."

Imagination.

The imagination is in most children the predominant faculty, and the importance of carefully watching and wisely directing its development is great. With the majority of children it may be more necessary to impose checks on its development than to furnish excitements. Yet, as this faculty will live and flourish in spite of all restraints, and, for this purpose, seek its food somewhere; and as the mode and degree of its development have much to do both with our usefulness and happiness, it will be important, in a work like this, to devote considerable space to it; and the more so, because, though our young people be much addicted to a sort of reading which over-stimulates and vitiates the imagination, we Americans are exceedingly deficient in the higher poetry of life, and much disposed to neglect as useless those methods of training by which the imagination may not only be made highly subservient to the sterner operations of the mind, but become a source of pure and vivid enjoyment. Our observations will again be taken chiefly from Schwarz.

Whatsoever is conveyed through the senses to the mind, and becomes its property, should be completely absorbed by the mind; *i. e.*, it ought to increase the freedom, the vigour, and the compass of the mind's activity. This activity is creative; excited by impressions from without, it develops them intellectually, and from what has been given it produces new images. This inward, creative power is often designated by the word fancy, which is, however, often misunderstood. Without this faculty, the mind is destitute of wings on which it may mount upward. Although, in the cultivation of the senses, the reason-

and the memory, that of the imagination is in a great measure involved, yet, in order that everything may be done to cultivate it fully and properly, it should receive special attention and exercise. Three points are here to be observed: 1. In the use of the senses, the reason, and memory, it is to give vitality to the observations. 2. It ought to be exercised independently. 3. It should pass over into purely intellectual activity, manifested in the production of ideas.

1. It is not sufficient that the material object merely deposite a picture in the eye or a sound in the ear; the mind is to add to these deposites something which it neither sees nor hears, without, however, disturbing or falsifying the impression made upon the senses; a something which employs the senses in the immediate service of the imagination. This takes place, on the one hand, in respect of the form of objects, considered from an æsthetic point of view, and on the other in respect of their material, considered as affecting the sense of touch in a variety of ways.

When the sight of children has become accustomed to distinguish forms and colours, their attention should be directed to the beauty which form and colour give to different objects. But this is not accomplished by exclaiming, "Oh, how beautiful!" or by teaching them to prate about beauty; for in this connexion mere words are entirely out of place, as they abstract the mind from all true enjoyment. They should be permitted *to see a great deal that is beautiful*, particularly in the vegetable kingdom, committing to a higher influence the time when their feelings will seek vent in words. Ugly and distorted objects, grimaces, shallow people, and other things, all calculated to smother taste in the germ, should be kept far from them. Do not inflict on them the analysis of flowers, the anatomy of insects, the shackles of system, ere they have contracted an affectionate intimacy with nature. For the best mode of treatment, we refer to the directions given in connexion with the cultivation of the sense of sight, where frequent walks amid beautiful natural scenery and exercises in drawing are recommended. If, with these, the frequent reading of descriptive poetry, and of tales and biographies, calculated to excite and nourish the filial affections, is combined, happy results will be witnessed, and children will frequently break out into expressions truly poetical. But great care should be taken lest the feelings which prompt to such expressions be perverted by your loudly testifying your admiration, or even exhibiting to others what you regard as extraordinary talent or sensibility in your children; these feelings are sacred and tender, and thrive only in the sweet repose of an affectionate family.

Amid the observation of the senses, the imagination thus becomes the guide to that higher world to which the mind is to be introduced. In this process, the understanding also is undeniably active; but there are some exercises which have a special and direct reference to the understanding, inasmuch as the creative power here spoken of conducts us from what has already been perceived and comprehended on to higher truth. Mathematical science exhibits this clearly in multiplication, in the theory of proportions, of the triangles, &c.; in the operation of finding, by means of certain given quantities, an unknown one, and thus bringing to light something new. A similar function is performed, unperceived by the understanding, in all its conclusions, but especially in the deductions of logical ratiocination; and thus the activity of the understanding depends, in its apprehension of truth, upon the active exercise of the imagination.

The young should not, therefore, be left to occupy their minds only with the objects which they see, and the thoughts excited by them, but they should be led onward to farther reflection upon cause, effect, connexion, &c. The mathematical and natural sciences will serve to accustom them to such reflection. Many suitable exercises, connected with common life, or demanding the examination of natural objects as well as works of art, the qualities requisite to their firmness and permanency, the accidents and destructive influences to which they are exposed, may be devised in order to direct aright their own independent investigations and observations, in the prosecution of which it is best to let them rectify their errors themselves, as any interference can only raise obstructions; for in this connexion the accumulation of knowledge is not aimed at, but the cultivation of the inventive power of the understanding.

The whole empire of supersensual truth would, without this power of the mind, remain utterly unknown to us. Without the ability derived from this faculty to mount above the gross elements of the material world, the soul would remain a stranger to religion, and therefore never find its real home. Hence, to lead the young to a deeper acquaintance with nature, may become, at the same time, a process of initiation into that which is above nature: and this great end may be attained on the development of the moral constitution, in which alone man can be assimilated to the divine nature; the cultivation, therefore, of pious feelings, be brought into such connexion with the study of nature, that the mind may discern in the material world the agency of a wisdom which its most sacred impulses lead it to adore. But, for this very reason, methodical training is necessary, in order that absurd and foolish imaginings may not be indulged in. Children should therefore learn, by comparing what has already been recognised as true, to proceed to the supersensual in unbroken and harmonious connexion, and hence with logical correctness. By means of these exercises, the creative power of the mind acquires its upward impulse, and yet remains the faithful handmaid of truth. Thus are prejudice and superstition not only avoided; the light that is poured into the mind does not convert it into an illuminated vacuum, but reveals to it its own depth.

But this training is complete only when it keeps, at the same time, the memory in activity. The stores of knowledge already accumulated must be perpetually brought to recollection, in order to form out of them new ones, to rectify errors, and to cause all that the mind has made the subject of thought to unfold itself in the mature blossom of One Thought. For example, let the children, when examining some extensive structure, bring distinctly to recollection what they have learned respecting horizontal and perpendicular lines, gravitation, the nature of wood, &c. With regard to machines, plants, &c., a similar course, adapted to the object, should be pursued. The more they have really learned, the farther will they advance in the perception of truth, and only in this way does knowledge become productive capital: "whosoever hath, to him shall be given." Provision is thus made that the young will not be robbed, by the capricious inventions of genius, of their true perceptions, nor become fantastical even when taking the largest and boldest views of nature, into which errors those are the first to fall who, in respect of the subject here discussed, are left to take their own course. But the proper training which the imagination, when called into activity by every exciting cause, and connecting its operations with those of the senses, the understanding, and the memory, will effect, leads to more profound and comprehensive views of truth.

We need but be observant of children to discover how powerful an impulse to the exercise of this creative faculty exists in the very constitution of our minds. If children are permitted unreservedly to communicate their own thoughts on various subjects, we shall often be astonished at the correct, though imperfect views which they will develop, without extraneous aid, on different matters, even of natural philosophy. And such observations will teach us how absurd is the practice of beginning with giving children instruction in everything, respecting its quomodo and its cui bono, without allowing them time, or affording them occasion, for prosecuting their own independent inquiries, as though, by the process of teaching, truth were to be driven into their minds. And surely, considering the rage for text-books on every conceivable subject, and the premature initiation of children in almost every department of science, which prevail at present in this country, this point is deserving of our most serious attention.

One direction, in which the imagination strongly inclines to exercise its powers, has been almost entirely neglected in modern times. We speak of its efforts to comprehend the hidden, symbolical meaning of things. While the symbolical character of natural objects possessed for the ancients an interest and charm which excited their liveliest attention, and had a great influence on their life and institutions; while, with them, it constituted an essential element of their education, the modern mind has, in a great degree, been closed against it; and this has had no little influence in producing the prevalent indifference to religion and its appropriate solemnities. But this tendency of the imagination is highly susceptible of cultivation, and for this cultivation ample occasion is furnished by many of the amusements of childhood. Little girls symbolize social life in their dolls, or ascribe to a wreath of certain flowers a peculiar meaning: boys make their canes the representatives of a variety of things, or seek to express a particular idea or sentiment by drawing a monument for a friend. Children should now be taught to read correctly the symbolical language of nature. Show them the oak as an emblem of strength; the slender poplar as representing aspirings and elevation to what is exalted; the violet, as the emblem of modest and retiring virtue; the tulip, that of a pleasing and agreeable exterior, &c., as in the Oriental language of flowers. But here, also, the independent activity of the imagination should not be too much forestalled. The best exercise consists in the reading of short poems, of tales *of a suitable character*, of fables, and parables. German literature is rich in exquisite parables, and our poverty in this respect might be relieved by translations. Those of Krummacher, of some of which an elegant translation was some years ago published in this country, deserve special commendation.

The principles already laid down will enable our readers to develop for themselves a suitable method for prosecuting this culture in harmony with the progress of the mind, and with a view to the more profound comprehension of nature.

The object to be attained by these exercises is the proper culture of the imagination alone. The understanding and the moral sense are cultivated by a different mode of instruction, only let harmony of development prevail. As additional exercises, we may mention the solution of riddles, charades, and the like; the invention of such; learning to understand some language of symbols; examining and finding out the meaning of allegories; the reading and memorizing of beautiful poems; the study of the fine arts; excursions of pleasure; and, lastly, every proper variety of study, if prosecuted with spirit. One of the most natural and elegant exercises, which is particularly appropriate for the gentler sex, consists in the cultivation of flowers.

The dreams of children are, in a measure, their poetry, and are generally more connected and vivid than those of adults; just as if childhood possessed an occult, inward world, which gradually disappears before the glaring light of reality. Who has not felt a lively interest when hearing children of six or more years artlessly relating their dreams? This pleasure should not be foregone. By encouraging your children to repeat to you their dreams, you obtain a twofold advantage; you will become acquainted with their dispositions, and thus understand better how they should be treated, and you will afford them a most appropriate exercise in giving expression to their poetic imaginings.

In respect to the subject before us, men differ from each other in that one has a very lively imagination, but deficient in order and stability; in another, the imagination enjoys a copious flow of images and thoughts, but is also usually deficient in arrangement and classification; again, in another, it is more active in inventing and in developing from within, but proportionably destitute of external resources; and in the fourth, its inventions are happy and its combinations correct, but it makes no forward strides, and remains poor. Now, that this intellectual power may acquire opulence and boldness through a copious influx of thoughts; that it may be quick in grasping and creating, and yet well-disciplined in forming beautiful combinations; that it may be persevering in execution, and that its energies may, on every fit occasion, vividly flash out—this is the object to be aimed at in its cultivation. By the cultivation of this faculty, the activity of the mind, in general, is to be strengthened and elevated, and flighty and unsteady heads are to be accustomed to persevering exertion. It is thus that distinguished thinkers are developed; and if nature come to the aid of the culture contended for, by gifts munificently bestowed and harmoniously arranged, we see before us a genius. If, during the development of the imagination, a docile and pious spirit be cultivated, it will have the most happy influence on the whole mental culture of man. It is, therefore, of the utmost importance, that, from the earliest period of its development to its mature bloom in the later years of youth, it be guided and disciplined by a proper mode of education.

Attention.

Attention, in the proper sense of the word, cannot be ascribed to children before their minds begin to become conscious of their independent existence and their capacity for exertion; their earliest consciousness has respect, not to their higher personality, but only to self. Our readers must, of course, be aware, that in our observations on the cultivation of the senses, the memory, and the imagination, the power of attention has already been largely treated of. The discipline, recommended under the just mentioned subjects, is in the highest degree calculated to awaken, to exercise, and to cultivate the attention. It will, therefore, not be necessary to expatiate much on this point here, and we shall merely add a brief sketch of the principles to be observed in leading the young to the exercise of attention. These may be divided into, 1. *Negative.* Do not require children to direct their attention to what must be unintelligible to them, such as purely abstract ideas, or such as are incomprehensible both from their nature and their magnitude; for example, the nature of God; but while their attention is directed towards subjects which their minds are capable of grasping, let all distracting influences be removed from them.

2. *Positive.* Positive means of exciting attention, and of promoting its steady and habitual exercise, will be found in the charm of novelty, of change, of contrast; and in ascending, by an appropriate and gradual progress, from lower to higher degrees of knowledge.

The great principle never to be lost sight of is, that the pupil should be able to make his own whatever is presented to him. Let, then, nothing be presented to his attention which he is utterly unprepared to master; which his mind is quite unable to digest, and which, therefore, cannot be changed "in succum et sanguinem."

When the child hears the oral communications of his teacher, or is made to see something, as it were, through the medium of the teacher's instructions, the subject communicated is as yet strange to him, but is now to become his own. The subject, therefore, awakens sensations new to him; produces an excited state, which is not at first agreeable, but demands a determinate effort for the exercise of the attention. Now, if the subject is to obtain entrance, and to engage the attention, it must excite an interest in the pupil, and enlist his desire of culture; it must transform, instantaneously, that disagreeable sensation into the pleasing consciousness of inward power; and by the apprehension of that which is given, that mental activity must be excited by which the pupil's own mind receives, digests, and assimilates the subject, so that what once was foreign now becomes his own. Here, also, one-sided culture is to be studiously avoided; neither too much nor too little direct instruction to be given. In the multiplicity of subjects which children are made to study in our day, there is entirely too much of mere verbal instruction; and youthful minds are often crushed under the weight of the external world, which is crowding in upon them through every avenue. How important is it that the old maxim be borne in mind: "Non multa, sed multum."

The Understanding.

It cannot be denied, that to the full and proper use of reason maturity of years is necessary, and that its factitiously precocious development, which displays itself in a certain knowingness and pertness, belongs to the most disgusting perversions of the youthful mind. Nevertheless, a great deal can unquestionably be done, from early youth, for the appropriate culture of the understanding. Our readers will not fail to observe, that much of what has already been said, in connexion with other subjects, has an important bearing, more or less direct, on the development and cultivation of the understanding. And thus the importance of *harmoniously* cultivating *all* the faculties of man, in such a manner as most effectually to attain the true end of his being, becomes more and more obvious the farther we advance.

Among the many points of difference between man and the lower animals, the first that particularly strikes us is the slow and gradual process by which he attains the full and perfect use of his senses. The cause of this is to be sought in the gradual development of the mind, whose servants the senses are. The higher senses, through which the soul receives its first impressions from the external world, and through which, therefore, the activity of the mind is first excited, are the first to come into vigorous and extended action, and the inferior senses are much later in coming to anything like perfection. But a long time is necessary in order to bring the senses to perform all their functions with that degree of acuteness and accuracy, vigour and compass, of which they are capable. And it is attention which gradually carries on and perfectly develops the energy of the whole sensual system of man, by detaining this energy in the different branches of that system, and by suitable practice giving it the mastery of each. These observations will serve to show how important it is that the cultivation of the senses, as recommended in this work, be carefully attended to.

We are here more particularly concerned with the understanding, as the *thinking faculty*. Yet here, also, we cannot immediately escape from the senses, because the thinking of children, in as far as they may be said to think, consists in observing by means of the senses, especially those of sight and hearing. The first instruction given to children should therefore treat of subjects which may be illustrated to the eye. Speak to children even ten years of age on any subject, however interesting, and, unless they have an image of it before them, or a clear conception of it, they will be listless and inattentive; but if you illustrate your narrative or explanations by visible objects, they will hang with breathless attention on your lips to catch every word that you utter. Yet are they not, therefore, slaves of the sense of sight; for, in the attention which their various modes of observing imply, the independent activity of the mind is already displayed, inasmuch as the attention passes deliberately, not only from one object to another, but from one form or colour to another; and even young children will develop abstract notions from all the various impressions received through the senses. The attention thus proceeds to form ideas of things, of their qualities, relations, and distinctive peculiarities; begins to accustom the imagination to distinguishing and classifying, and thus to conceive of things different from the reality; and acts, therefore, with perfect independence, both in perceiving and imagining. These operations are displayed in the constant search after something new, not yet seen or heard of by them, in which we see children engaged. This vivid play of the attention, passing from perceptions to the formation of ideas, and vice versa, increases until about the fourteenth year, when the attention withdraws more into the inner world, which the morning-star of love begins to illumine, or fixes itself more on some particular object in the external world.

With children of seven years of age the fancy will already far outstrip the realities of the material world; their narrations of what they have seen will be less faithful; they will omit points that failed to interest them; they will exaggerate those which excited their liveliest interest; they will delight in marvellous stories and accounts of superhuman beings; and as this is clearly the age of play, their plays and amusements deserve particular attention. Regarding them as an essential means of not only intellectual, but almost every other variety of culture, they ought not to be left to mere accident, but should be treated as a most important part of education. Games which exercise the patience, the ingenuity, the imagination of children, or require some acquaintance with geography and history, are to be highly recommended. If the age of childhood and early youth is the season for play, care should be taken to give meaning and character to the games of the young. Games which contribute nothing to the development of the body and the culture of the mind, or even promote indolence and sensuality, ought to be discountenanced as utterly worthless. But the veriest trifle becomes important as soon as it contributes to the attainment of higher purposes. All games are liable to degenerate, and to be perverted to mischievous purposes: all games of hazard are evil and only evil, and those who indulge young persons in them are guilty of downright wickedness.

During childhood the receptiveness and retentiveness of the memory are greater than at any subsequent period. The boy of fourteen years will have to make greater exertions in committing to memory than the boy of seven years. But now the inward activity has increased in freedom and strength. The boy sees and hears more acutely what he wishes to see and hear, and impresses it more distinctly and firmly in the mind. Determined to see and hear correctly, he will make greater exertions to commit the subject to the memory, but it will be done in such a manner as to ensure distinct recollection. But, as the inward activity of the mind keeps pace with the progress of youth to maturity, in feeling, in developing ideas, in forming purposes, whatever is immediately connected with this inward faculty will be more easily and better retained. The youth who, in his boyhood, most readily and distinctly remembered the forms of words and the scenery of his home, will now be occupied with the meaning of words, and with the rights, the advantages, the improvement, the adornment of the paternal estate, and seek rather to acquire thoughts through the medium of language, and to become acquainted with the relations of human affairs. Thus the memory is gradually diverted from observations to ideas: in earlier years its business is chiefly to receive impressions through the senses ; in youth it becomes the servant of thought in recalling ideas: and thus, also, the power of recollection is strengthened; for the many accumulated impressions are now more and more frequently reproduced, classified under various forms of thought, or interwoven with divers feelings, so that it is frequently the favourite employment of youth to look back into the paradise of childhood.

The highest activity of the thinking faculty is exhibited in the process of reasoning, and in this respect the understanding is the power or impulse to strive after what is greatest and highest in thought. Its first manifestations are witnessed in the attention with which children observe, by means of the senses of sight and hearing. The constantly increasing desire to conceive and create by means of the imagination, is nothing else than the understanding progressing in its development. Children will connect two conceptions with each other, and form out of them a third; and for this process they soon develop a rule, which refers all individual conceptions to that one entire product of connected thought which we call truth: this rule is the syllogism.

The reasoning faculty will early give evidence of the decided convictions which it has attained; and even children of three years of age will imagine possible cases, and make provision for that case which they regard as the most probable to occur. The subjects which occupy their minds are mostly such as employ their physical energies and their senses; but, as they advance towards youth, they rather compare conceptions (or perceptions) with each other, in order to separate the true from the erroneous, and to obtain a correct apprehension of everything. This striving after unity of thought, this thinking of many things in order to develop and apprehend the truth, which is the object of all thought, is denominated reflection.

Another mode in which the activity of the thinking faculty is manifested, is contemplation. The mind here employs itself in thinking of an object in such a manner as to elevate this inward process of thinking into an operation of unlimited compass, and resembling vision in its nature and clearness. Thus we contemplate nature and the traces of the Deity. This operation of the understanding is originated by the imagination, which seeks to present the subject under a variety of conceptions to the soul, but, not satisfied with this alone, enlarges them ad infinitum.

Reflection and contemplation constitute that activity of the reasoning faculty which is manifested in the earliest process of thinking, and its product is thought. A thought beyond which the thinking faculty cannot go in respect of any particular object, is termed an ultimate truth. The child has notions, the boy gets thoughts, the youth obtains ultimate truths.

The understanding is designated by different terms, according to the particular direction in which it is pre-eminently active. When it correctly and easily combines the general and the particular, it is called a sound judgment; if it perform this operation with acute discrimination, we call it profundity; and if with happy associations of ideas, we name it sagacity. Even in young children possessed of a healthy understanding, these mental qualities may be observed. They will, for example, note the difference between two animals; they will play upon words; they will draw rapid conclusions from the expression which they observe on the countenance of an acquaintance; or they contrive how they may most effectually prevail with their parents to grant them some wish; but, of course, all this is done unconsciously and without design, at least throughout the second period of childhood. Not until the season of youth can sagacity and penetration be deliberately exercised, and the pleasure arising from them aimed at, at least if their minds have not been perverted in childhood. The boy of ten, or even fewer years, may easily solve riddles, or discriminate between two significations of the same word, or translate into well-chosen words, and with correct application of rules; but the boy of fourteen years is not likely to invent riddles, or to write original essays, or to form a critical judgment of anything, because he does not yet possess the power of abstracting his mind from the objects themselves, nor of exercising his mind with reference to rules, ideas, and connexion of ideas. Before the fifteenth year, it will, therefore, be necessary to exercise his judgment, penetration, and sagacity in observing: practice by means of original productions belongs to the subsequent period.

In attending to the mode of treatment recommended for the cultivation of the senses, the memory, the imagination, the attention, and the understanding, the complete result will be the proper culture of the mind for the healthful and energetic performance of its various functions. You will thus arouse children from the dreamy habits into which they are apt to glide, and habituate them to the deliberate control of their thoughts. You will accustom them to form clear conceptions and correct perceptions, and the consequence of this will be, that they will express themselves clearly. You will train them to independent efforts in thinking and judging; and you will excite them to the exercise of penetration and sagacity. You will essentially aid them in the attainment of clear conceptions and perceptions by giving them accurate definitions of objects and observations, and by practising them in defining; by letting them closely compare and distinguish, which will particularly practise their penetration and sagacity; by explaining to them the origin and use of things, and the mode of using them; by directing their attention to the connexions subsisting between things, such as those of cause and effect, of means and object, &c., and by practising them in arranging and classifying their observations. On the other hand, you are sure to suppress the independent activity of the understanding by exposing them to influences which distract the attention, and by undertaking to accomplish too much at once: for example, by giving them too many and too extensive lessons; by proposing to their minds what they cannot comprehend; by habituating them to that slavish reliance on the authority of others which the poet repudiates, when he describes himself as "nullius addictus jurare in verba magistri;" and lastly, by despising, or treating as ridiculous, their opinions or judgments, which, though objectively wrong, are yet subjectively correct; *i. e.*, such as, from their point of view, they necessarily must be.

Penetration and sagacity may be perpetually exercised in the daily intercourse of life, and especially, also, by certain amusements, which we have specified, and which demand an effort of the understanding.

The reading of the young is a point of the utmost importance in respect of their entire culture. That this should be carefully and wisely controlled and regulated, we need not urge. Although excellent juvenile books of every description are now exceedingly abundant, furnishing to the young nourishment for the mind and heart, this well-founded rule remains unshaken in its authority, that small children should scarcely read at all, and boys and girls but little; and that, even in youth, reading should not be extensive in quantity.

Our young people now read incalculably more than they can digest ; and such reading, which in our day is a downright mania, exerts an inconceivably pernicious influence on the mind. When we consider the mass of trash and miserable twaddle which, in the shape of tales, &c., is daily thrown from the press, and see with what voracious appetite children and youth devour this noisome stuff, we stand aghast at the consequences which loom up out of this muddy atmosphere.

In conclusion, we observe, that the entire intellectual culture thus treated of is not designed to form the future professional scholar, but is that development of the understanding which is equally necessary to all, and ought to characterize every sound mind.

CHAPTER III.

ÆSTHETIC CULTURE.

Cultivation of the Feelings for the Perception and Enjoyment of the Beautiful.

For the sense of the beautiful, in the widest signification of the term, *i. e.*, taste, the best foundation is laid by observing and promoting cleanliness, order, and simplicity, in the arrangements and concerns of external life. These requisites should be procured for the sense here considered, even before it awakes in the child, which does not, indeed, usually happen very early. The favourable influence of cleanliness and order in the interior and exterior of dwellings, and of everything around them, on the development of æsthetic feeling, is amply attested by experience.

As the beautiful itself is necessarily divided into two varieties, namely, 1. *sensuous*, as an object of observation,* and 2. *intellectual*, as employing the judg-

* This word, which is often used in the present work in its popular meaning, is here and elsewhere (as the reader will have noticed) employed in a manner somewhat peculiar, in order to express what the Germans call Anschauung. By observation we therefore mean the acquisition of perceptions by means of sensations produced through any one of the senses, or the acquisition of knowledge by the inspection of objects through the medium of any of the senses.

ment, there will also, in this respect, be a twofold education.

With respect to each variety, the necessary culture should be immediate; *i. e.*, partly with direct reference to observation, and partly with a direct view to feeling; yet with this culture no theory of the beautiful should be connected; for such theory cannot belong to popular life, but only to the learned world.

We here again observe, that much of what has been said in relation to the cultivation of the senses and the imagination has a direct reference to the æsthetic culture here treated of, embracing both varieties of the beautiful, but more particularly the first. The following brief observations will therefore be sufficient on this subject.

The first important requisite for the cultivation of the taste for beauty in perceptible objects, in its widest sense, is, that the external dispositions of locality, which daily meet the child's eye, be of a beautiful, tasteful, and exalted character. This requisite applies with peculiar force to the dwelling and its ornaments; to furniture, utensils, toys, and pictures, from all which objects the child receives its first sensible impressions: but the most important point to be considered is the character of surrounding nature. It is much to be desired, that, in the choice of a locality for institutions of education, the beauty of the circumjacent natural scenery might meet with far greater attention than has generally been the case. The grounds which surround academies and colleges ought to be laid out and planted according to the dictates of refined and elegant taste. Alas! that in this country the destructive propensities of college students are so extensively employed in marring the beauty of such arrangements by hewing or breaking off young trees, and in many other ways. This very fact proves a deficiency in the early education of our young people. When an American scholar of eminence, during his travels in Germany, expressed his surprise that the public grounds and gardens were not injured by the populace, and his regret that such was but too much the case in his native land, the German, who asked him the simple question whether we had no education in America, had obviously the correct view of the matter. Early education must cure the disgraceful habit, which so generally prevails in this country, of cutting, and in various ways defacing and injuring, whatever is accessible to the public.

Frequent excursions into beautiful and romantic mountain scenery, particularly if accompanied by suitable conversation on the part of the parent or teacher, calculated to awaken and guide the attention of children in observing the beautiful characteristics of the landscape, both in mass and in detail, will do much towards developing and cultivating their sense of the beautiful. This and other exercises, recommended on former pages, will lead children to the unaffected enjoyment of nature. This enjoyment should arise from the actual perception and correct appreciation of what is truly beautiful; and hence every mode of culture should here be avoided which can be productive of pedantry, or an *affectation* of pious feelings, in contemplating the beauties of the Almighty Creator's works.

Parents who desire to cultivate in their children a capacity to perceive and enjoy the beautiful, should be careful to select their toys with taste. The majority of these things, as well as most of the little books for children, which are generally disfigured by uncouth and gaudy daubs, exert an influence most prejudicial on the future development of the child's taste; but, on the other hand, by affording children early and frequent opportunities of learning to admire beautiful paintings, a most effectual and salutary educational influence will be secured.

It is the opinion of some, and among them of Rousseau, that a taste for the beauty of forms and of nature is promoted by early teaching children botany, in a manner suited to their young capacities. To this we can only assent if but little of the details of botanical anatomy (for such is the analysis) be introduced, and the attention chiefly directed to the wonderful variety of forms, of colouring, and habits exhibited in the vegetable world.

When the power of observation has acquired acuteness and vigour, and the understanding begins to display a degree of judgment, children should have frequent opportunities of observing (see note, p. 233) works of art; of painting and design; productions of the plastic art, strictly so called; of music and architecture. Without intending to practise professionally any of these arts, every man should, in his youth, cultivate his observation; in general, his power of perception, by suitable practice in several of these arts, if not in all. This should be treated, not as a branch of school-instruction, but as an amusement; at least where the educator has learned to manage amusements in a manner suited to the attainment of higher ends.

We are aware that on this point education will thus come into conflict with the spirit of fashion, inasmuch as the modern arrangements of life exhibit very little that is truly beautiful in all these arts, but much, on the other hand, that directly corrupts the taste. Much might be done in our seminaries of learning for the promotion of a better state of things, by judiciously cultivating in our youth a taste for all that is beautiful in nature and art.

The point of transition from the purely sensuous beautiful to purely intellectual beauty we find in the beautiful human form, with its intellectual expression, in bearing, motion, and features.

The observation of beautiful human beings, whose exterior announces excellence of character, is directly the most effectual education for the perception and appreciation of intellectual beauty, which can be apprehended only by the judgment.

We need not here attempt to show how desirable it is that children be placed in situations where they would remain entire strangers to the dregs of human society, while enjoying the genial influence of refined and virtuous society, both male and female.

The chastening and refining influence of female

society on the young of the other sex is a subject on which elegant pens have largely written, and which needs no recommendation here; yet here, also, how necessary is caution! how baneful is the influence of females who have nothing to recommend them but personal beauty, and the frivolous gayety, the trifling worldliness of mere fashionable life!

Not before the age of puberty should young persons begin the *study* of intellectual beauty as presented by the poets, in order *by* it to cultivate themselves *for* it; but more particularly, and first of all, should they cultivate acquaintance with the poets of their own native land, in order that at length the absurd prejudice may be eradicated, that there is *no* real beauty except the antique or classical, and that learning, or even pedantry, is necessary to the apprehension of the truly beautiful.

A gradation should here be observed from the more easy to the more difficult poets.

1. Authors more distinguished for pure versification than poetic depth, and who cultivate the taste more by the melody than by the meaning of their song: under this we include also hymns, narratives, ballads, and fables, where *simplicity* is the highest grace. Such are the productions of Mrs. Barbauld, Watts, H. F. Gould; certain pieces of Wordsworth and of Cowper; Gay's Fables, &c.; Mrs. Hemans, Mrs. Sigourney.

2. *Pastoral Poetry*. Shenstone, Pope, Thomson, Crabbe, Collins, Dryden's Eclogues of Virgil, Beattie.

3. *Epic Poetry*. Pope's Homer, Dryden's Virgil, Milton's Paradise Lost, Spenser's Faery Queen, Sir W. Scott's Lady of the Lake, &c., Southey's Thalaba, Don Roderick, &c.

Tragic and lyric poems are scarcely adapted to the culture of youth, as they are not sufficiently understood until maturer years have been attained, though they be not injurious, as comedies and satires undoubtedly are.

It is deeply, inexpressibly to be deplored, that poetry also has been prostituted to the service of lust and licentiousness How carefully should the sanctuary of the young heart be guarded against the polluting influence of such vile works of art! Yet the fastidiousness of those who confound love with lust will do little for æsthetic culture, by forbidding the young all but grave, didactic poems.

The very impossibility of understanding many of our best English poets without some classical culture, demonstrates the necessity of an acquaintance with the classics; but this necessity presents itself from a higher point of view when we consider the poverty of modern life in everything poetical and beautiful: these elements are crushed amid the crash and clamour of business, the rush of railroads, and the clatter of money. The beautiful aspects of classic Greece should therefore afford our youth an ideal background upon which after times may throw their darker colours of reality.

Children merely observe, they do not reflect. Hence an additional reason for making them acquainted with the Greek classics arises from the objectiveness of the Greeks, so observable for children; and this will serve as a counterpoise to the highly reflective subjectiveness of modern times. The study of the Greek classics should not, therefore, be regarded as belonging exclusively to the culture of the professional scholar, but treated, as it is to a considerable degree in England, and in some measure also in this country, as constituting an important element in the general culture of man. It serves as a lever to raise men from the *common* class (common as regards culture) to the educated or cultivated.

From these observations it will appear that classical culture should be attainable without the study of the Greek language. It is the *enjoyment* of the beautiful, as exhibited in the Greek classics, which ought to be accessible to all; and for this purpose *good* translations should be put into the hands of those who are not instructed in the Greek language.

It is desirable that this classical culture might commence at a very early period. Among the first picture-books and stories put into the hands of children should be mythological representations. These will also have a favourable influence on the imagination, as well as the taste for sensuous beauty; and thus, through the pleasures of its world of amusements, the child will domesticate itself in the mythological and historical world of the Greeks. The writer recollects, with pleasure, that in his early days such things were furnished for children: and to them he feels himself, in a great degree, indebted for such familiarity as he has with the mythology and history of the Greeks. Has it contributed to the improvement of the age that these classical toybooks have been superseded by Merry Jack, et hoc genus omne, with all its daubs and unmeaning rhymes?

Next, then, let translations of the Odyssee and Iliad be read to children, so that they may, at the same time, feel the pleasure arising from the charm of rhythmical numbers. Unfortunately, this charm, as it belongs to those glorious Greek epics, is entirely lost in the English translations of Pope, while in the German translations of Voss the easy and graceful flow of the hexameter appears as perfectly as in the Greek. But, as the English language (some authorities to the contrary notwithstanding) is incapable of hexametrical verse to any considerable extent, we must be content with what we have. No reflections on Pope's elegant translation are intended; we speak merely with reference to the beautiful metre of the original.

The children should themselves read geographical and historical representations from the Grecian world, which ought to be illustrated by suitable engravings and maps.

A book of travels for youth, in the style of Barthelemy's "Journey of the younger Anacharsis to Greece," would be a desideratum.

In later years this difference arises, that by far the smaller number of pupils only have an opportunity to study the ancient languages, with which the majority of our youth remain unacquainted. It therefore only remains to furnish, for the use of the unlearned of both sexes, translations, giving not only the sense, but the spirit of the originals. The literature of Germany and France has long been rich in such translations. Is there no encouragement for American scholars to supply the deficiency of English literature in this respect?

The following order may be observed in making the young acquainted with the classics. Next to Homer should follow translations of Ovid expurgated; next, of Virgil; and, lastly, of Horace's Odes, which must also be subjected to an expurgatory process. At the same time might be read an English version of what Herder has translated of the Anthology; also, a selection from the poems of Theocritus. Equally to be recommended are translations of prose writers, such as Herodotus, Plutarch, Xenophon. We have already said that the ancient tragic and comic writers, though the former be not actually injurious, are not directly suited to the course of education here treated of.

The design of this whole æsthetic culture is not to educate future artists or scholars, but to produce that culture of the feelings which is equally necessary for all men, and should give to the judgments of all the refinement of taste.

CHAPTER IV.

Practical Education, designed to develop the Character in general for the Public and Practical Affairs of Life.

1. *Practical Education in general, or Education in Business Habits, and in the Proprieties of Life.*

The first point here is to give the young correct and salutary views of human life, which occupy middle ground between rudeness and effeminacy, and, being at the same time liberal, will counteract the prejudices of contracted minds. It is, no doubt, a difficult matter to contend against a corrupt public sentiment; and when this is so, the children will be so also. It is the business of a wise system of education to remedy this evil.

The young should be taught to entertain a health ful self-respect, which lies midway between false humility and foolish pride. No less should a generous desire, and a dignified pursuit, of distinction be inculcated, which again keeps the middle course between a stupid indifference to the opinion of others, and a vainglorious passion for shining. In these respects the habits of the popular mind will present no small obstacles to education.

The virtues of active or business life, by means of which property is acquired, are, industry and economy, midway between habits of drudgery and a passion for dissipation, and between avarice and prodigality.

The young should be taught to value labour and property as means for the supply of wants, and never to regard them as the end or object of life. The importance of these considerations to our thrifty and money-making community is frequently recognised by writers and public speakers who have the good of the public at heart; but still the mighty throng rushes on in the pursuit of wealth, and the voice of the preacher is scarcely heard amid the buzz of the eager multitude. It behooves, then, the educators of youth to assail this evil at its root.

In connexion with industry and economy, the young should be habituated to a love of order, which comprehends regularity and punctuality, and occupies middle ground between rude insubordination and a listless pliableness, indicating a total absence of an independent will.

In these highly important concerns of human culture, the example of the educator must furnish the most suitable and efficient process of education. Without this, neither instruction nor admonition will be of any avail. The earlier you begin with habituating the young to these virtues, the more easily and completely you will succeed. Bad habits, in these respects, are not easily shaken off in later life.

To the proprieties of life, which comprehend personal cleanliness, posture in sitting or standing, and to politeness, the young should be accustomed in early childhood; but never should nature be sacrificed to the conventional rules of politeness, or, in other words, artificial forms or affected manners should never usurp the place of that gracefulness of deportment, that studiousness to gratify and anticipate the wishes of others, to promote by even the most trifling attentions their comfort and enjoyment, which are dictated by an amiable disposition, or, more correctly, by a thoroughly and well educated heart. In this particular, also, example and habit will be most effectual. But, from what has just been said, it is evident that examples should be chosen with care. The notion that *by intercourse* with society the young should be educated *for* society, is an absurd prejudice. It is the business of a good education to raise the young above the follies and caprices of fashionable life, and to give them strength and independence of character, to adopt such manners as are dictated by a sound judgment and an elegant taste, however those, who are slaves to conventional rules, may sneer.

The design of this general culture for life is insensibly to habituate the young to those virtues which constitute the basis, not only of the culture necessary to any particular profession, but of every higher development of character.

As the subject here discussed is, in general, well understood, we have considered ourselves justified in treating it quite briefly; the more so, as it is one on which much valuable matter may be found in the writings of Dr. Franklin, Blair, and others who have laboured for the general improvement of men

2. *Practical Education for some particular Calling.*

Not only is it with most men a matter of necessity, but, with regard to all, it belongs to the beauty of life, that they devote themselves to some particular calling; for this alone can give to life form and stability of character, without which it can present nothing to the view but shapeless confusion. The life-ideal of the rich, which consists in restless but passive change, in alternation between country and city life, and in travels undertaken solely with a view to pleasure, or to run away from the ennui of home, is as contemptible as it is false. The most wealthy ought, without any regard to gain, to seek the most important offices in the state.

Education for some particular calling, which consists in the cultivation of a capacity for business (professional or mechanical) and usefulness, is thus an essential element in the culture of the understanding for the development of intellectual grace or beauty. A capacity for business is not the highest object at which education should aim, but it is that most important element, without which all that is higher can have no fixed centre, around which it may perform its steady and beautiful revolutions.

If the cultivation of useful qualities has, in modern times, been neglected in other countries, either from effeminacy or through the influence of false theories, this reproach does not affect the inhabitants of our free states, where, on the other hand, the practical predominates, to the exclusion, in a great measure, of the beautiful and ideal.

Every human being ought to be free to choose his own calling, in accordance with his talents, which are wont to manifest themselves at a certain age by favourite inclinations and tastes. Few are so happy as to enjoy this privilege; in the exercise of which, however, the young should be guided by the counsels of experience and mature wisdom.

Education should therefore do all in its power to effect this object, as far as it may be attained: its business is to inquire, with the utmost care and impartiality, into the talents of the young, and, according to the result, to fix upon their future calling. A child ought never to be compelled to embrace an occupation against which all its inclinations revolt. Such coercion can only have a pernicious effect on the whole course of life, by diverting powers, which might be most successfully exercised in some other sphere, into channels where they are sparingly expended in unprofitable exertion, and by destroying the individual's contentment and happiness. Nothing can be more foolish than to *compel* young persons to study with a view to some learned profession, and nowhere is this folly more mischievous, than when it introduces an unwilling drone into the Gospel ministry.

The callings of human life are divided into two classes, which may be contrasted as the higher and lower; the ideal and practical; the elevated and common; or the intellectual and sensuous.

The former constitute the learned or literary world; the latter, the world of the people, or of common life. They are opposites; yet not hostile, but friendly opposites: certainly the most amicable relations ought to exist between them, for they really stand related to each other as the flower to the stem. The learned world has in the public its root and stem: hence only when popular life, the life of the community at large, is healthful, can health and vigour pervade the learned world; but it is the duty of the latter steadily to advance the improvement and culture of the former in all things essential to the well-being of the individual and the state.

The scholar is, by virtue of the special calling to which he is bound to devote himself, a member of the popular world; for only in connexion with this can the ultimate objects of his calling have real significance and importance. But this relation cannot be inverted. The common man is not to intrude himself into the learned world, for he does not belong there—he is unfit for it; and, however desirable the general diffusion of useful knowledge undoubtedly is, there is in our modern culture too much of that perverse tendency which amalgamates the two opposite callings, degrading learning into a trade, and making a scholar of the mechanic.

Popular callings are such as are rendered *necessary* by the wants of our nature, but which are valuable only as means for the attainment of higher purposes.

The learned callings, on the other hand, are those

which are truly free (liberal, ἐλεύθερα), and have directly in view the genuine, the highest purposes of man's existence — truth, virtue, and beauty. The Greeks divided society into freemen and slaves. This distinction cannot coexist with the doctrines of the New Testament, which represent all men as brethren; and, according to these doctrines of Christianity, the scholar, though in intellectual culture he rank far above the community at large, ought to be the faithful servant of society, and, as such, labour earnestly for its good.

Preparation for any future calling is effected by suitable instruction and training. The science which presents a system for the *instruction* of youth is called Didactics, and is necessarily divided into two parts.

A. *Popular Instruction, or Education for the Callings of Common Life.*

What the popular callings chiefly require is skill in reading, writing, and arithmetic. It is too late in the day to urge the importance of these acquisitions, more especially in our land of common schools; yet recent statistics have shown the shameful extent to which even these primary branches of knowledge are neglected in different sections of our country.

In this earliest instruction of youth, the wants of the people and of the professional scholar coincide.

The question, whether the Bible be a suitable reading-book for schools, has been often discussed and variously answered. We certainly think that there are serious objections to this use of the Bible. It seems inconsistent with the reverence due to this Divine Book, while, at the same time, much that it contains should not be read by *children*; yet the imperative necessity of extending the knowledge of it, and the frequent difficulty of accomplishing this in any other way, seem to require its introduction into schools; and, in order that it may not be reduced to the level of common schoolbooks, we would venture to recommend that the teacher himself devote about an hour each day to this exercise, by reading aloud to his whole school judicious selections from the Old Testament, embracing especially the historical and devotional portions, and the New Testament entire; and, in order that sectarian jealousy may suffer no alarm, let him do this "without note or comment," excepting, perhaps, the explanation of such words as the children cannot be expected to understand, and such elucidation of ancient manners and customs, as may be necessary to a correct understanding of what is read.

No human calling ought to be of such a nature, that the occupation or trade which constitutes it must needs injure and degrade, physically, intellectually, and morally, him that practises it; hence popular instruction ought to impart such knowledge, also, as will not only protect against immersion in sensuality, but make those whose employments are sensuous, who live in the material world, susceptible to the higher interests of humanity, to beauty and virtue.

On the second step, also, of the instruction of youth, the wants of the people, and of those who are looking forward to a learned education, coincide; and, as regards the latter class, this second period furnishes the best opportunity of showing whether they possess the requisite talents for the course which they have in view.

The subjects belonging to this second period of instruction are geography for children, with which natural history adapted to the capacities of children may be profitably combined; history, Latin, and composition, all conducted in a manner suitable for children. In general, instruction in language, judiciously adapted to the capacities of the pupils, belongs to this second stage of scholastic study.

In the geographical course, the natural productions of different countries will furnish opportunity for the introduction of a judiciously adapted course of instruction in natural history. But scientific inquiry and systematic arrangement are, of course, as yet out of the question. It is indispensably necessary to exhib it to the observation of children the different natural productions treated of, as well as animals peculiar to other climates, either real or in plates. If possible, good coloured plates should be obtained for this purpose.

In every course of historical instruction for children, everything will depend on the selections which the instructer makes, and the mode adopted by him of presenting that which he wishes to communicate. In both respects, he must, of course, be guided by the capacity and the destination of his pupils.

Children should not learn history from books, but from the viva voce narrative of the teacher. In order to suitable selection, the teacher should therefore possess a copious fund of historical knowledge; and, in order to his presenting what he has selected in a suitable and interesting manner, a peculiar talent for narrative is requisite. The younger the child, the more should he be instructed by narrative suited to his age and capacity, and not in the style of books, least of all by reading to him. At a later period, detailed accounts of particularly important transactions may be read to the pupils; but the general plan should continue to be that of viva voce narrative, with which suitable conversation, suggested by the subject, may often be very profitably combined. For the first course, the best plan will be not to teach universal history, but prominent sections separately, as,

1. Biblical: 2. Grecian: 3. Roman history.

Instead of teaching the young American what is called Middle History, or even modern history in general, it will be best to instruct him in that of his native land, with which all that is essential in the history of other nations will either naturally connect itself, or may be easily brought into connexion.

In every historical course, it is imperatively necessary to present what has been selected in a manner as much as possible adapted to the keenness of youthful observation; *i. e.*, to bring out the individual points definitely and vividly: in the subsequent repetition or recitation by the pupil, only the leading facts and the most important dates should be called for; but, in respect of these, the greatest accuracy should be insisted on.

A survey of universal history, or even a comprehensive view of particular periods, is less to be expected of children than a thorough acquaintance with separate details. The former is more easily acquired at a later period, than the latter, if neglected in childhood, can ever be made up.

Particular instruction in language is a consideration of a higher character, and therefore a matter of less general or imperative importance. If the above-named subjects of instruction ought to be taught in our common schools, the higher schools, designed for those whose employments and social position call for a more elevated and liberal education, should be prominently characterized by the addition of that study which is here treated of, namely, the study of language. And here the acquisition of some knowledge of the Latin grammar and vocabulary is particularly desirable, for two reasons: 1. Because the Latin is inseparably interwoven with numberless terminologies of common life, of every science, and even of our own grammar. 2. Because the study of a foreign language requires closer attention, and leads to a more intimate and thorough knowledge of the entire structure of language.

It is desirable that those who expect to take the course usual at high-schools and academies should become acquainted with the Latin language previous to studying grammatically their native tongue, or other modern languages, which may be useful to them in after life. Great care should be taken not to burden the pupil with too much at once.

With this early instruction in language should be connected exercises in the expression of ideas; *i. e.*, in style. These may be either oral or written. As regards the former, all affected declamatory utterance should be guarded against; but great attention ought to be bestowed on correct and natural declamation.

The design of this popular instruction is not to make of the people, in general, unripe and foolish scholars (σχολαστικοι), and thus to advance them to an unsatisfactory grade of learning, but to communicate to them, besides those acquisitions which are necessary to the ordinary pursuits of life, those nobler and more purely belles-lettristic attainments which develop and elevate their perception of beauty and moral excellence, to which life itself must cultivate them after their school education is completed.

B. *The College, or Instruction preparatory to the Learned Professions.*

Our collegiate institutions are chiefly designed for those young men who intend to devote themselves to one or the other of the learned professions. They may indeed be, and no doubt are, frequented by those who have no such intention, yet this is the great and principal object, in view of which they must be regulated and conducted. Their great design is this: the pupil is to be made sufficiently acquainted with antiquity, that, in his future learned profession, he may be able to learn whatever is known in that profession, so that in its cultivated class, whose office it is to exert a cultivating influence, the commonwealth may possess men who have possessed themselves of these treasures of humanity, of human knowledge, which have hitherto been accumulated. It is necessary to adopt this exalted aim, even though it still remain an ideal; and, if this be the goal to which our colleges are to conduct the young, their chief concern is the ancient classic languages, and, besides these, history; yet, as a matter of course, the other usual studies can be the less dispensed with, because every one who desires to enter and occupy the higher rank of the cultivating class, must indispensably possess whatever belongs to general culture, and is expected from every other class. On the importance of the ancient classic languages to the attainment of this purpose we shall treat farther below. They are indeed indispensable. Seek a substitute for them in whatever quarter you please, and you will find nothing that will, in like manner or degree, give to the cultivating class that culture which is illustriously distinguished from that which every individual in common life may obtain, and which, therefore, alone elevates him to the rank here contemplated.

From this also follows, that the pupil is bound to bestow a much greater amount of time and exertion on his college studies; not more, indeed, than his strength will bear; but let him who is destitute of that energy which this higher intellectual rank calls for, and which must, of necessity, be capable of no ordinary efforts—let him, in the name of conscience, not obtrude himself into the halls of colleges.

The daily hours of study to be observed by the pupil must, of course, be gradually increased in number. From the age of eight or nine to the age of eighteen years, the study-hours in general, including hours of recitation, should be gradually increased from eight to nine, to ten, to eleven, to twelve.

In the beginning his labours are performed in school-hours; subsequently he is expected to *prepare* for recitation, and, in general, to study in private, at an increased ratio, proportionate to his progress and advancement. The hours of private study should be to those of recitation in the proportion about =6 or 8 : 4. The entire period of this scholastic culture may, on an average, be estimated at ten years, six of which will be spent in preparatory schools, and four in college. It may, however, be expected, when a suitable mode of instruction is pursued, that even slow heads, or mediocrity of talent, will sometimes pass, in a manner perfectly satisfactory, through the whole course of study in eight years; and as only the higher order of minds should aim at this highest eminence of culture, the time may sometimes be even still shorter. Yet, as every good thing requires time, a minimum must here be adopted.

The most suitable age for entering college is the beginning of the sixteenth year, provided that the preparatory course of instruction has been passed through with complete success, so that now the higher may be essentially the philological school, the lower schools having first communicated a profound and thorough acquaintance with the grammar.

In a good plan of instruction for colleges, regularity of progression should be carefully observed. The different classes should be so graduated, and sustain such a relation to each other, that the best students in the one may, with the best students in the next above, constitute a continuous succession of strictly progressive advancement.

Hence it will be necessary to be exceedingly strict in admitting students to college. When pupils enter unprepared, it is at no time an advantage to them, and always an injury to the institution. The course of instruction should resemble the clear, unruffled current of some gentle stream. Every pupil ought to be capable of vigorously co-operating in one common work; each one should bring to it powers sufficient to go through with the work; each one should stimulate the other, and contribute to his intellectual growth. To the attainment of this object, a plan like the following, for conducting recitations, will be found highly conducive: let one student go through a portion of the lesson assigned for recitation, say in translating from the Greek or Latin; let another be called upon to suggest alterations; a third to rectify these; a fourth may be invited to make observations; a fifth will perhaps contribute a voluntary remark, and thus all become, at length, accustomed to take an equal interest and share in the business in hand, and learn, sine ira et studio, to co-operate in eliciting, in working out fully the sense of a passage, to correct each other's mistakes, to communicate ideas: they mutually stimulate and are stimulated, and with liveliness and cheerfulness the work advances: fervet opus. From this, however, it follows, that the classes must not be crowded. By strictly adhering to an elevated standard with regard to qualifications for admission, the evils arising from classes being unduly large may in a great measure be obviated.

To the above observations on colleges, which have

been substantially derived from Schwarz, we add the following on the importance and uses of classical studies.

We consider the advantages arising from the study of the ancient languages under two aspects. The study is important, 1. As a means for the culture of the understanding, or of the thinking faculty in the widest sense. Memory, imagination, abstraction, sagacity, judgment—in short, all the lower and higher intellectual powers are most appropriately and happily exercised and cultivated by a spirited study of the ancient classic languages. Even the art of expression (style) is much more suitably practised in this manner than by so-called exercises in composition, which the higher classes in college *ought* to be prepared to dispense with. It is this study of the classics which will afford the student occasions for presenting his own thoughts and those of others in the greatest variety of essays; and thus these essays will combine with his other studies in the formation of a complete whole, and not be a lame accompaniment, consisting of disconnected and unsuccessful hors d'œuvres. Thus will the study of language be the best preliminary training and preparation for the learned world, for this is the world of thought.

2. The second advantage attained by these classical studies is found in the subjects which are presented in the ancient languages, and with which this study is to procure us a familiar acquaintance. The collective mass of these subjects may be termed the classical world. The study of the classics, regarded from our present point of view, is therefore designed to afford us a comprehensive and complete view of the world, or the life, of the classic nations of antiquity, for the reason that these nations present to us an *ideal of beauty*. Classical studies thus constitute the best preparation for the highest purposes and pursuits of the scholar; for the learned are, first of all, to promote the ideal of a truly beautiful public or popular life.

Considered from both these points of view, the

proper study of the classics will require some particular rules, according to which it ought to be conducted.

1. *As a means of Mental Culture.*

a. The most natural course would be to begin with the Greek, rather than the Latin; but, in most cases, custom is averse to this.

b. With the grammar, application in translating should at once be connected by using elementary books; also, written exercises in the language studied. The deficiency of suitable books for this latter purpose has long been felt.*

c. The higher art of *Latin and Greek writing* retains its value as a beautiful or fine art independent of every practical purpose to which it may become subservient. Our youth would acquire a new taste and spirit for this art, if once they learned to penetrate deeper into the spirit of the Romans and Greeks; for it is only by learning to think, in the spirit of the Greeks and Romans, that the art is acquired of expressing one's thoughts in the genius of these nations; and in this respect the art of writing Latin and Greek verses is of great importance.

d. Without, therefore, endeavouring prematurely to instruct the student in the art of writing good and elegant Latin, a very rigorous grammatical method should be adopted and steadily observed. This must, of course, be adapted to the natural development of the pupil's mind. In every class the student should be taught no more than he can distinctly survey and perfectly understand, but so much he should be absolutely required to make entirely his own. The introduction of too much of the philosophy of language should be avoided, while the powers of the memory

* Since the above was first written in 1842, the consummate ability of an eminent American scholar has been, and continues to be, indefatigably employed in supplying the deficiency referred to, and the writer can not forbear expressing the great pleasure which the appearance of Dr. C. Anthon's voluminous series, to aid students in the study of the Greek and Latin classics, has afforded him. By his unwearied and invaluable labors in every department of classical learning, Dr. Anthon has secured the lasting gratitude of all who love the literature of Greece and Rome, and appreciate its influence in the culture and refinement of the mind.

should be constantly and heavily taxed, without, however, permitting the mode of instruction to become inane and lifeless. The method of the ancient humanists and grammarians deserves to be, to some extent, revived, particularly as regards their metrical and rhyming rules of Latin grammar.

e. Of the utmost importance is a suitable selection of the authors to be read in class, which selection must be the result of an extensive and profound acquaintance with classical literature.

2. *As a means of acquiring valuable Knowledge.*

a. The great point here to be aimed at is, that the young become suitably and profitably acquainted with the *whole* of classic life. We do not mean that the students are to become archæologists, veteran antiquaries, but that the instructers should be perfectly at home in antiquarian lore. The value of such knowledge will become manifest, both in the business of selecting authors for the class, and in the improvements which its application will produce in the methods of teaching ancient history which have hitherto been in vogue.

b. Let such authors only be selected to be read in class as will essentially contribute to present a complete picture of the ancient world, and let the list of such authors be as full as possible. But they should only be read carptim, selecting such parts as are essential to the grand object in view. The student ought, of course, to feel sufficient interest in the matter, and to possess industry enough to read in private the parts omitted. Only by adopting and strictly adhering to a method like this, will a full and satisfactory knowledge be obtained of what is essential, in the originals, to a complete acquaintance with classic life.

c. Suitable instruction in ancient history and geography constitutes the indispensable basis for the study of the authors of antiquity. In both a vivid light should be thrown upon physical, artistical, statistical, and political relations; but, in order to do this successfully, it will be necessary for the instructer to have completely digested and assimilated in his own mind the writings of such men as Heeren and Barthelemy. Maps, and drawings of whatever is not actually represented in modern life, are indispensable for rendering classical affairs observable to the student.

d. This entire process of introducing the young into the beautiful world of the ancients should always be a direct one; *i. e.*, adapted and corresponding to the feelings; it ought never to be mediate, *i. e.*, presenting theories and dissecting views and ideas already developed. It should be accomplished by the intelligent and spirited reading of the originals themselves, accompanied by such explanations, and illustrations, and other reading as may be necessary to bring out their meaning clearly and fully, and to put the student, as far as possible, on the same standpoint with his author.

This latter course would in Germany belong to the University; with us it will have to be mainly left to the private reading of the student, after having completed his academic course; and, therefore, the way to the perfect comprehension of the ancient world should also be opened by immediate æsthetic impressions of the plastic arts. A most important exercise for the student would consist in observing and copying with his pencil antique statues, temples, porticoes, and colonnades. Instruction in drawing may be almost entirely limited to representations from mythological and Biblical history, and from the later life of the Romans and Greeks.

e. In general, a *thorough* and *profound* acquaintance with the ancient world should be insisted on: this will be the best preventive of pedantry, and of all *affected* admiration of the beauty of Grecian life and literature.

Those young persons who design to devote themselves to some one of the learned professions ought, while at college, to regard themselves as laying a foundation, broad and deep, for that learning which it will be their subsequent business to accumulate, in connexion with their professional studies and pursuits. Indeed, our present collegiate course does little more than lay such a foundation. If in this course the classics are first in importance, we yet cannot refrain from expressing our deep regret at the superficial and unsatisfactory manner, in which certain other highly important branches of knowledge are usually treated. We speak of geography and history. It is evident that the memory ought to obtain indefeasible possession of a copious stock of geographical and historical knowledge. No one will pretend to deny that such knowledge is indispensable to the professional scholar; yet our colleges make little or no provision for these important branches of scholastic education. The student is expected to have done with them, so far as instruction is concerned, before he enters college; or, at most, a little is done in history during the freshmen-year.

We will admit that an adequate amount of geographical knowledge may be acquired during the course of instruction which prepares the pupil for college; yet, even in geography, a subsequent course of a higher and more scientific character would be desirable. But in respect of history, the case is truly deplorable. The schoolboy is made to recite, memoriter, some author on the history of the United States, some catechism on English history, and Tytler's Universal History. It is a mere task, and, usually, no palatable one to the pupil; while, in fact, this study might and ought to be so treated as to engage his keenest interest. When the instructer teaches by viva voce narrative, communicates in an interesting and spirited manner his own accumulated stores of historic lore, schoolboys will wait, as we can bear witness, with the most impatient eagerness for the hour of history to return. Of the portion communicated during the hour, the teacher can furnish an abstract, to be transcribed and committed by the pupils. But, while much may be accomplished by the adoption of such a course in academies, history, in its widest compass and its highest meanings, ought to constitute a prominent branch of college study, and we would venture to suggest that every college should have a professor of history: a man of large and liberal mind; one possessing in a high degree the faculty of treating his great subject, mankind, in its varied aspects, developments, revolutions, and activities, in a lively, spirited, and sensible manner; in a manner every way calculated to lead to those important and valuable results which an intelligent and profound study of history is confessedly alone competent to effect; and we would farther suggest that ancient history be thus studied in the first two, and modern history during the last two years of the collegiate course.

It is farther important that instruction in modern languages should be continued and completed in college. It is, perhaps, difficult to point out the extent to which this instruction should here be prosecuted. The only suitable mode, however, of conducting it is through regular teachers of their respective native tongues, who will, by private lessons, and conversation out of school, effect vastly more than can ever be accomplished by instructers to whom the language is foreign, and who are therefore under the necessity of treating it according to the established scholastic method.

The æsthetic exercises in drawing and music, which had been practised in childhood more as an amusement, should now be cultivated with a more direct view to the high calling of the scholar, by a more thorough and rigorous method. Both these fine arts should be practised by every pupil, at least until the teacher himself, and not his own disinclination, has pronounced him destitute of talent for either. A correct and rigid method of instruction is no less important than it is rare.

For every variety of music, the foundation must be laid by instruction on the piano-forte, with which singing should be connected as early as possible.

Vocal music ought also to be extensively cultivated in our common schools; and we rejoice, not only that the experiment has been made in the public schools of Boston, but that it has been attended with results so highly satisfactory as to furnish every inducement and encouragement to other communities to imitate so praiseworthy an example.

Another matter of great importance in college-instruction is that preparation for higher scholarship which is obtained by means of mathematics and logic, *i. e.*, for perception and conception.

These two branches of education will require very different modes of instruction, which will coincide only in this, that in respect of both, independent effort, and not mere memorizing, should be insisted on.

With respect to instruction in mathematics, we wish to ask attention to a few remarks, which the mode of treating this science among us has suggested. It will strike every one conversant with our colleges, that students generally regard mathematics as a difficult study; that they dislike it as dry and uninteresting. Now it appears to us that the difficulties of this study and its unpopularity arise, in a very great degree, from its being commenced too late, and being then, from necessity, treated in a manner too abstract. The student's mind, which has already, in a great degree, formed its tastes and partialities, is expected, without having acquired any interest in this study by early and entertaining methods, at once to jump in medias res, and while pursuing, at the same time, studies far more inviting in themselves, to grapple with all the abstruse details of this sober science. The difficulties and the consequent unpopularity which so generally attach to this study would, we conceive, be very much diminished, by commencing it much earlier than it is at present the practice to do. In this science, also, Pestalozzi adopted a method which is in harmony with his general system, and which was more particularly developed and applied with eminent success by some of his disciples. Through their instrumentality it has been extensively introduced in Germany; and although it has met with considerable opposition, it has, in genial, maintained the field; and as the following observations, which we translate from the work of Schwarz, imbody the principles of Pestalozzi's method, we make no apology for introducing them here.

"The abstract consideration of space and time furnishes matter of instruction which is of unlimited extent, and calculates spaces, times, powers, and laws, in relation not only to our earth, but the universe; and the Greek word mathematics indicates that in this science the process of learning is preeminently performed. It exercises the thinking faculty in its primary functions and efforts; but, when properly treated, it exercises also the fancy, by giving impressions (imaginando) of pure form, which is at the foundation of all sensuous observation, and thus it exercises the thinking faculty in its legitimate activity. In this respect, then, it may be truly termed gymnastics for the mind. This, therefore, is its great use in the culture of the mind; and for this reason it constitutes a principal department in the instruction of education. But its use in respect of what it really and directly gives, adapts it no less for the purposes of general culture, and, therefore, some of its branches have, in their application, also become necessary for the young.

"Instruction in mathematics begins with the exercises for the cultivation of the sense of sight, particularly in estimating distances, as also in the drawing of lines and figures, and then pursues its regular course, and cultivates the faculties concerned during boyhood; so that, towards the fifteenth year, the pupil reaches that point where he may proceed to the scientific method.

"In the first stage, then, he will learn to comprehend the doctrine of space and of number; in the second he will study geometry and arithmetic strictly as sciences, and, not before this period, algebra and mixed mathesis. The educator will instruct, 1. in the doctrine of figure (or form) and of magnitude; and, at the same time, 2. in the relations of numbers, or in calculation. This instruction must be conducted mathematically, *i. e.*, not merely in the way of observation, but also to produce comprehension, and a real understanding of the doctrine of equality, of similarity, of the different relations of angles, figures, proportions, &c.; so that the difference between the instruction here spoken of and the scientific instruction, both in geometry and in algebra, exists only in the method pursued, while the same things are actually learned to a certain point.

"1. *The Doctrine of Form and of Magnitude.*

"By form we mean the limits of space, in all its various phenomena; and, contracted into what is infinitely small, it is conceived of as the mathematical point. It can, therefore, be exhibited in two ways, either by proceeding, as seems to be the natural course, from the former, *i. e.*, from what presents itself to the eye in space, or from the latter, the point, of which a conception only can be formed by the mind. The question here arises, Which course would furnish the best method for education? The former, it may be thought; yet it is only seemingly the best; for, in fact, this course would have to proceed from the entire field of vision, inasmuch as the individual object in it, or, rather, its outline or surfaces, must first be sought out and distinguished by the eye: thus some skill in observation is already presupposed, while this is, in reality, to be acquired in the manner prescribed. Moreover, the field of vision is something so indefinite and confused, that there can be, in relation to it, but the smallest degree of clearness and simplicity of conception; and, in addition, it requires a power of abstraction very considerably cultivated, in order to form an abstract conception of the mathematical instead of the material figure, of its surface and its limits, of the lines and points. This course of instruction, therefore, presupposes the power of the pupil to possess what he is first to acquire by instruction, and is, therefore, only objectively, and not subjectively, elementary.

"But the second course, which is diametrically opposite to the preceding, leads from the internal to the external, from the most simple in conception to the most extended in space, according to its three dimensions; and its starting point is the mathematical point. It is true that this is, in the first instance, visibly represented, and is therefore, however diminutive it may appear on the board, in so far a material point; but this i: is only symbolically, as the teacher requires the pupil to imagine it so small as to occupy no space at all. And this *can* be required of him; for to the child of seven or even more years, this is more easy than the process of abstraction, demanded by the other course. And this is the real beginning of mathematical thinking, which imperatively demands the flight of the imagination in order to the conception of pure form; it is the easiest beginning; and by exciting the mind to observe through the medium of what is figured to the eye, it leads the mind immediately onward, in perpetually progressive succession; for the teacher will now let his pupil mark two points on his slate, and notice the possible directions between them; then three, pointing out the different possible lines between them. The pupil may for some time be exercised in finding the possible cases of the relative position of several points to each other, until he has acquired considerable readiness in pointing them out; but to exhaust them all would, with more points than four, lead to enervating diffuseness. The pupil should now rather be taught to distinguish between straight and curved lines. The possible directions and combinations of two straight lines, and thus, at the same time, the possible angles, are to be sought, then those of three, afterward of four lines; by which process a notion is acquired of triangular and quadrangular figures. After a while the pupil should proceed to the combinations of several straight lines, the teacher having first drawn for him a number of curved lines, and dwelt at sufficient length on the most regular curved line, the circle. Meanwhile the pupil should be induced to exercise himself, in private, in combining straight and curved lines, and in inventing various figures, these employments serving to exercise the creative power of the imagination both for mathematics and for æsthetic feeling, while the hand, at the same time, becomes skilled in drawing.

"If the teacher can devote about an hour daily to this course of instruction, his pupil will find himself in the midst of geometry ere he is aware of it; for these progressive exercises will of necessity lead the pupil, when engaged in drawing or examining figures, to measurements and comparisons; to the perception of equality and of similarity; to the comprehension of reasons; to the clear exhibition of demonstrations; so that it will only be the constant business of the teacher to direct the pupil's reflection to the subjects before him; and thus the demonstrations are devised by the pupil himself, and have a real existence in his own mind: he sees at once the origin of figures and their relations, and the reasons for everything. This, then, is a very different affair from that contracting and cramping operation which mathematics is so generally made the instrument of inflicting on the mind. Here the mind expands; conceives of magnitudes as they produce themselves or continuously increase, and thus enters the field of their natural powers and their laws, and therefore proceeds to philosophy.

"It may therefore be expected that the pupil with whom this method has been pursued will, at about fourteen years of age, have comprehended what is called elementary geometry, besides stereometry and trigonometry. The mode of instruction is chiefly inventive (*i. e.*, the pupil is required to invent demonstrations himself), sometimes catechetical, and succeeds best with a number of pupils whom the teacher can stimulate to competition in inquiry. He should himself speak but little, merely exciting investigation, and requiring its results to be properly expressed."

2. As regards the relations of numbers, or calculation, we deem it unnecessary to translate the re-

marks of our author, partly because, in this instance, the difficulties spoken of in connexion with mathematics do not exist; but chiefly because, in teaching calculation, or the relations of numbers, the method here recommended has, in a great measure, been very generally and successfully adopted in this country.

LOGIC.

Instruction in logic should never be commenced before the last collegiate year, and even then only what is easiest and most general should be dwelt upon. There should be two courses of logic distinguished: one for the college; the other, which would in Germany belong to the University, ought in this country, while our present academic arrangements continue unchanged, to constitute a part of the strictly professional course of study. Only in the latter can the science be treated in its completeness. The former should aim only to elicit self-observation, to produce a correct understanding of the nature of abstraction, to incite to its practice, and to teach the first elements of the language and terminology of philosophical speculation. Accordingly, it will be necessary to adopt, not the *progressive* course of some particular compend, but the *retrogressive* course of some analysis, which should be followed up in all suitable collateral *digressions*. A complete survey of this science is here not at all to be thought of; for the object in view is that the pupil may begin to learn to think. The mode of instruction should be conversational; but it must be borne in mind that in this science it will be impossible to elicit the truth from the pupil by questions, as it may be done in mathematics; he can only be invited to the observation of it.

Hence arises the unfrequency of logical acuteness, because the fondness for it is very rare. In mathematics much may be forced, in logic nothing.

As respects the didactics for this higher academic instruction, the following two general but necessary observations will suffice:

1. Whichever of the three learned professions the

student may intend to embrace, he ought on no account, for the sake of the studies of his particular calling, to neglect that general learned culture which he has commenced in college, and which is rendered complete by the suitable and judicious study of the natural sciences (natural history, physiology, experimental physics, and mixed mathematics); of philosophy (logic and metaphysics); mathematics (of which the collegiate course may communicate sufficient knowledge, but, at all events, no scientific survey); and history, in its higher aspects.

2. In general, it is desirable that the mode of instruction in college should, in no branch of study, be too acroamatic; yet in history it must of necessity be more so than in other sciences.

It is much to be desired that, for the comprehensive scientific culture which our colleges ought to supply, the ideal of the Greek academy might be restored. This, indeed, could not be attained by insipid and stale catechization or puerile questioning, but only by free conversation, or disputatio in the sense of the ancient Romans. With this might be connected, at suitable points in the different sciences, general recitations, or repetitions of what has been gone over by the class, which would both furnish the student a general view of what he has learned, and, at the same time, teach him the meaning of independent study.

And only when the student has been led to make independent efforts can written communications (essays in composition, or by whatever name they may be designated) to his professor have any real value; and they are not, therefore, to be treated, either by the teacher or the pupil, as college-tasks.

These ideals of educational methods in academic instruction can, of course, only succeed, when the professors sustain to the students the relation of elder friends. To what extent the spirit which prevails among our youth at literary institutions, and which often manifests itself in developments little to their credit, would be favourable or unfavourable to such relations, we shall not here attempt to determine.

All farther theory respecting academic instruction would be more suitably treated as a part of some particular science of academic life; and such a science would serve to show that, by means of this higher general culture, the scholar is to become superior to the rightly cultivated man of common life only in point of intelligence, and not in moral worth.

SECTION II.

MAN EDUCATED FOR SOCIAL LIFE, OR IN THE SOCIAL AFFECTIONS.

CHAPTER I.

Education in the Sentiments of Private Friendship, Love, and Benevolence in general.

THE rational life of man in society must, in order to present a beautiful aspect, be a life of friendship; a life adorned by the practice of all the so-called duties of philanthropy, love, and benevolence. As regards education in this respect, everything will depend on the distinction made between what is essential to our character and what is merely ornamental. Private friendship, family affection, and public spirit, should be the ideals of every human being of high and generous culture. These ideals are destroyed as soon as they are dictated as duties. It is, therefore, the first business of the educator to be well satisfied in his own mind respecting the following views:

The nature of friendship consists in that pure affection for another, which, being an unconstrained, a spontaneous satisfaction or delight in its object, can never submit to the authority of prescribed rules, though it will ever be dependant on the degree of culture, especially the judgment. This pure affection is either love for an ideal, for every moral ideal, or love for some individual person. The former constitutes the higher or ideal friendship; the latter, the lower or common; both combined constitute the highest ideal of friendship.

Affection which is felt for some particular person

combines within itself delight in that person, good-will towards him, and the performance of kind offices for his good. Such affection can therefore be exercised only towards an object that is really amiable; but this amiableness is either mental; *i. e.*, it consists in the peculiar characteristics, in the temper and disposition of the individual; or it is sensuous, *i. e.*, the amiable deportment of the individual in his intercourse with others.

The opposite of this is hatefulness, or the repulsive or odious qualities of individuals, existing, like the foregoing, under a twofold aspect. The man who cannot hate, cannnot love: he is a superficial, sweet, soft, pleasant sort of person. There is much misconception relative to that love of our enemies inculcated in the New Testament: the nature of this is purely religious, and not ethical.

Personal affection is, in the first instance, felt only by one: it must become mutual, and thus it ripens into friendship. Affection, and mutual devotedness to each other's welfare, exhibited in every possible kind office, constitute for every relation of life an imperative requisite to the realization of the beauty of benevolence and gratitude, which has its true foundation in the sentiment of universal philanthropy. For the product of the spirit of friendship, expanded, diffused over all, and graduated according to the manifold relations of human society, is that sympathetic, purely philanthropic fellow-feeling, which produces towards every man (for the sake of his humanity, which always deserves our love) good-will and benevolence, which will not fail to meet with gratitude and return of affection on the part of truly noble natures capable of friendship.

Benevolence that assumes an air of graciousness and condescension, however inseparable it may be from peculiar civil organizations, is utterly worthless and contemptible when actually characteristic of the person who practises it.

As we are here considering friendship and benevolence, not from the stand-point of religion, but as belonging to the beautiful developments of human life, we cannot refrain from inviting the recollection of our classical readers to the delightful results produced, in respect of these virtues, by the παιδαρτάσις of Pythagoras. Damon and Pythias were Pythagoræans. Many other beautiful and affecting instances of the noblest and purest friendship, which grew out of this school, will occur to the scholar.

Opposed to these philanthropic virtues are the misanthropic vices of malevolence, jealousy, envy, and mischievous or malicious delight in the misfortune or misery of others. If they be not in themselves vicious, they always become so as soon as they exert an influence on deliberate designs and matured purposes, in which case they are justly designated as fiendlike vices. Now, as a disposition or propensity to love and friendship, with all their subordinate virtues, has its appropriate abode in the human heart, education, in view of their development and cultivation, will have to proceed chiefly in a negative manner. Let it beware, above all things, of extinguishing love in the human breast, which takes place especially by the expression of contemptuous judgments respecting others uttered in the presence of children. The ear of childhood should be regarded as a sacred depository; and thus, also, it is of great importance, in this connexion, to prevent children from becoming selfish; to see that their ego do not acquire an undue importance and prominence.

Education will exert its positive influence in this matter by producing in children a respect for life, or living beings in general; and, first, a tender regard for animals, and then for inferior persons, however poor; for example, towards beggars; especially, also, for the domestics of the house, and for children who are poor. The first point is of far greater moment than men are wont to regard it: he that is unfeeling and cruel towards animals, will never be a kind friend of man; and children who are permitted to treat animals with cruelty, will be pretty sure to ill-treat and tyrannize over their fellow-men in after life.

In respect of the culture here considered, the most important influence will proceed from the example of the educator.

The powerful influence of Christianity in promoting real love to mankind, true philanthropy, will be considered on a subsequent page.

Particular care should be taken to cultivate the love of ideals: it is true that this also exists in every man, but it is more easily extinguished by the realities which come into conflict with it. Education ought to recognise youthful ideals as necessary, and even to educate for ideals. With regard to this, no particular rules are necessary, if those who educate are themselves in possession of noble, exalted ideals; if none such exist in their minds, all rules are useless. But, in addition to the example of parents and teachers, we may mention history and poetry as highly important means in the culture of the young for ideals. This subject will be farther considered in the progress of the work.

Educators and pupils often confound ideals and productions of the fancy with each other, and therefore mistake a fantastical or romantic for an ideal temperament. The inseparable characteristics of enthusiasm for ideals are considerate seriousness, and sobriety of thought.

It is necessary here to warn against that vital mistake, so frequently made by those who have the education of children intrusted to them, of valuing natural goodness of heart, good-nature, or bonhommie, too highly, and of undervaluing insensibility or coldness of temperament, which is, indeed, of less frequent occurrence than the other. Both are in themselves only natural qualities of the disposition or temperament, which are yet to acquire their real value, in and through that rational self-control which is the work of culture. The former is apt to be allied to preponderant sensuality and an inclination to licentiousness, and generally to weakness of character, and under the latter is often concealed the most profound and vigorous love, which embraces all the relations of mankind, and which no vicissitudes nor passions can prostrate or extinguish. Such opposite natural temperaments will require very different modes of education, in order that the true beauty of affection, of genuine human love, which lies in the middle be tween all extremes, may be attained. It is an evidence of the effeminacy of modern culture, that there exists a prejudice against characters called cold, and in favour of good-nature.

The design of this education for friendship is therefore, by means of culture, to give to the life of the individual, in his relation to others, a beautiful (in the narrowest sense) character and aspect; and this in a twofold respect: 1. In the closest relation of friendship, properly so called: 2. In the wider and the widest relations of universal philanthropy.

CHAPTER II.

Education aiming at the right Development of the Sentiment of Love, in its narrowest Sense, as the Love of Family and Kindred.

A DISTINCT species of private friendship, not only, but its highest manifestation, is conjugal love, the love between man and wife, whose friendship-ideal is found in the common object of the procreation and education of children. Matrimony being the highest beauty of social life for the individual, is the destination of every human being. As such, and as a virtue, it occupies middle ground between the mischiefs of coarse sensuality, or fornication, and fanatical spirituality, or monachism. It may be right and praiseworthy if, for the sake of exalted ideas, which demand the utmost self-consecration, this noblest blossom of human life is sacrificed and foregone: this resignation or renunciation of the most sacred and happy of human connexions may, if made for the sake of objects or purposes truly noble and good, be regarded as sub lime; but it should never be other than voluntary, and never be required of any man.

The beauty of family-life is perfect only when it can be regarded, 1. As an individual manifestation, or individuum, in the collective mass of the great family of the state; when the private interest of the family is not at variance with the public interest of the people, *i. e.*, with public spirit; but when, on the other hand, it rather promotes the latter by the development and cultivation of all truly human virtues, which are first to acquire tenderness, beauty, and strength in the family circle, *i. e.*, in the friendship subsisting between man and wife, parents and children, employers and domestics, but are then to manifest themselves in the public life of public friendship, *i. e.*, of public spirit; or, in other words, in the family must be nursed, cultivated, and established those affections, those kind and benevolent sentiments, which ought to adorn a nation's public life, and minister, in every proper way, to the common good. In the life of the family must be sought the pith and marrow of the state.

To the perfect beauty of wedded life belongs, 2dly, the free choice of matrimonial companions, which must proceed from pure love, and develop itself into firm friendship. For this choice of love, and for subsequent beauty and perpetuity of matrimonial friendship, everything will depend on the following three virtues: chastity, faithfulness, and the mental culture of both parties, for which it is the business of education to provide.

1. Education in purity of mind, or in true chastity of heart, presents, in accordance with nature's course of development, the following three aspects:

1. Accustom or train the child to modesty;

2. Carefully protect and rigidly discipline the child's fancy;

3. Direct the child's fancy upon what is spirituous or ideal; for by this means the sternest contempt of mere sensuality, effeminacy, and lust is effected. For chastity is not merely to be external, as manifested in outward conduct, but internal, as constituting a disposition of soul. The latter ought to be, and

can be, retained, even after acquaintance with real life has put an end to the *innocence of childhood*, and substituted *experience* in its place.

It was the opinion of Aristotle, that the intercourse of young persons of both sexes should, at the time when the sexual instinct is developing itself, be subjected to the closest supervision; and many modern pedagogists have expressed the same view. But unchastity very generally owes its origin to the premature development of the sexual instinct, induced by various causes. This may, in a great measure, be prevented by proper attention to the physical education of the young. But the great point, is to keep at immeasurable distance from the young everything that can pollute the heart and corrupt the imagination. Watch over the eyes and ears of your children as you would over a sacred deposite, that nothing unclean may approach them, or even taint the air in which they exist. Here, if anywhere, prevention of evil is worth all the cures that human ingenuity can invent, and which seldom effect much, and can never restore what is lost. But where the preventive, or negative education for chastity, recommended under the three aspects specified above, is consistently and carefully practised, the desired result can scarcely fail to be attained; and with respect to young persons of both sexes, thus educated, it will not be necessary to watch, with timid solicitude, their social intercourse; yet, of course, the supervision of parents or other educators should never be withdrawn from this intercourse. But young persons, correctly educated, and having nothing to conceal, will not seek concealment. The pure, the virtuous, *never* shun the light; and the young man who has retained his innocence through boyhood, and whose soul has never been polluted by so much as an unchaste word, or by early initiation in the knowledge of sexual relations, will bring modesty and self-respect with him into that period, in which new impulses begin to manifest themselves in his organism, and he will have that within him which will impel him to shun companionship with the unclean, and to spurn pollution with indignation from his presence.

And if we say that, in relation to this important matter, our boys are everywhere exposed to evil influence, we need but refer to the evidences of impurity of heart and corruptedness of imagination so copiously exhibited in various ways, wherever boys frequent, in order to convince those who have the interests of education at heart, that in this particular a great reform is necessary. But how and where will you begin to reform, when impurity is everywhere rife, without condemning children to monastic seclusion? Better, indeed, would this be than pollution. But, of course, the reform must begin at home: *i. e.*, parents must attend to this matter, superintending the education of their children themselves, not exposing them to promiscuous companionship, but excluding from their intercourse those whose character is suspicious, or even unknown; giving them more of their own company, and using every conceivable precaution to secure them against evil communications.

If it should be thought that we have dwelt at too great length on this subject, we can only reply, that having, for many years past, been in various ways and at different places employed in the business of education, we know full well whereof we testify, and speak only from actual knowledge of the necessity of the case.

2. Faithfulness in love has its basis in general excellence of character; in that nobility of soul which shrinks from no sacrifice as too great, when required by honour and justice. Nothing can be more indicative of weakness of mind and littleness of soul than fickleness in love: nothing more base and despicable than trifling with the affections of confiding woman. There is reason to fear that the frivolity and lax morality, which characterize the social condition of some European countries, are making progress among us also; and to the influence of education we must look for the erection of a barrier in the hearts of the rising

generation, and hence in public sentiment, against the spread of this and every other moral pestilence.

3. We add a few general observations on the different mental culture required by the young of different sexes; and we premise that in the education of females there exist two grand mistakes, the one more practical, the other, as yet, chiefly confined to the lucubrations of theorists, which call for the judicious but very decided interference of education. The first of these mistakes is founded in the prejudice, which has become so general among the rich of this country, that it is disgraceful for *ladies* to have any knowledge of domestic economy, not to say practical acquaintance with the ordinary affairs of housekeeping, and the daily routine of housewifery. In consequence of this certainly very extensively prevailing prejudice, we see that many rich families, and many that are *not* rich, educate their daughters in a manner calculated to fit them only for the boudoir, for gossip, and for parties, for fashionable assemblies, and to unfit them for all real *usefulness;* for all those domestic *duties*, whose faithful, and intelligent, and *cheerful* performance is so essential to substantial domestic happiness—so important in order to secure stability to earthly happiness; while the sterling virtues, and the ready tact and skill in management which qualify for the discharge of those duties, are alone competent to supply expedients and resources, when vicissitudes, reverses, nay, poverty, come to those who have been bred in the lap of affluence, as, indeed, they often do come, when least expected, in a state of society so fluctuating as ours.

The second mistake is that which has of late years made no little noise in theory, through the sexual public spirit (perhaps, more correctly, esprit-de-corps) of Miss Martineau and a number of others, and which consists in wresting from woman the crown of modesty, the lovely virtues, and the sweet charm of that noiseless, retired, unobtrusive life and activity which constitute her appropriate sphere, and thrusting her into the busy thoroughfares, the noisy assemblies, nay, the political arena, where men jostle each other, and contend for gain or distinction.

On neither of these mistakes do we deem it necessary here to expatiate, because the first argues a lack of common sense, which many exceedingly pertinent productions of some of our most gifted and popular female writers have hitherto failed to remedy, and because we believe the second to be confined chiefly to a few monomaniacs, against whose baseless pretensions and preposterous demands we have no doubt that the right feeling, and correct taste, and good sense of the sex will ever revolt, to the frustration of assumptions that are obviously contrary to nature.

The due differential relation between the respective mental culture of boys and girls must be determined according to the nature of the intellectual capacity of the different sexes. Man's mind finds its sphere in action, woman's in feeling: to man, therefore, belongs the practical, to woman the meditative sphere of life. The man, therefore, is to be educated for the busy stage of the world by manifold knowledge and skill, and his highest callings in the scientific and the artistic world have already been pointed out.

Woman's calling is to the more retired sphere of domestic life, for husband and children, and her distinguishing virtues should be prudent housewifery, *i. e.*, order and economy combined; feeling sympathy, tender care, cheerful affection, and vigorous patience. For these ideals should woman, *as such*, be educated, *but without prejudice to all other general human education.* It is the *latter* only which, in respect of females also, fixes the different degrees of mental culture. In this general education of the female sex, as well as in that special culture which has direct reference to woman's peculiar sphere, the process, as in all popular education, should not be mediate, *i. e.*, proceeding from theories and scholastic systems, but everything should be adapted immediately to the feelings, so that the example of the educators, whether male or female, will be of the highest importance.

Girls should be educated only in the social circle, and by their mothers. Yet, for the time being, female boarding-schools appear to be a necessary evil.

To this general sketch we subjoin the following more extended discussion, which we translate from Schwarz:

"*From the beginning of the eighth year.*

"From the beginning of the eighth year, the two sexes require, in almost every respect, a different education. With respect to boys, it is scarcely necessary to add anything to the general directions which have been given on a former page, and from which the necessary special rules are easily deduced. Their principal concern are the studies of school, alternating with bodily exercise. Their amusements are, at an early age, of the more active kind: chasing the butterfly, and scouring the plain with other boys: at a later age they should engage in pedestrian excursions and bold undertakings, and enjoy the cheerful company of their equals; taking care, however, that their playmates be of the proper character, and that their hearts be cultivated for what is noble and generous. This vigilant supervision should follow them to the later years of youth, and guard them against all bad company. Their propensity to imitate other young persons, older than themselves, which, among other evil practices, so often leads to the early habit of smoking, and the like, should be enlisted on the side of what is good and praiseworthy, by constantly managing their entire education in accordance with sound principles.

"On the subject of early female education it will be necessary to go more into detail. And here we must, first of all, deprecate a most unhappy error, which appears, in our age, more and more to extend its mischievous operation, without receiving the attention which its progress calls for. In former times girls were *too much* buried in domestic life, and forgotten; whereas now they are too early advanced to a many-sided culture; and the attention of the whole family, and of visiters, is to such a degree directed to the little daughter of three or four years of age, that we need not wonder if the girl of seven expects to be noticed before all others, and at fourteen pretends to the dignity of a lady; and if, in the end, the married woman must be allowed to regard herself as the principal person in the family, if she is not to pine away as though under the influence of a slow poison, and thus to poison the whole sphere in which she moves.

"It is true that we speak here, primarily, of the so-called cultivated class; but the evil appears to be already extending itself to those who have no pretensions to culture.

"It should be well considered what female culture is, and how high, when it is of the right character, it is capable of elevating a being which, without it, either sinks from its own weakness, or succumbs under the storms of life. Nothing should girls learn earlier than to take delight in manifesting their affection towards the whole family by artless, noiseless, well-regulated activity; to anticipate their wishes by courteousness, reflection, and good sense: in the happiness of those around them they should seek their own. This is, in general, the end to be attained. Let us consider more particularly the manner in which education should contribute to its attainment.

"Girls require chiefly the guidance of the maternal hand, in order that their tender nature may not be rudely handled, their purity not invaded, and the appropriately female direction of their development not interfered with. Their understanding and their feelings should be exposed to no rude touch, that, like the rosebud, they may develop themselves purely from within, and like the chaste mimosa, shrink from every the least contact. Maternal gentleness can alone administer such treatment. Man is incapable of giving up the more rigorous process of forming or determining, according to his own purposes; and when he does this, as we so frequently witness when fathers have to educate their daughters alone, he rarely succeeds in finding the right method, and then generally prefers doing nothing at all. That the mind of woman has so often fallen into error, or lost its purity and truth, is chiefly to be ascribed to the preponderance of external influence upon her culture: girls are instructed and treated like boys, and the peculiarities of the female character are too much overlooked, and handled with too little tenderness. Girls should therefore always and chiefly enjoy the gui dance of the mother; and she should more carefully attend to their health and bodily vigour than is usual; and physicians should be consulted on this point: so that, in the place of feeble women, suffering from sundry nervous affections, future mothers of healthy offspring may be educated. Mothers should rather pride themselves upon blooming than on elegantly dressed daughters.

"The employments, whether designed for instruction or for amusement, with which little girls are furnished, should all be of the gentler character. They will be easily amused by silently observing flowers or human beings; they will, indeed, take delight in jumping and running about with others of their age, and they should be encouraged to do so, yet taking care that they do not acquire habits which are more becoming boys; for much that would not be unbecoming in boys might acquire for girls the unenviable name of hoidens. In their case, therefore, greater care will also be necessary in the choice of companions and playmates; and, in general, they will want fewer than boys, because otherwise they are apt to fall into what is called gadding about, while their inward beauty and tenderness of feeling are injured; and to this cause it may, perhaps, be owing that there are so many heartless women and coquettes. The little garden out of doors, and the little doll-closet within, will supply little girls with entertainment, and with exercises suitable to their future sphere, for hours. They must, by all means, be furnished with a doll and its paraphernalia; but not with more than they can well manage and make use of, in order that they may learn to take care of their little concerns, and accustom themselves to good management. They ought to have a few playmates, whom they may see daily, and with whom they will contrive little dramatic entertainments of various kinds. At the same time, however, they should have a fixed season for certain female employments, such as knitting, for hearing something instructive, or for relating something themselves. This stated time for actual employment must, indeed, at first be short, but it may soon be extended to the length of some hours; and in connexion with this, little commissions should be frequently given them to perform, in order that they may become habituated, in all respects, to order and punctuality, and to noiseless, domestic activity.

" Girls are more fitted than boys to mingle frequently among grown persons; but they should not be too much noticed and praised, and, in general, not be permitted to contract a desire of notice. But their habits of domestic industry should not become such as to confine them too much to their room, and thus to deny them the enjoyment of nature and exercise in the open air. They ought, at a very early age, to be introduced to the world of flowers.

" Girls of seven years of age should already possess a decided fondness for domestic employments, and from this period onward they ought themselves to learn all the active duties which belong to domestic life: they should derive pleasure from active employment in the different departments of the household, the kitchen, the nursery, and in needlework, &c., in order that they may become well-informed and skilled in all these affairs. It will be necessary to continue the exercises designed for the cultivation of the senses. At this period, also, they must become acquainted with books, since these are inseparably connected with modern culture: they should, therefore, be gradually instructed in writing, natural history, geography, civil history, &c., and perhaps, even at this age, already in the French language; but, in imposing any such exercises, it will be necessary to proceed with caution, and to observe the utmost moderation ; the more so, because girls are, at all times, too prone to confine themselves too closely to pursuits of this kind. How many young girls have become diseased in body and in soul by reading! how many have lost their health by close application to ornamental needlework! They ought, therefore, to be directed, at all suitable times, to engage in free bodily exercise, and even in some of the more quiet and gentle gymnastic exercises ; they should enjoy frequent opportunities of appropriate amusement in the society of others of the same age. It is particularly desirable that they should have several little friends, with whom they may keep up an interchange of less frequent visits, in order that their tenderness and freshness of feeling towards beloved persons may on no account be blunted, as is so frequently the case in consequence of daily intercourse. In general, too great care cannot be taken that that cheerfulness which is so lovely in all should not be lost by study, or application to any other pursuit. It is delightful to hear every part of the house resound with the young maiden's sweet song : delightful is that vivacity which so often enlivens home and cheers all its inmates.

"Modesty, cleanliness, propriety in all respects, as well as all other female virtues, will indeed manifest themselves spontaneously in young maidens who have not been neglected or spoiled in childhood ; yet they must be earnestly cherished and carefully cultivated ; and it is precisely at the age commencing with the eighth year that this is most necessary, because at this age an excited state of mind with reference to social relations supervenes, by means of which the artlessness of childhood is apt to suffer. Hence, even in the playful age, some *positive treatment* is necessary, *i. e.*, treatment by which the inward soundness of character is secured by external influences, which favour the firm retention of good habits. It is difficult here to find the proper medium or middle course, so that, on the one hand, that simplicity and artlessness (*naïveté*), which are such beautiful features in the character of young females, be not impaired and dissipated, and that, on the other hand, nature be not left to run wild, at a time when its second impulse is developing itself. It is only the tender mother, herself free from vanity and egotism, who can truly understand and appreciate the delicate organism of her child's mind, and succeed, by her beautiful tact in treating the elements of childhood, in awakening its slumbering powers. Intercourse with rude companions, and, still more, every public exhibition of young girls—for example, in public musical performances—would directly contravene the object aimed at; and in this respect even boarding-schools have their disadvantages. When it is borne in mind how easily the mind's simplicity and purity are lost by shallow gossip, by ungentle, injudicious treatment, and by fondness for shining and public display; when the many examples of female flippancy, vanity, and coquetry, that meet us everywhere, are taken into consideration, it will be obvious to every reflecting mind that the treatment, or, rather, absence of proper treatment during the period of which we speak, is in fault. Girls, in short, require treatment of such delicacy and tenderness, as to cherish in their minds a prominent and acute sense of personal sacredness.

"But they are not, on that account, to be brought up to be fragile, sensitive, or ornamental plants. Girls also have their path of life to run, which is often enough thorny, and the asperities of whose atmosphere they must be prepared to bear, while in their home they let their softening and warming light shine. But, in order to this, exalted self-denial is necessary, and nothing is so sure to communicate this as a Christian education. Their school for life will therefore be home, with its joys, and, perhaps, more frequently, its sorrows; and this school will be the best for developing their tender feelings, and to induct them gradually into their own beautiful activities. One of the most beautiful of these is the care of smaller children, particularly of brothers and sisters, in which girls may be the assistants of their mothers.

"The tone of the house, and of the entire mode of treatment, should be, both for boys and girls, the same even, natural, sober, and friendly family-tone, if education is to be successful. Nothing affected, nothing stiff and constrained, nothing pedantic; but throughout, unconstrained cordiality, cheerfulness, and good-humour, combined with due sobriety and firmness in all things, which the educator must require: this is what the nature of children and of parents demands. But, in all respects, parents, educators, and others should live before children as in the sacred presence of God, and thus accustom them thus to live. This may become, at the age here treated of, the fixed habit of the whole life; and what could be more desirable? If the omnipresent God dwelleth in the heart of the child, it is already in the path of wisdom.

"*From the beginning of the fifteenth year.*

"It will not be necessary here to say anything more on the subject of physical education. The proper mode of life, with all its good habits, should by this time have become second nature, and be identified with moral accountability. On the direction of this, by means of instruction, we have only the following observations to add:

"1. *The education of young men* is best conducted on the principle of leaving them to choose the good for themselves, and to avoid the evil. Even in the monkish Middle Ages this principle was recognised, and Vincent de Beauvais has some excellent remarks on the subject.

"The young man may be expected to make the right choice, if he has, up to this period, been trained up, and continues to be guided, according to the directions which we have given. On the one hand, his reason must, by means of his scientific culture, become the ruling power within him; while, on the other hand, his heart must be elevated by noble and generous feelings. Happy are the influences of affectionate intercourse with his parents, his brothers and sisters; of tender attention to his younger brothers and sisters; especially, also, of friendship, and even of love, which should be allowed to develop itself and bloom in the youthful heart: it is a guardian angel, that protects in many temptations. Thus will he enter armed into life, and consecrate himself to God and mankind. The guidance which he will still require should consist not only in the directions of sensible counsel, but also in protection against evil influences. Youth cannot, as yet, dispense with a certain degree of rigour. Thus, for example, he should not so much as desire bad company; and on all occasions entertain the firm resolve not to be misled. He may yet, in various ways, break his resolutions, and run into excesses; and here he will stand in need of a Mentor, who will come up powerfully to his aid, and, if need be, not spare him. Even the young man of eighteen ought not to enjoy absolute liberty, but a degree of rigorous Mentorship should still be exercised over him. Thus, in every good institution of learning, there ought to be inexorable statutes against card-playing, and every game of chance, and against certain classes of meetings. An all-important point is, that young men repose confidence in their counsellors; and, in connexion with this subject, we refer to what has been said concerning the early cultivation of enthusiasm for ideals.

"We should encourage youth of this age in the development of truth; in giving an account, at least to themselves, of their actions; in cultivating habits of reflection; and we may do this, among other means, by exciting doubts in their minds, when we observe that they are too hasty to assume things as true; yet, in so doing, it will be necessary to keep within due bounds, and to treat with respectful tenderness that youthful heart which pursues and embraces with ardour.

"The youth's heart should glow for whatever is good, and true, and beautiful. Hence it is the office of education to provide that his active or moral principles, having developed themselves with his growth, having been disciplined by instruction, and practice, and displayed themselves in the various virtues of early life, may be strengthened. The sphere in which he moves, example, scholastic instruction, and religious culture, all will co-operate in this; but serious admonition and counsel must not be wanting. Science, indeed, leads directly to truth, but there must be a steady influence to excite a thirst for truth. His taste, as the sense of the beautiful, must be protected against whatever may corrupt it.

"The utmost cleanliness and unaffected neatness in dress should be insisted on. While you seek carefully to preserve him from foppery and all fashionable follies, use every suitable effort to give predominance within him to a sense of what is becoming, beautiful, and dignified. The cultivation of the taste must, in the mean time, make gradual progress; every attempt to force out premature fruit must be avoided, otherwise the young man will learn to criticise before he learns to admire and to love; he will become a shallow babbler, who will prate about matters of art in the phraseology of popular periodicals. No, let not this be; let him first learn to feel healthfully and naturally; then, as his taste becomes more and more developed in the study of nature, and in progressive artistic culture, he will, in due time, have a healthy, sound judgment, which is scarcely to be expected of the youth of eighteen; for he is still, at this age, in too excited a state to possess it. Let, then, no conceit be indulged in him, which would rob him of his greatest ornament, his modesty.

"And then, when the youth receives into his soul the true with the good, and the good with the beautiful, his most exalted idea will dawn upon him in its glory. He will find happy hours in devotion: he will desire, with some dear friend, to strive upward to the divine: he will resolve to consecrate himself to the promotion of human happiness: he will long to see a heaven upon earth, and to labour for the evolution of better times; and if, amid these high impulses, he should begin to indulge in fantastic schemes, and threaten to run into extravagances, he will need, not only a calmly reflecting friend, but also that *αγᾶθοδαιμων* within him, which will admonish him modestly to attend to the corrective counsels of his older and maturer teachers. Yet only when the culture of the mind and heart, in its whole compass, advances stead ily, can that which is highest in humanity, however mightily it may struggle within him, be actually developed in the youth. Our age is, in the highest degree, unfavourable to the education of young men. They are too early left to themselves; an emancipation utterly at variance with nature. Among the more cultivated, everything tends to excite in the youth more of pretension than of modesty, more egotism than affection, more fantasticalness than thirst for truth, more idolatrous devotion to the prevailing spirit of the age than fear of God: and a high-souled youth is a phenomenon that men stare and wonder at. Among the uncultivated, the state of things is even worse. What rudeness and licentiousness characterize great numbers of apprentices and journeymen in our cities and towns, and extend even to the sons of our yeomanry, is but too notorious."

What a commentary on the state of education among the mass of our people do we read in the progress of insubordination, in the ferocious exhibitions of a riotous and lawless spirit, which have, for some time past, been more and more frequently witnessed in our land! What does the police—what can it effect in our peculiar political organization? The schools do little enough; and fathers also, even though they be sensible and wise, can accomplish scarcely anything, since the spirit of the age has so much enervated parental influence, and the current of unrestrained license is hurrying along so many even of the more cultivated and better class. The influence of the Church, of religion, is indeed great, so far as it reaches; but how vast the multitude of those who spurn its authority! When, therefore, we look abroad, and contemplate the condition of our youth, we see that, precisely at the age which requires the strongest inward efforts of virtue, they are not only sent ou helpless into the world, but exposed to the most frightful dangers to the soul: not much better than if the newborn child were exposed in a wilderness inhabited by ravening beasts. If better provision be not made, both in city and country, for the education and discipline of the young, both in and out of school, in domestic and public life, no good is to be expected from education among a cultivated people; nay, the evils deprecated seem to keep pace, at a fearful rate, with culture itself. Of this we have evidence in all the information we possess on the subject respecting our large cities and towns; and, alas! that we should say it, abundant proof is furnished even by our colleges. And we cannot but hope that our state legislatures, as they see these evils increasing with fearful rapidity, and evolving the most lamentable results, will be induced not only to make more ample provision for the education of the people, but will inquire more closely into its nature, and adopt a system that may be calculated to train up the youth of this great republic in such views of life and of human duty, as may fit our people for the right and profitable exercise of those political rights and privileges of which they so fondly boast.

In conclusion, we may add, that if our legislatures are too indifferent or too impotent to extend, both as to time and space, the operation of education, and to adapt its character to our wants, as this is the age of societies, a society might be formed which should aim at reforming the existing system of education, and developing and establishing principles indispensable to the discipline of a free people, and adopting and introducing a plan and method, by which the evils which exist and are increasing among us may be assailed and remedied at the root, in the mind and heart of the young, and the true, the right, the beautiful, and the good become the objects of the people's love and pursuit.

"2. *Female Education from the thirteenth year of Life*

"At no time of life does the sanctuary of the female

heart require more vigilant protection, than at the age when the young maiden begins to develop herself to womanhood. Not only should the mother, with the utmost solicitude, guard her against improper company, and against evil communications of every description, but she should herself be more than ever her daughter's companion. Her own heart should more intensely glow for whatever is pure, and generous, and good; and thus will her maternal conversation and example exert an influence which cannot fail to produce fruits of greatest excellence. At this period the young female should engage more extensively in domestic employments, and make greater exertions both in acquiring accomplishments and in cultivating the understanding, being, at the same time, gradually introduced into social life, and taught to accustom herself to the harsher and rougher elements of human intercourse. Education must provide that she meet with nothing corrupting to the soul, nothing destructive to faith, and hope, and love. It is at this period that conversations on religion and on other subjects, not only with the mother, but with the father also, will be most desirable and profitable.

"Whatever peculiar destinies may await the young maiden, something should be learned by means of which, even though she remain unmarried, she may be able to lead a useful and dignified life. Every talent that makes itself manifest should be suitably cultivated. In the cultivated class, every young woman should, at least to some extent, learn drawing and music, for these fine arts are favourable to the development of inward truth in thought and feeling, and subserve the attainment of other female accomplishments.

"But, because such should be their influence, females ought never to be called upon to make what may be called exhibitions in these arts: it is only among friends that girls or young women should sing and perform on an instrument; and then not for the sake of applause, but to give pleasure. Performances before large and mixed companies have a tendency dangerous to some of the most beautiful traits in the character of well-educated woman; and young women should never engage in them, except they be really above all vain desire of admiration and praise.

" Moderation and dignity in all suitable amusements should be strictly insisted upon, and all fashionable folly and impropriety in dress carefully guarded against. The present aspect of social life would stamp with absurdity all declamations against beauty and elegance of apparel; but surely every well-educated woman should not only be above mere worldliness in anything, and the follies and frivolities of fashionable life, but ought to exhibit the purity and nobleness of her character by seeking the beautiful and elegant in what is modest and becoming, simple and dignified, and by making all her accomplishments subservient to the true and the good.

" Although boys should be chiefly educated by men, and girls by women, the two sexes should unite in the education of both boys and girls. The boy requires the mild and gentle treatment of the mother, in order that his sensibility may not become callous; and, besides, he will always need some intercourse with persons of the other sex, both young and adult, as it is found in families, because otherwise he will contract habits of rudeness, without developing a susceptibility for the finer feelings of humanity. Without such influence, the youth would become coarse and rude in his manners; for, as the youth is less disposed than the boy to submit to positive treatment, and his educators are, consequently, under the necessity of influencing him chiefly by instruction, there would be reason to apprehend that his feelings would be deficient in cordiality and fervour; or that he would be less capable of expressing them suitably and well; or even that he might enter on evil courses, and fall into the excesses of ambition or of lust; for it is in intercourse with cultivated, noble, and virtuous women, that virtue presents itself to the youth in its most amiable light; and while this, therefore, will most readily make him complaisant and modest, nothing is better calculated to overcome the first movements of impure desire than such society, for it has even been effectual to the reformation of dissolute characters. If, then, the uncorrupted youth is so happy as to have access to such society, this will not only give his manners a pleasing exterior, but will increase the enthusiasm of his soul for everything noble and good. In certain situations, in which he needs some one to whom he may confidingly open his heart, we would recommend to him to seek some judicious maternal friend.

"Not exactly in the same, but in a similar manner, it is necessary that man should co-operate in the education of females, from its earliest stages, in order that they may not become too effeminate (if we may be indulged in this *seeming* paradox), but acquire energy of mind without prejudice to the graces of the female character. We may particularly observe that girls will, in general, learn better with a male than with a female teacher.

"In human life, at least in our European culture, the two sexes are, as they ought to be, associated: hence young women must be accustomed to the society of men; and, if so, they must not be excluded from it in their earlier years. They will then, if their education have been of the proper character, be the less liable to be deceived by the exterior of shallow or unworthy young men, and they will be better prepared to appreciate, in all its forms, whatever is noble in mankind; and this, surely, is necessary to completed culture. It is important to consider that the young female's mind will more beautifully develop itself, and attain higher elevation, if the communications of a gifted man instruct her on those subjects, of which she has formed only remote or obscure ideas. How much may a father thus do for his daughter!

"We see, then, in the arrangement of nature, by which the child is given in charge to both parents, the directions of wisdom, indicating, indeed, that men are to be chiefly engaged in educating the young of their sex, and women those of their own, yet showing no less clearly that both sexes are to unite in the complete education of each. The energy of the male sex would launch out into wild excesses, if the influence of the gentler sex did not calm and restrain; the powers of the latter would too much live and lose themselves in the inward world, if they were not roused and elevated by the influence of man's energy."

CHAPTER III.

Education for the Community or for Public Life, whether of the Church or the State. Patriotism.

The highest degree of friendship is the universal national bond of public spirit in public life; but this presents itself under two forms, according to two ideas, for which public friendship may be formed—religion and love of country. In the former case, friends unite for the realization of that cosmopolitan ideal which is set forth by Christianity alone; in the latter, they unite for the attainment of that political or civil ideal, which gives to the patriotism of each particular nation its own peculiar form. If, then, the life of the young is not to be destitute of the highest mental beauty, they must (irrespective here of all imperative duty) be educated also for Christianity and for patriotism. As both Christianity and individual nations are historical developments in mankind, the development of both will have to proceed from history, and derive its life from it; each of the two, of course, according to distinct and peculiar relations.

Christianity must *live* among the people: *i. e.*, it must,

1. Be known from the Bible and from history; and,
2. Practised in the manners and customs of life, and in the forms of society. To provide for this Christian *life*, is the business of the Church or the clergy. For the first requisite above specified, Christian teachers and pastors; for the second, Christian institutions of life, are necessary. By means of both these instrumentalities, a society is constituted within

the state, which ought to be entered voluntarily and from conviction. The institutions of life will have in view partly the regulation of affairs, partly the solemnization of religious rites and exercises, in meetings open to all. To the former institutions belongs a constitution or Church discipline; the latter shows the subserviency of art to Christianity, in beautiful public representations for the eye and ear, and in the worthy celebration of Christian festivals.

We learn from history that the Catholic Church has not only aimed at exhibiting this subserviency of art to the purposes of Christianity, but that she claims the exclusive credit of success in this attempt; yet her great defects, and especially her heathenish superstition, are obvious to every unbiased observer.

The Protestant Church, in returning to the simplicity of the apostolic times, and to the paramount authority of the Inspired Volume, has brought back religion from the region of fancy, and the empire of superstition, into the daily life of man, and restored to her that influence which she is designed to exert over his mind, and heart, and conduct, in order that in all the pursuits and relations of life he may be a servant of the living God. Christianity in the Protestant Church, particularly in this country, is, as it ought to be, eminently practical; and the great object to be had in view, in connexion with the regulations and institutions mentioned above, is, therefore, their influence on practical life—on man's habits of thought, feeling, and action, in every position he may be called to occupy in life. We regard the institutions of Protestantism as in the main scriptural, and hence decidedly calculated to effect the desired object; yet we would venture to suggest whether the Protestant Church has not, in part, been one-sided in its course, in rejecting those more solemn festivals of the early Church which have been retained by some Protestant denominations. We regard the stated commemoration of the leading historical facts in the redemption of mankind and the establishment of the Christian Church, as founded in reason and sound views of human nature. We feel persuaded that, when these festivals are celebrated in the right spirit, unaccompanied by superstitious notions and empty observances, their influence will and ever must be highly salutary. And believing that their abandonment has mainly arisen from causes which can no longer operate, we should rejoice to see these solemn celebrations of the prominent events in the history of human redemption restored, in all their early simplicity and solemnity, throughout the Protestant Church. We regard their influence on the young as peculiarly happy.

The farther consideration of religious education belongs to the following division, to whose third chapter the reader is referred.

Education for patriotism is much less difficult than that for Christianity; first, because its ideal is one that is easily comprehended; secondly, because patriotism is not based upon a history which is in part foreign, but upon that of the people itself.

Patriotism may exist among every people that possesses a history of its own; national customs and forms of life, which are mostly the results of the former, or of the peculiar nature of the country, contribute greatly to its advancement and growth. General desiderata for the cultivation of patriotism in the young are the following:

1. An intimate acquaintance with the national history, which should be taught in the schools, and kept before the public mind by the celebration of important events, *i. e.*, by national festivals.

2. Habituating the young to national peculiarities. This object will be attained without difficulty or coercion, if,

3. The public life of the nation is animated by patriotism. If a people at large be destitute of lively patriotism, it may be best cultivated in narrower circles of friends, whose patriotic life will diffuse its spirit by the force of example. These points are essential to the cultivation of a patriotic spirit. But the subject before us is vast in its extent, and of incalculable importance, especially under a political constitu-

tion and government like ours; yet it is difficult to mark out a course of education in view of a result which so greatly depends on the spirit by which a nation is actually animated, and upon influences which are as fitful in their course and as uncertain in their operation as the wind. In general, we may say, that when the young are properly educated in all other respects, and especially when they are brought to a due sense of their religious obligations, they cannot fail to become sound and conscientious patriots; yet, in order that their patriotism may be, *politically*, according to knowledge, the desiderata which we have mentioned demand due attention; and we may farther say, that every father should consider it his duty to instruct his sons, as soon as they are capable of understanding and appreciating such instruction, in the Constitution of this country, in the nature of the privileges which its citizens enjoy, and in the grave and important duties which these privileges involve. He should make them acquainted with the principles and the design of a government like ours, and point out the motives and purposes with which the elective franchise ought to be exercised. He ought to instruct them respecting the necessity, the nature, the scope, and the object of human laws, and inculcate a spirit of reverence for, and submission to, institutions without which order would be subverted, the bonds of society rent asunder, and all the affairs of men unhinged. It may here, indeed, be objected, that the great majority of fathers are destitute of such knowledge themselves, and hence incapable of communicating it. True; but it is, and it must be, the object of that common-school system, which is rapidly gaining ground among us, to diffuse that sort of knowledge among our people which shall fit them for the proper exercise of their political rights, and the rational enjoyment of their civic privileges. Our schools, then, must begin the work; and we earnestly recommend that in all our common schools a course of instruction be introduced, whose general subjects and features we have presented above; but for this purpose, and to aid teachers in the performance of this duty, we need a text-book or political catechism adapted to the use of schools; and we hope that this desideratum may be, ere long, supplied by some one of our learned civilians who is both a patriot and a Christian. If the children who frequent our public schools should be thought to be, in general, too young to comprehend the whole subject under consideration, a course suited to their age should be adopted; and we would add, that it is precisely at this early age, which, as we all know, remembers better than any other, that the inculcation of correct views and principles with regard to all human relations is pre-eminently important. The more extended course might then belong to higher schools and seminaries of learning. We regard this subject as one of great importance, and recommend it to the serious consideration of those to whom the direction and management of our scholastic institutions are intrusted

---

DIVISION II.

MORAL EDUCATION.

CHAPTER I.

The Moral Education of Man, considered as an Individual. Cultivation of the Sense of Honour.

THE traits of character which are to be cultivated in view of the proper education of man in his individual capacity, may be briefly stated as follows: Every man should regard himself individually as the equal of every other. This feeling of self-respect constitutes the true sense of honour. It is necessary carefully to distinguish self-respect, as well from self-confidence, as from self-love (egotism), and from self-esteem. When self-love and self-esteem are combined, they constitute, in their union, the true and noble love of honour. That self-respect, which is here insisted upon, has for its office merely to maintain inwardly the individual's own dignity, and manifests itself in the capacity of what is termed generous pride only negatively, in repelling all arrogance and presumption In contradistinction from this self-respect, we find, in human life, the following vicious qualities: false or feigned humility, self-contempt, or baseness of disposition, and a grovelling or cringing temper; also, the following perversions, or rude and harsh manifestations of the sense of honour, viz., insensibility, arrogance, and ambition or vaingloriousness.

The educator must here observe two stages of development in the pupil, and regulate his treatment of him according to his years. In the merely sensuous child or boy, who is yet far from being conscious of real personality, this personality should yet be prepared for its development; should be, in anticipation, gently treated and respected, as certain to manifest itself in future. This will be effected, 1. By cultivating the child's bodily health and vigour, which will, at least, produce a sort of physical self-respect, whose office it is to maintain its ground in the external world, as will subsequently the sense of honour in the world of mind. In this connexion it is also important to accustom boys to hardships and the endurance of pain; in short, to develop that genuine stoicism in which our effeminate age is so deficient. Boys should not be prevented from courageously using their fists in cases of real necessity, and in general they should, as far as practicable, be allowed to settle their childish quarrels themselves.

2. By the proper treatment of stubbornness or self-will, which is not in *all cases* to be entirely condemned, but which ought, in every instance in which it is clearly wrong and evil, to be repelled and resisted with inexorable severity and the utmost calmness. On this point the great majority of mothers betray the most culpable weakness. The evil here spoken of is one of the greatest magnitude; and, as it begins to manifest and develop itself in earliest infancy, this is the proper, and the only proper period for resisting

and subduing it. When we consider the injudicious manner in which we usually see children treated in this respect, and the weakness and mistaken fondness which lead so many parents, and particularly mothers, to oppose remonstrances and coaxing to the stubbornness and the self-will of their little ones, and even to give up to their *violent* explosions of temper, we feel that no apology is necessary for the introduction here, from the work of Schwarz, of the following discussion of the subject:

A. Abnormal Developments: their origin and prevention.

The first abnormal manifestation of the newborn child is its excessive screaming: this must be distinguished from the first scream, which is produced by the reaction of the system against the numerous excitants to which it is exposed. But screaming is to be regarded as irregularity, when it betrays the incipiency of selfishness; and this is betrayed when, by screaming, the child offers resistance to its mother and others, and strives to invert the established order of things by attempting to rule. As yet, the child has no other means of making resistance except the use of its voice; but this unruly disposition will subsequently manifest itself by striking, stamping, and the like. Such screaming may be distinguished by those who are about the child, not only by its angry tone, but also by its increasing in violence until the desired gratification has been obtained; and with this successful attempt, an association is formed between unruly conduct and the attainment of purposes, which will last through life. The child very soon discovers that by this means it can obtain its object; it knows this at first, as the animal does: for example, the dog, which asks its master for what it wants by barking; but it gradually learns, by experience, to effect by screaming whatever it desires, and to rule, by importunity, over those around it. For such a child it becomes very difficult to acquire, at any time, the feelings of love, of gratitude, of cheerfulness, of confiding attachment; it will always command—always regard those about it as tools, and even, in the end, regard itself in the same light. It will neither enjoy its own life, nor allow others rightly to enjoy theirs. If, then, at any time, a man, in whose childhood such abnormal manifestations were developed and indulged, should feel a desire for anything, or a want (and how few hours of life are free from wants!), he is peevish and morose, even before he seeks the gratification of his desire; and this temper naturally grows worse by the experiences of each day; and out of it grow ill humour and suspicion. If any desired object has been obtained, he is not satisfied with it; and far from feeling grateful to those who do him favours, he talks of nothing but the additional demands which he might make, and thinks only of rights and claims where he ought to think of duties. If he have need of anything, or if any of his efforts be unsuccessful, he becomes a burden and torment to those around him and to himself. He is always dissatisfied with things as they are, and never at peace with himself; and though he should have the semblance of religion, yet would he use God himself only as an instrument, and is constantly quarrelling with Providence. If morals be at all his study, his conduct is, in all things, artificial. In a person of this description, it is in vain to look for affection, and even his parents must not expect any from him. And thus the child, that is indulged in the unruly habit of effecting, by means of screaming, whatever it desires, may become an intolerable egotist; and if this should not be the result, it will be because the circumstances of his life have prevented it, and for this parents may feel thankful to God. We meet, in the intercourse of life, many persons, whose ill-natured conduct will justify us in saying, "they have, in their childhood, made trouble in the family by their screaming." Varying with different dispositions and circumstances, such children become malicious, headstrong, irascible, spiteful, crafty, liars, sycophants, deceitful, cruel, tyrannical, &c.

The existence, then, of this unruly habit, involves a

serious charge against parents. No child is, indeed, so entirely possessed by it, that better features should not be now and then exhibited; but it is bad enough if once the habit has struck root. We should see a great many more children of good dispositions, if that evil habit were not permitted to form itself in the infant.

The principal remedy for this evil is to repel the very first attempts of the child; not to give up to it, but to let it scream; but to make it a point to satisfy its natural wants before it has occasion to demand gratification by screaming and importunity. In other respects it should be treated in as kindly a manner as possible. This is the so-called subduing of the temper.

It is a mistake to suppose that this must be effected by a sort of force; for, if this has actually become necessary, it only proves that much of the evil already exists. This is, indeed, usually the case, as the practice of yielding is the most common, and thus the perverseness of the parents descends to the children. When, however, the evil really exists, nothing is left but this subduing of the temper; and the sooner this is accomplished the better, otherwise the evil will increase with each day, for the association becomes established and deeply seated in the organism. It is no better, or rather worse, if the child is remonstrated with; for, by so doing, a sort of dominion is conceded to it, and in the end, a pernicious struggle is the consequence, which stimulates to increased unruliness. "But," it is objected, "the child will cry too much, and perhaps injure itself." You may safely run the risk; or, is the injury less if it becomes daily more headstrong? When shall the temper be subdued or the will broken? Will you leave it to time and circumstances? This would be cruel; for the stern Nemesis never omits to come, and she is a stranger to sparing gentleness. If the child sustain a bodily injury, this may be cured; or it may become happy even with it; but an ill-tempered child will certainly become an unhappy man. Nor is there great danger of injury arising from screaming. When its exertions are destructive to itself, nature soon becomes sensible of it, and the child will scream no longer than it can bear it, at least not in early infancy: it will grow weary, and rest the more sweetly; and perhaps this exercise of the voice will even serve as a wholesome excitement to its animal organism; but when the unruly child has been, for once, allowed to scream to its heart's content without effecting its object, all is gained; that evil association is broken up; it will not carry its second attempt so far, and nature is freed from its bonds; for, according to nature, the child feels itself dependant on the will of others, and finds itself well at ease in this sense of dependance; much better than in its position of unnatural domination. I know an excellent mother, whose acute observation detected the beginning of this unruly tendency in her infant daughter when only six weeks of age. The child screamed in order to be taken from its bed; she let it lie, and it screamed more violently; it continued to scream for about fifteen minutes, until it could scarcely be endured; but the mother had firmness to persevere. The child screamed until it was weary, then fell asleep, and awoke in the best humour imaginable, and never made a similar attempt, but became a most obedient and amiable girl. Although it had been born with an umbilical rupture which had scarcely been healed, its screaming had not had the least injurious effects upon it.

As the breaking from any habit always produces a disagreeable excitement, and that the more sensibly the more the evil habit has become confirmed, and the more it feels the restraint imposed upon its violent manifestations, so every means employed to correct the evil here particularly treated of cannot but leave a disagreeable impression in the child's mind which can never be effaced; an aversion to the person who subjects it to restraint, which can only be prejudicial to affection and cheerfulness. The longer, therefore, the subduing of the will is put off, the more violently will the child be exasperated against those who ultimately attempt to curb it. Hence arises the universally prevailing propensity of children to disobedience, and even aversion to education; for a child, that has not been more or less neglected in this respect, is one of the greatest of rarities. All have, in some degree, to suffer for this early neglect, and never is the penalty completely cancelled; for, in suffering for it, it is always again renewed, though it be but to a small degree. And, therefore, the disobedience of children is to the parents who complain of it, the penalty of sin; and the same is true of all the bitterness and ill-will of the younger generation towards the elder, which suffers from the effects of these feelings and tempers.

In extreme cases it will be necessary to resort to chastisement, and then the rod is a remedy, as an emetic is for divers diseases. In its bodily pain, the child feels the displeasure of its parents; and this feeling resolves itself into the association that such attempts must in future be abstained from, in order that such pain may be avoided. But the child's heart is, at the same time, excited to humility by its own sense of the justness of its suffering, and the displeasure of the parents now becomes the displeasure of the child with regard to itself. This mode of treatment, though severe, strengthens the child's capacity for self-government. It is true that, if the course thus adopted be not persevered in, the case becomes worse than it was before; for then the child has been exasperated, and becomes malicious; and, what is more, feels its own superiority to the will of its parents. But if the child is really brought to feel the superiority of its parents (and how can it otherwise, except they themselves be weak?), in that moment nature resumes its prerogative; the child's heart has been softened, and its will become pliant; and as soon as the hand of affection is again held out to it, it will cling the more fondly to its parents. It is inherent in human nature that he who is the weaker, and needs the support and guidance of others, should cheerfully content himself when he is made to perceive the strength of his guide, and perhaps even to become sensible of it by means of suffering in his own person.

When chastisement is administered, let it be brief, and severe in exact proportion to the necessity of the case, lest it degenerate into worrying; and let all scolding be abstained from, for this only exasperates. One single severe word, *e. g.*, "silence!" uttered with a commanding voice, is better than many. But let all be done without passion, for an angry face can only produce a frightful impression on the child. And now, when the child is content and yields, let him at once again see a serene brow and an unclouded face, and talk with him about other things; this will operate like the warm sunshine after the first thunder-storm in spring. The unseemly habit of which we speak is exhibited, in an inferior degree, by children who are prone to much weeping. This occurs most frequently in sensitive natures. By violent dispositions it is manifested in a higher degree by striking indiscriminately at all around; and in morose tempers it is displayed by vexation, which boils and rankles within.* As tears may injure the eyes, care should be taken that they be soon wiped away.

If the child should cry from ennui, it is, indeed, to be also regarded as an impropriety, but it is, at the same time, an indication that the child is not sufficiently employed; and nothing is more easily remedied than this. Give the child something that will entertain it, before ill-humour can intrude and gain a footing. When the child cries because there is something to irritate it, let it be quickly brought into a different position. If its crying be occasioned by bodily pain or sickness, sympathy should be manifested towards it; but if this should provoke a desire in the child to attract still greater attention and compassion, it will be necessary to drop all expressions of sympathy, and rather to encourage and cheer up the child, or to direct its attention to something else.†

* The following passage from St. Augustine strikingly illustrates this sort of disposition. "Vidi ego et expertus sum zelantem parvulum. Nondum loquebatur, et intuebatur *pallidus amaro adspectu* collactaneum suum."

† For those who are conversant with children, it will not be difficult to

As this species of misdemeanour, the worst that appears in the first months of life, is generally exhibited on those occasions which are inseparably connected with the earliest training of the child to order, *e. g.*, when it is washed or laid down, &c., all that can be recommended here is, do not suffer the child's screaming to interfere with your operations; it will soon accustom itself, and cheerfully submit to them.

If the child be sickly, both physical and mental culture will, of course, suffer. In such a case, nothing can be done but to indulge it, as far as the disease renders indulgence necessary, but, at the same time, to guard it, as much as possible, against ill humour. Many parents indulge their children, under such circumstances, more than is necessary. If, in giving them nourishment, in washing them, &c., they be subjected, on those days in which they enjoy a better state of health, to the usual order of life; if they be not too timorously treated, nature will always assist in curing the inward evil which she has herself occasioned. I once saw a boy who passed the first years of his life in constant suffering from sore eyes; so much so, that he could scarcely see, and was confined to a dark corner. Whenever he heard the other children playing joyously around him, he would sometimes stamp on the floor from pain and vexation. The parents were apprehensive lest he should become a malicious and envious boy. I advised them to take no notice of his displays of temper, while they continued the application of remedies to his eyes; to persevere in habituating him to regularity in the reception of food, and otherwise to treat him kindly and gently. This was done; they neither spoiled him, nor treated him with neglect; and when, after some time, he was cured of his ailment, he manifested none of those evil dispositions which had been apprehended, for they were not in his nature, and his sickness had not led to the formation of any unruly habit. He became one of the most cheer-

distinguish and properly to treat the different varieties of crying. Jean Paul Fr. Richter has, in his Levana, many excellent hints on this subject.

ful, good-natured, and amiable boys. Nature always makes amends for whatever evils she is alone accountable for.

In proportion as the child's self-consciousness is developed, self-will more and more advances its claims and this takes place to the detriment of good impulses, just in proportion as the particular virtues suffer The first of these is complaisance, a kind regard for the happiness of others: egotism is opposed to this at one time in the shape of obstinacy, at another in that of indolence. These, then, are the first definite forms in which degeneracy is manifested in children; and each of these produces a series of new ones, which, in the progress of time, enter into a variety of combinations with others. Obstinacy springs from the nascent consciousness of the freedom of the will, and consists in a striving for independence of control, without reference to any particular purpose, but merely in order to be independent. The contemplative temperament exhibits this degenerate trait more in pure obstinacy, as a feeling which submits with repugnance to foreign control, and therefore repels such control without any farther reason. Natures, whose tendency is to activity in the external world, will manifest it more in the form of self-will; they seek to rule, and refuse to be guided by others; and when the will of such children is to be subdued, and to be subjected to that of the parents, they will strive to assert their own, and sometimes to carry it by violent efforts.

Boys, therefore, are in general more self-willed, afterward impatient of contradiction, and lastly refractory; girls more frequently obstinate, peevish, and ill-humoured; but both will then be disobedient, and may become intractable and headstrong. Indolence is egotism in its feebleness, *i. e.*, when the natural powers refuse to exert themselves for their cultivation. In lively and susceptible dispositions, this will manifest itself by an easy surrender to every impression, by levity and frivolity; in firm and reflective dispositions, by retirement into themselves to the extent even of thoughtlessness and idle revery. Both these generic corruptions are hostile to attention: the first will not receive, the second will not pay attention to anything; the first has lost the cultivating energy (love) by an irregular resistance, the second by an excessive submissiveness.

The three virtuous tendencies of children are obstructed in their specific manifestations by egotism. It opposes industry, on the one hand, by a determination to be idle, which, when carried to extremes, is called laziness; but, on the other hand, by a mode of life which has neither method nor fixed aim, and is called instability. It prevents true cheerfulness, either directly in the form of gloominess, or in that of extravagant hilarity, and it contravenes the development of pious feeling, either in the shape of selfishness, which repudiates every feeling of dependance, or in the form of sensuality, which abandons itself to sensual gratifications.

And thus these marks of degeneracy develop themselves progressively to the age of youth, when they become passions, and lead to deeper corruption, and everywhere throw obstacles into the way of virtuous self-government, of ideal culture, and of everything that belongs to good character. Before we trace the farther development of these corruptions, we shall present a few general observations on the means which should be employed to combat them.

Of such means there are two classes, constituting either a negative or a positive mode of procedure. The first mode anticipates, prevents, and corrects; the second interferes, expels, and eradicates: the former belongs mainly to the entire plan of education; the latter consists in single, occasional measures, to be designated as rewards and punishments; and it is this of which we are here to speak.

A single remedy, which is applied as a medicine, operates as a stimulant; and it is necessary here to attend to the psychological principle, that such remedy ought to be neither too stimulating nor too relaxing in its operation; its quantity or potency should be well weighed, in order, at the time and place, and in the manner necessary, to produce that stimulus which will restore health, *i. e.*, restore the patient's powers to their equilibrium, so as less and less to require stimulants or medicines. If we were to adopt a different course, and to create an increasing necessity for new and stronger stimulants, we should resemble the empiric, who cures his patient of one disease by poisoning him, or, at least, so treating him as to bring on another disease. Do not expel one demon by another, nor leave the door open for him to return after he has taken to himself seven others, so that the condition of your pupil has become worse than it was before. In the treatment of corruptions, parents and teachers usually commit the greatest faults, and do, perhaps, more harm than is done in the use of medicine by quacks. Only in the way indicated above may rewards and punishments be employed, *i. e.*, according to the laws of stimulants; but the former should be less frequently administered than the latter, because praise operates, as is well known, more powerfully and deeply than censure, and therefore induces, more easily, the evil of vanity.

Punishments, in the pedagogic sense, are means of discipline; and they differ essentially from the punishment of crime by the civil magistrate in this, that they aim only at the reformation of the person punished. They consist in the endurance of deserved suffering, which the educator inflicts in order to bring his pupil to self-knowledge, and to effect his reformation. They ought to resemble Divine chastisements, in that the person who punishes manifests indignation, virtuous wrath, which, to the heart of the person punished, should be an evidence of love. Through the rigour of severity, the kind intention ought to be discernible; but if, on the other hand, the smallest degree of vindictiveness, of hatred, of injustice on the part of the educator is displayed in the infliction of punishment, its wholesome operation is not only lost, but it becomes a poison. Even if it be unaccompanied by due seriousness, it will operate unfavourably, inasmuch as it will cause the child, or young person punished, to hold in contempt the punishment and him who administers it. It must, therefore, be adapted to the age of the child: smaller children feel only the rod; older ones are more sensible to wounds inflicted on their sense of honour than to bodily pain.

The end of punishment is best attained if the child can find in it the restoration of its inward peace; a sort of expiation to which it will gladly submit. Children of good dispositions will sometimes, of their own accord, offer themselves for punishment; and, after the pain is over, such are usually more cheerful and more affectionate towards their rigorous guide. This effect should be aimed at; but never should the sufferer be induced to kiss the hand which has inflicted chastisement, for this makes hypocrites: nor should natural punishments be contrived, as Rousseau recommends; for in him who inflicts punishment the child should recognise a sacred authority of will, but not be tempted to act a part.

It is unnecessary to add any more particular rules; and we merely subjoin the general observation: Let punishment always be just, suited to the evil which is to be removed, and really calculated to effect its cure, according to the rules for the progressive application of stimulants. Larger children should accordingly be first reproved, then, for a season, deprived of liberty, and lastly, if the offence be again repeated, let the rod be administered; but, when the punishment has been inflicted, do not give the child reason to believe that you bear it any farther ill will.

We proceed to the application, taking up the corruptions above specified in due order:

1. *Obstinacy and self-will.* The child wishes to rule, and to treat the persons who are about it in the same manner as it does the little articles which are given to it: thus, for example, it will command the mother to give it something to eat, and if she does not instantly comply, it will cry; nor will it become quiet until its commands are complied with. To refuse pos-

itively, and to persist in the refusal, while all other proper attention is shown to the child, this is the sovereign, universally known, domestic remedy, but which is, unfortunately, so little employed. It is a remedy that *must* be effectual. For why does not the child storm against nature? Why does it not command the tree to hang itself full of cherries, or to hand them down to it? Those persons with whom it has to do are, indeed, a complaisant nature, upon whom it can more easily make demands; but if they were as inexorable, whenever it is necessary, as external nature in refusing, the child would submit to its dependance with regard to them as well as to nature, and refrain from fruitless wishes, entreaties, and efforts, particularly if its natural wants are, at the same time, duly attended to. Should the child be unmanageable, and its conduct become outrageous, it ough to be shut up by itself; *i. e.*, it should be removed to a secluded, but not dark or disagreeable place, where it will feel the privation imposed upon it; and there it should be left until it has again become quiet and submissive. If the son of Themistocles could say, "My will is the will of all Athens; for what I will, that my mother wills; and what she wills, my father wills; and what he wills, that the Athenians will," we need not be surprised that this son became unworthy of his father. Socrates could hold him up as an example, proving that virtue cannot be communicated by instruction.

When the child has acquired a taste for ruling, it will be fond of making experiments in the exercise of dominion, at one time out of pride, at another from caprice; for the child which is fond of executing, and strives directly forward to its object, while it has an eye, not to the object only, but also to itself, and delights to say to itself, "I must, at all events, have my will," such a child will sport with its will. But from such conduct proceed that ennui and chagrin which are called ill-humour. This is a disagreeable state of mind, which self-willed obstinacy will seek to remove by setting others in activity on its account, in order to enjoy the consciousness of authority and power. After all the child's demands have been complied with, it is still dissatisfied with everything, and is then usually peevish and fretful if it cannot think of anything more to demand; and, in the end, it desires only to torment all with whom it has to do.

Self-will is perseverance in external action; obstinacy, in refusing to receive or admit influences from without: the latter is, in its nature, more deeply seated and permanent, but the former is more violent and unruly. In both, it is not the perseverance which is to be regarded as evil: nor should the self-regard peculiar to the former, nor the proclivity of the latter to sensitiveness, be viewed as such; but in the former, the desire to rule, and in the latter, the propensity to contemplation, should be suppressed in season. The suppression of the former is effected by positive, that of the latter rather by negative treatment: for example, your little boy insists that you shall mend his whip for him, and none but you, his mother, shall do it; you have positively refused, but he becomes more importunate; he screams, stamps on the floor and repeats his demand: "But you *shall* do it." (Who has not, time and again, witnessed such scenes?) Others have offered their services, but that is not to his mind. Say nothing to him, except at the most, with perfect calmness, "No! Be still." If he becomes too noisy, assign him a seat by himself; and when he becomes more quiet, think of something that is to be seen or done, and direct his activity towards it, but without directly requiring his action, in order that he may not lose his sense of freedom, and yet be sensible that no one else bows to his will. Though this method may not always be successful in the first paroxysm, it will yet, in most cases, succeed after the first heat has passed off; and if your attempts should then still be unsuccessful, let him sit, even though he should have to fast for some hours. As self-will proceeds from impetuosity of temper, seek to give this a different direction, and, at all events, oppose to its efforts the firmest resistance, by which it will not fail to be broken in the end.

Your little girl pouts because she has not been first attended to. and now she makes this a matter of complaint. When you have told her to be quiet, she complains of something else; you endeavour to remove the grievance, but her peevishness increases; she demands first one thing, then another, and refuses to move. What is to be done? Nothing. Take no notice of the morose child; let her stand; let her not interfere with your pursuits; and if she becomes too noisy, put her by herself. Let no one, in the mean time, speak to her, least of all irritate her; in short, deport yourself as though she were not present. Thus she not only fails of effecting her object, but discovers that in this way nobody manifests any concern about her; and in the end, while nothing has been done to blunt her sensibility or to weaken her firmness, she will be obliged to yield, and to use entreaty. As soon as she has, in any degree, become pacified, give her, without any artificial management, some commission, which you know beforehand that she will take pleasure in executing.

The more affection there is in the child, the more painfully sensible will it be of its unruly conduct, if in this manner it discovers that those whom it loves cease to concern themselves about it when it misbehaves. But if these persons should add reproaches, or appear hurt by its conduct, they would, on the one hand, permit the child to partially attain its purpose, and thus nourish its evil dispositions, and, on the other hand, they would exasperate it. By entering into long remonstrances with the child, they would only protract the longer its evil state of mind; but, when its misdemeanours are resisted in the manner recommended, it will be soonest restored to its cheerfulness. Your treatment tends directly to effect this. When the paroxysm has passed off, you should allow your child to consider all as forgotten, and treat it with your wonted kindness. With such treatment, it is scarcely possible for obstinacy to make any progress;

nor would these displays of temper ever have occurred, if you had not, from the beginning, indulged your child in commanding. Such exhibitions of temper should not, however, be overrated, for children of an energetic or sensitive temperament cannot remain entirely free from them.

From this tendency to domineer, *i. e.*, from the natural feeling of self-importance, there proceeds yet another very prevalent irregularity, namely this, that children determine to pursue a certain line of conduct simply because it has been forbidden them. To this there is a propensity in all men ("nitimur in vetitum semper, cupimusque negata," says Ovid); not, however, consisting in a deliberate purpose of wrong-doing, but in the struggles of selfishness beginning to advance its claims. The energies involved in this struggle are bent upon exertion. The first excitement to this is given by prohibitions, and it is these which make such efforts possible; but inasmuch as they also obstruct their exercise, they furnish an additional and stronger excitement. The child sees the possibility of maintaining an ascendency over those who have imposed on it a certain prohibition, and through whom it therefore finds itself restricted, and this discovery gives new force to the excitement. Thus every prohibition excites to at least secret transgression, by exciting the selfish desire of independence, in the consciousness of energy which belongs to our nature. Now if parents are gratified by such demonstrations, and foolishly regard them as marks of a noble disposition, then wo to their child. The case of frank, upright, and honest children is then the most hopeful, because with them the evil will break forth in undisguised rebellion; but others feign obedience, while their temper secretly rebels against the prohibition, and they long to be delivered from their chains. These are hypocritical and truly disobedient children, and they become deceitful, cunning, and spiteful. As this evil is once seated in the heart, and cannot be entirely prevented, it should rather be suffered to break forth openly, in order that it may, as far as possible.

be combated. This may be accomplished in the following manner: when anything has been forbidden the child, let something else be pointed out to it which will excite its activity, and cause it to forget that which it is not allowed to do; and it will then be better if the prohibition be so pronounced as to almost escape its attention. In general, it would be best not to multiply prohibitions. But what is accomplished by it? In all legislation against rudeness, against irregular conduct, we trace the evidences of the perverseness of human nature, and it is nothing but indolence in discipline that calls forth a countless multitude of prohibitions, of which each renders a new one necessary. The educator should keep in view the method adopted in the beginning by the Creator in the discipline of man.

Every attempt to remedy this evil by reasoning or argument, designed to demonstrate to the child the necessity of the prohibition, would only aggravate the injury already done; for the child has, as yet, no capacity to appreciate argument, and ought not to have any. You will, therefore, only excite it to entirely unnatural attempts; for it will begin to make stipulations, and endeavour to maintain its ground against those whom it ought only to obey; it will acquire an absolute aversion to obedience, contract habits of falsehood, and other evil practices, and thus its state is one of many untoward excitements. "But the child must subdue its temper, and learn to act according to duty." Yes; but do not, as yet, expect this of the child, if you would not train it to be a hypocrite or an impudent rebel, destined to become a moping and disagreeable man, whose soul is in perpetual strife with itself. To lead the child into temptation is no better than prematurely accusing its artless heart of evil; it is to create cause for offence; it is monstrous wrong-doing.

A kindred manifestation of degeneracy is that of teasing; it is a mode of acting, in which children betray their growing selfishness when they strive to carry their own points in opposition to their equals, in order, by means of trifling, but provoking tricks of irritation, to make their superiority felt. This practice, at the same time, nourishes the obstinacy of those who are thus teased; and hence, when this ambition of the weak to domineer has once fairly established itself among a circle of brothers and sisters, there will be no end of intolerable struggling and wrangling. The older children of this description are apt thus to tease the younger ones; and if they be more vigorous than the latter, they are prone to exercise authority over them. They attain this purpose the more easily, as they have frequent occasion to assist the younger children, without regarding them in the same light in which they do grown persons; without feeling towards them the natural impulse to obedience which they feel towards their parents. If their efforts are successful, they become completely imperious, insufferable to their playmates, and, under certain circumstances, tyrannical, cruel, and malicious. How shall this evil be arrested in its incipiency? Above all things, avoid all argumentation, all efforts to convince your children of relative rights, if you would not make them hypocritical, disputatious, and hateful; but do not allow their injurious efforts to succeed for one moment. If you observe anything of this kind, deprive the little usurper forthwith of his violently obtained spoils, and give him a smart rap on his fingers. If a general dispute should arise about the object which has caused the difficulty, take it away from all the children without farther parley, or adding, at most, two or three peremptory words, and endeavour to direct their attention to something else.

2. Children become *indolent* when their attention is either too little taxed or only occasionally exercised. In the former case, inactivity of mind, and even stupidity, are the result, even though there may be physical activity. In the latter, children become trifling, incapable of connected thought, intractable, and averse to persevering exertion. They learn nothing well; they will sit still and listen to instruc-

tion, and even be fond of reading; but they will accustom themselves, in all things, to be supplied with employment by others; and even in the play of imagination, in which they seem to display talent, they will be merely passive.

3. *Laziness* is the expanded form of the preceding evil, in its positive annihilation of industry. This is induced by indulging indolence, and nourished by idleness and want of excitement. It will often be found where the routine of business is slow and drowsy, but not unfrequently, also, in families where the children are not sufficiently excited to activity. It affects either mental or bodily exertions alone, and often both at once. As the natural impulses will incline to mere enjoyment, in proportion as they are diverted from active exertion, lazy children will usually become gluttonous, uncleanly, thievish, given to lying. Contemplative natures, particularly effeminate ones, or persons of phlegmatic temperament, are the most likely to contract habits of laziness.

Nature herself points out the remedy for this evil, for necessity compels man to work. Let, then, lazy children suffer the want of one thing or another which they may happen to desire or stand in need of, and that so long until the sense of this want becomes painful, or until they have earned, by some active exertion, the object desired, even though it be their necessary food. This treatment has proved effectual both in families and in houses of correction. In the case of children, a perfect cure can be more certainly effected than with adults, because nature still prompts them to activity, and the evil habit has not yet become fixed. But labour should not be made unpleasant to them, by giving them more than they can accomplish; they should be gradually accustomed to greater exertion, and to this they should be encouraged by moderate praise and kind treatment.

Uncleanliness is nothing more than laziness supported by the absence of a sense of propriety. Nothing will here avail except inexorable firmness in cultivating the opposite habits.

4. *Instability* proceeds from not fixing the attention, particularly of more active children; from leaving them too much at their own disposal, and not habituating them to perseverance: hence arises a restless and fickle activity; the boy undertakes with ardour, but soon abandons his undertaking, and commences something new; at length he becomes averse to begin any serious employments; he runs about, plays, amuses his fancy, &c. Thus this sort of activity is converted into a passion for amusement, and even into intellectual laziness. This evil is not unfrequently found in the cultivated class, when many studies are commenced with children, but none perseveringly prosecuted; and an easy, entertaining mode of instruction serves only to establish it. In schools and educational institutions, the same evil is often produced by the adoption of too great a variety of studies. It usually does not fully display itself until the youth enters college, or the maiden is brought out into society; the absence of all inclination for serious employment then betrays itself completely, as also a decided propensity to idle gossip and amusement.

It is not easy to cure this evil, if the child has been given up to it until it is seven years of age. It will be necessary to return to the starting-point of judicious education, by exercising the child's attention, by giving it easy tasks of progressive difficulty, just difficult enough to leave a certainty of their successful performance; whatever can distract the attention, should be removed; instruction itself must be exceedingly simple, one subject only being undertaken at a time, and completed before another is taken up; and when once the child has tasted the pleasure of really accomplishing anything, it will thus receive a powerful impulse to perseverance; but the victory obtained must be resolutely followed up.

As the indolent, although averse to serious and profitable employment, would not be totally idle, a multitude of evils spring from indolence; and they are such as we hear most frequently animadverted upon Awkward postures of the body, clownish and clumsy manners, noisy conduct, boisterous laughter, silly and stupid remarks, gluttony, pilfering and junketing, &c., are physical or mental activities, produced by a combination of sensuality and indolence, and making a most disagreeable impression on all around. For these there is no other remedy than to accustom the child, in general, to the proper exercise of its powers, and to assail the evil habits by the infliction of severe punishments. But with punishments it is necessary to be economical, lest, coming too often, they blunt the better feelings of the child. Nothing is more injurious than constant chiding, or to be perpetually scolding at the child on account of some evil habit: rather let cautious physicians be imitated, by removing one evil ere you attack the other.

As regards, 5, gloominess, or habitual moroseness, and the other extreme, 6, excessive levity or frivolity, we may remark, that the judicious treatment of children in their general education, especially in view of the corrupt manifestations already considered, will serve also as a preventive against these. Yet moodiness or gloominess must sometimes be directly assailed by urging children to exertion and the exercise of courage, without noticing their foible, and by increasing your demands upon them when they are ill-humoured. Even punishments are in this case effectual, by effecting a revolution in their state of feeling. Yet, if indulgent treatment, or cockering, can only increase the moroseness of children, continued harsh treatment would not be less injurious. The great point will be to provide them with cheerful company, to treat them kindly, to employ them regularly, and, in case of necessity, to use severity. A tendency to levity and frivolity must be seasonably checked by very similar treatment. An indirect, but perhaps the most effectual remedy against it consists in cultivating the sense of hearing, and the memory, by frequent exercises.

7. *Selfishness* is a development of egotism which dissolves all pious feeling. A general want of affection, particularly towards the parents, feebleness of

filial feelings, produce a transition from egotism to disobedience, and in more energetic natures, to rebellion. These corruptions, therefore, appear in those families where parents do not respond to the young affections of their offspring, and inspire their children with neither love nor respect; and the evil develops itself equally, though in different ways, among the rich and the poor, the cultivated and the rude. And where there is no respect for religion; where the young are not brought up to prayer and the fear of God, all pious feeling will expire in the early years of life, and the welfare of the family, and that of the nation, is destroyed. There is no practical truth older or more sacred than this, that reverence and love towards parents brings a blessing on children and children's children, and that there is no wisdom without the fear of God; but if once the young have been neglected in this respect, they are not easily reformed, and never completely so: hence all corruptions belonging to this category must be smothered in their birth. The more mature manifestations are, dogmatical churlishness, rudeness, harshness, deception, and violence.

The remedy is simple, if it be early applied. The entire treatment of the child, and perhaps its external position, must be changed. It must learn to respect and love those that are about it. All unseasonable indulgence must cease, and rigorous firmness be opposed to the disobedient child. The treatment recommended under previous heads will be effectual here also. In addition, we observe, that the child should not receive many commands, and at first chiefly such as it may be expected to obey willingly and cheerfully; and then an affectionate recognition of its active proofs of affection will exert a good influence. If the child be destitute of grateful feelings, it should not be attempted to elicit these forcibly, by means of censure; for this would procure the benefactor nothing but hatred, and expressions of gratitude would only be base lies. But the child should be occasionally instructed respecting the odiousness of ingratitude, and, at the same time, treated rather coolly, and with bare justice, in order that it may learn to appreciate benefits as such. If it lack confidence, this may be gained by kind treatment and little kind offices. The selfish little mortal should be frequently made to feel his destitution and dependance on others. The necessary instruction in religion should on no account be neglected: this will awaken filial feelings, and revive, as far as possible, the deadened germ of good. All this should be done early; if deferred to the later years of boyhood, or even of youth, the difficulties are multiplied a hundred fold. The father, who would then yet recover the confidence of his son, must first thoroughly ascertain by what means he formerly alienated the confiding affections of his child, and now studiously omit all such measures, however he may be able to justify them, such as anger, chiding, moralizing; let him manifest the greatest kindness towards the youth, and show that in all allowed and expedient things he sympathizes with his youthful joys.

8. Sensuality consists in the child's self-abandonment to the gratification of the lower senses, and therefore chiefly to the consumption of confectionary, dainties, &c. Thus arises immoderation, lustfulness, daintiness; and out of these irregularities proceed developments of still lower sensuality. To these evils contemplative natures are most inclined. But generally such irregularities are found where children are too much indulged, where there is too much good living in the family, and where the children thus become accustomed to consider luxurious living as important. The principal preventive remedy for all such sensual and effeminate irregularities consists in adhering, from childhood, to a healthy, regular, and active mode of life, in which the child must be brought to accustom itself to obedience, industry, and simple diet, in connexion with innocent pleasures suited to its age. Where these evils actually exist, a regular course of training for their remo-

val must be adopted, and a rigid school of self-denial and endurance of privations instituted.

All the abnormal developments exhibited in the ramifications which have been specified, form a multiplicity of combinations with each other; thus mutually strengthening each other, and degenerating farther into corruptions, which usually manifest themselves in the age of youth. But it will not be necessary to descend into greater detail, as the necessary mode of treatment has been sufficiently developed under the preceding general heads.

B.

Treatment of Corrupted Youth.

All men are more or less under the influence of selfishness, which subjects one more particularly to sensual gratification, another to avarice, a third to ambition, but each, at the same time, to vanity and pride These two, vanity and pride, are the generic tendencies, and stand in opposition to the virtue of youth, even though the more specific corruptions should have been prevented or subdued. Pride is a feeling of independence, which is unaccompanied by enthusiasm for the ideal, which may otherwise have already been attained, and it therefore destroys modesty and humility in the root. Vanity is that sense of self-importance which is sought and acquired by means of accidental, external, trifling things, and, therefore, by adopting the manners and ways of the world. To the former fault young men are more exposed; to the latter, young females; but the foundation is laid at an early age. Parents exaggerate the merits of their children, so that they learn to think of their own importance; when they speak and act, they are no longer entirely free from the purpose of putting forth claims to consideration; they become more and more arrogant because their advances are not resisted; thus they at the same time become cold and indifferent to the interests of others; they become dogmatical; are easily offended, captious, disputatious, and unyielding; grow rude, and deal out blows, or refuse to listen to others; and seek to fix upon themselves alone the attention of the company. We often meet with young men or women who, when in company, will scarcely deign to bestow an answer, or so much as a glance, on those persons whom they esteem of little importance. In such young persons pride has already attained its full development; whether in the form of pride of station, or of wealth, or of intellect, or genius, or of pedantry, &c., or of a self-complacent conceit of their superior refinement. Obviously as this sort of pride is more at home among the more wealthy, and those (often by a sad misnomer) called the more cultivated class, because parents, as it were, inoculate the children with it, especially when motives of ambition are employed as spurs to learning, or when the young are early introduced in the social circles of adults; it is no less certain that it obtains, to some extent also, among those who have no pretensions to refinement.

The vanity of young persons manifests itself in their passion for admiration. Children become vain by learning to draw upon themselves the attention of others. There is too much notice taken of their pretty ways and their graceful bearing; they are toyed with like dolls, adorned, and admired; they are called upon to repeat sayings or actions which are considered fine: by these and other practices they are trained to act a part, to do everything, as it were, before a glass. No wonder if they fall into absurdities in speaking and acting, by which they aim at making an impression; and by fondling and dandling them the evil is aggravated. Young men thus become shallow votaries of fashion, and young women dressy coquettes; and if there be a want of love for the ideal, the true, and the good, they will severally, according to their peculiar dispositions, give themselves up to vanity and the world. It has been remarked that this tendency prevails chiefly among the wealthy and the (so-called) refined; but no one much conversant with society in our country can be ignorant to what extent male foppery, and female competition in dress, prevail among the poorer and less cultivated portion of the community. But among the rich there is little to check, and everything to foster the evil. The public distinctions which children receive among them; when, for example, their musical performances are admired and applauded; when they are taken at an early age to festivities, and even balls; when they are permitted to act their own part in company: these irregularities, which obtain in refined or fashionable society, can only promote the idolatry of vanity.

We must not omit to notice that form of selfishness which we can only designate as covetousness. This is developed among all classes, especially through the example of parents, and their practice of everywhere making their children observant of their own advantage. At first the children desire to possess what they see others have; then they will deprive the latter of whatever pleases them; or they are unwilling to communicate, especially in respect to eatables; but soon this degeneracy gains ground, and, if suitable caution be not used in allowing children the use of money, they will, at an early age, become covetous of money; and hence we see so many selfish young persons, prodigal on the one hand, but on the other so rapacious, that they are not ashamed even of mean and dishonourable means of gratifying their cupidity.

The means of counteracting selfishness in all these ramifications are inherent in the soundness of the entire course of education. Children must be removed from the position in which those faults were seen to grow up and flourish, otherwise all counter-efforts will be fruitless. They should, at the same time, be taught to acquire real, substantial distinctions, and thus, through the entire age of youth, to make progress in genuine culture. Against pride and vanity there is no remedy, except in the consciousness of being engaged in striving after real excellence; and thus, also, in opposition to covetousness, the ideal to which the mind is elevating itself must gain the ascendency. The more man consecrates himself from childhood to an idea, the more will he deny self. But this he will not aspire after, except he be brought to feel the gentle but powerful influence of love (in all its appropriate developments); and hence no effort should be spared to develop cordial and fervent affection in selfish children.

That each of these corruptions is adverse to the pure and right culture of man, is obvious, and universally admitted; and yet education, as now practised, takes one or the other of them into its service, and effects great things through their instrumentality. How much may be accomplished through ambition or the love of distinction! how much by fostering vanity in the pupil!

These incitements need only be set in motion and encouraged, and you may raise him to a degree of culture which will attract universal admiration: but it is such a one as the world honours. He that covets this culture has but to enter the service of that spirit which rules in and by worldly-mindedness, and he will usually attain his purpose; this spirit rewards his servants, even in the business of self-culture; but let him, who would be a cultivator of mankind, forswear that demon which is hostile to the divine image, though he should profess to work miracles.

A confirmed inclination or propensity, which has obtained the predominance over the divine in man, we call a passion; and the ebullition of feeling, which interrupts the sobriety of reflection, an excessive emotion. The passions are in themselves cold, but may produce fervidly ebullient emotions; for example, the love of distinction will thus excite violent anger: moreover, they are generally connected with reflection and great penetration, and hence they are deeply-seated corruptions. True culture must therefore prevent all passions from asserting their power; and young persons of both sexes, when rightly educated, are entirely free from them, though not from general depravity. To excessive emotions even the best are subject; but when passions invade the soul, an evil spirit enters with them; and where education finds these, she can do little more than mourn, for there is, generally, not much to be done against them; but against excessive emotions there are remedies. We find here two varieties, similar in their nature to others which have been considered.

The first, which may be termed excessive emotions of effeminacy, are those of fear, or terror, in its different degrees. On this subject the German reader will find admirable remarks in Jean Paul Fr. Richter's "Levana." Children of a lively imagination are most subject to excessive fear; but it is generally awakened and nourished by tales of terror, by the timidity of older persons, and the like. Everything unknown is calculated to excite it, as well as darkness, or, perhaps more frequently, twilight; and children who have never heard of ghosts become alarmed, when in the dark or in a solitary place, even by the gnawing of a mouse. In this we see an arrangement of Divine wisdom, that things uncertain or mysterious in their nature should excite such feelings in order to awaken caution; and this is what ought to be produced, but not timidity, or even cowardice. Children should therefore never be allowed to hear ghost-stories and other tales of terror, except they be accompanied by a clear exposition of the illusion experienced by the senses; delusions of the fancy should be made to lead to a comprehension of the reality. Children should also be made to accustom themselves to be in the dark or alone. Let their courage be strengthened by the cultivation of general energy of character.

The emotions of the second class are of a vigorous character, and operate more outwardly, being exhibited in different degrees of anger. Persons of ingenuous character are precisely those who are most easily provoked to anger, inasmuch as their indignation is strongly excited by the wrong and unjust deeds which they witness; but lively dispositions, having an admixture of the contemplative or vigorous, and therefore, the ardent, the impetuous, the bold, and daring, are much subject to anger. In general, the female sex is less so than the male. In contemplative natures anger rankles more deeply within, and generally betrays itself by the pallor of the countenance.

The principal remedy against anger consists in removing, as much as possible, whatever is calculated to excite it; so long, at least, as the power of resistance is too weak. But it is of the utmost importance to make internal provision against it, by eliciting self-knowledge, by representing its sad consequences, by strengthening the resolution to resist it. While the paroxysm lasts, let the child be very calmly and dispassionately admonished. The well-known remedy of repeating to one's self a suitable maxim at the moment when anger is rising, deserves to be recommended.

Two vices incident to childhood are, lying, and, especially in boys, unchastity. They have been called the besetting sins of childhood. The latter has been cursorily considered under physical education and elsewhere. On the former we subjoin the following observations, which are taken from Schwarz:

" Addictedness to lying, which branches out into deceitfulness, dissimulation, exaggeration, hypocrisy, knavery, &c., has already been referred to, in connexion with other depraved manifestations, out of which it is apt to grow. There must be a great deal of mismanagement before a child will lie: for 'God hath made man upright;' and if a child be guilty of this sin, it has certainly been taught to lie; for, at the period of life in which it does not yet distinguish between truth and fiction, it does not as yet consider whether it can accomplish anything by lying; and it does not really design to utter a falsehood, even when it says what is not true. Now, if anything of this kind is magnified into importance; if a purpose is imputed to the child which, as yet, it cannot have; if the child's attention is thus directed to the circumstance, or, if care be not taken to prevent its accomplishing anything by an untrue statement, the child is actually taught to do what otherwise it would not have learned—nay, what its natural instinct would have led it to abhor, *i. e.*, to speak untruth designedly; it is taught to violate its own self-respect by lying. And now, if children do things for which they are censured; if they be subject to several abnormal developments of character; and if the parents do not command their entire confidence, or if they be even subjected to harsh treatment, they will contract a vicious habit of lying, under the auspices of example and of desired success, and stimulated by manifold opportunity.

"There is here no other remedy than that of closing up the sources of the evil in the other corrupt tendencies, and of obtaining the implicit confidence of children. Children should, in no instance, be allowed to get out of a difficulty by a falsehood; never permit yourself to be deceived by them, but give them due credit for a frank confession, and never punish them for a fault which they spontaneously avow. If they have once been brought to repose full confidence in their educators, all is gained; and in this course it is necessary to persevere. The first real, intentional, deliberate lie should, without a moment's forbearance, be punished with sorrowful severity of manner, and likewise every subsequent falsehood, according to the necessary gradation of punishments. When once lying has become a confirmed habit, the young person will not be easily reformed, perhaps not till after the lapse of years; nevertheless, the necessary course of treatment must be consistently persevered in. It will, at the same time, and especially in the case of hardened liars, have a good effect if they be made to feel, on all suitable occasions, the baseness and odiousness of this vice. The least inconvenience to which they can be subjected is, that they are *never* believed; that they receive no credit, under any circumstances, until they give evidence of amendment."

We shall take leave of this entire subject by adding a few general observations. Throughout this course of education for man as an individual, it will be important to aim at exciting, from early childhood, a sense of what is honourable, decorous, and beautiful; *i. e.*, by exciting a desire of *honourable* distinction, but not ambition; and, where punishment is necessary by shaming and humbling, but not by disgracing Due praise should be given where it is deserved, yet, as we have said, not too frequently: yet we cannot but protest against the practice of giving premiums in order to excite ambition and competition: it gives to effort a wrong basis and a pernicious motive. In the place of it, we would strongly recommend to teachers the practice of giving their pupils certificates respecting their progress and conduct, in order to present them to their parents. This gives to exertion the firm basis of duty, and adds, as a powerful motive, the desire of giving pleasure to those whom the child ought to love best.

In proportion as the understanding of the child or youth is developed, education should increase its careful efforts in cultivating and respecting the sense of honour. The pupil should be treated with respect and confidence, and his feelings never be injured by undue harshness, or lacerated by the scourge of sarcasm. In spite of the modern doctrine, so subversive of all civil and social order, "that it is wrong for one human being to exercise any physical control over another, and that hence even children must be governed, if at all, by moral suasion," submission to authority and law, obedience to parents and instructers should be distinctly insisted upon, and, if necessary, peremptorily and energetically enforced; but, though all commands should be positive and unalterable, and though all reasoning and argumentation with children should be utterly eschewed, no *slavish* obedience should be demanded. In order that obedience may be a rational and cheerful submission to authority, let but the educator *have* good and maturely weighed reasons for his commands, and then the pupil will not find occasion to ask what those reasons are, or to call them in question. Thus, also, the young ought never to be required to practise any obsequious forms of politeness.

In the management of pride and vanity, and particularly of that self-conceit for which college students are so often distinguished, the educator will be most frequently tempted to wield the scourge of satire; but let him forbear, except in rare cases, and rather operate upon the young by his own noble example. The history of ancient and modern times affords the most ample materials for holding up to the pupil's observation the excellence of a truly honourable character, and for enabling him to distinguish it from the false glory of a character merely ambitious; and thus observation and instruction may be beautifully combined.

The objection so often raised against Christianity, that it blunts or destroys the sense of honour, can be most effectually refuted by true portraits of the most distinguished characters in its history.

CHAPTER II.

Moral Education of Man considered as a Member of Society.

The sense of honour belongs to man as an individual; a sense of justice fits him for intercourse with others, and adapts his personal virtue to the intercourse of life. Hence common usage speaks of justice as virtue par excellence, and of its behests as duties.

This virtue, then, in its narrowest signification, as a sense of justice, is based on the following relations, which determine the specific forms in which it is manifested. As honour makes it my duty not to postpone my own dignity to another, and to regard myself as the equal of all others, so justice requires of me that I respect the moral dignity of every other member of the human family, and treat him as my equal. This respect for the dignity of others we designate, 1. As justice in its narrowest sense. It embraces the virtues of modesty, peaceableness, equity in our judgment concerning others, and the republican spirit. Opposed to these virtues are the following vices, viz., arrogance, contempt, slander, and derision.

In the possession of this sense of justice, man is prepared to associate with his fellow-man. The relations of human intercourse then farther enjoin, 2. The virtue of veracity, which is violated by every species of deception and fraud, and by all injurious encroachments on the rights of others. Writers on ethics distinguish a variety of falsehoods. We deem all specifications superfluous, as every deviation from truth is wrong in itself, and violates both the sense of personal honour and of justice towards others. 3. The virtue of good faith, *i. e.*, my obligation, on the one hand, to be true to my given word or promise, and on the other, to submit to the laws under which I live. This obligation embraces all the requirements of justice.

4. As regards the merely external dealings of men with each other, irrespective of their inward disposition and intentions, justice requires, both in public and in private life, an adequate compensation for services or value received, and reparation for injuries inflicted. It is very common to make this merely external consideration a test of inward character; and persons are often heard to claim credit for virtue, because they render to every man his due, and do their neighbour no wrong, while, in fact, their conduct has no other basis than their love of ease, no other principle than self-interest. But here we must insist upon the truth that virtue is estimable for its intrinsic beauty alone, and asks no reward; vice bears its own condemnation within itself, without being punished.

Justice, then, in its essential character, is based on that consciousness of inward dignity which I respect in others, in the same manner in which I desire that my honour should be respected by them. To this ennobling consciousness, which gives me that degree of self-confidence that renders the practice of virtue possible for me, is opposed that consciousness of personal unworthiness, that proclivity to evil, which humbles me in my own eyes and in the sight of God, but not in view of other men, respecting whom I know that the same is true. Hence this humiliation is purely religious, and not ethical, in its character. From the preceding considerations we derive the following elements of the moral education of social man: the first is negative, and consists in counteracting the propensity to evil; the second is the positive promotion of virtue; and the third consists in the establishment and maintenance of moral discipline, and in securing the predominance to good habits.

A.

Negative or preventive education must, first, protect the young against evil examples, both in real life and in books. As regards the influence of living example, the necessity of this caution is universally admitted. But in view of the popular and light literature of the present day, which contains so much that is frivolous and corrupt, we cannot too earnestly urge upon parents and educators the duty of exercising a constant and wise supervision over those whom Providence has committed to their care. This supervision should be rigid in its scrutiny, but not oppressive in its manner, and ought to adapt itself to the progressive development of the pupil's understanding. The laxity of many parents and educators as regards this necessary supervision, and the indifference of others as respects their own example, deserve to be severely censured and rebuked. They are unfit for the trust committed to them.

But, secondly, this preventive education must be vigilant in its care to preserve the yet uncorrupted child from falling into corruption. It should be the earnest purpose of its educators, as long as practicable, to keep its heart from pollution, to preserve its innocence, and that not merely in respect of certain peculiar impurities. This object may be attained by promoting cheerfulness in children; by constantly engaging them either in useful employments or play, for idleness is the beginning of all vices; and by exercising constant supervision over them. We need but point to the boys who are suffered to run at large in the streets of our cities and elsewhere, and the necessity of the treatment here contended for is abundantly illustrated.

B.

Positive education must aim at training the young to good habits in all respects, and therefore by requiring obedience, the true principle of which is faith, *i. e.*, affectionate confidence in parents and educators. Everything will here depend upon the educator's obtaining due authority, and possessing a good tact for government. Rules are easily given, but a certain degree of native talent is requisite for their successful application.

Above all things, the educator must possess, in the highest possible degree, the respect of his pupils, in contradistinction from their affectionate regard, which is only the second element; for without the former the latter cannot really exist. This respect he will directly obtain if he manifests the most conscientious faithfulness in discharging the duties of his office; if he possesses the requisite talents and information; if he practises the strictest impartiality towards all his pupils; and if his entire conduct gives evidence of excellence of character. Those who are deficient in any one of these points, or in all, and seek to make up for the deficiency by treating their pupils with great kindness and affection, will, of necessity, utterly fail. Nor will those succeed better who assume the appearance of authority, when the respect on which the reality is based is wanting; and least of all can such respect be extorted by excessive severity or tyranny. A reign of terror is the worst of all in education.

The manner in which commands and prohibitions are given is of the utmost importance. The following principles should be carefully observed: Let there be as few commands or laws as possible; but what has once been prescribed ought to be irrevocable. If altered circumstances should require the abrogation of any rule that has been given, it should be as formally abrogated as it was enjoined. No rule should be permitted to become an obsolete statute, for which nobody has any farther respect. Hence it will be necessary to reflect maturely before any rule of conduct is prescribed; and no order should be given, to enforce which the will or the ability is wanting. By neglecting these several principles, great and extensive mischief is done by many who undertake the business of education.

Rules for the conduct of children should be given in as few words and with as much distinctness as possible; and no flattery, or any other mixed motives which would derogate from the authority of the rules, should be employed.

No commands should be given in the excitement of passion. Hence irritable persons, who are easily provoked to anger, should be careful not to betray their foible to their pupils, and in all cases refrain from speaking until they have recovered their command of themselves.

After punishment has been administered, all reserve and austerity should disappear, and kindness and love towards the pupil be exhibited as before. The educator should much less indulge himself in pouting than even his pupils. A heart softened by punishment is often the more easily and directly influenced for good. Disobedience need not, *in all cases*, be punished; nor should obedience be always rewarded. If the latter were done, there would be danger of converting all morality into mere legal obsequiousness.

As respects the former, that is, the omission of the punishment of disobedience, this may be admissible when, in order to avoid excessive rigour, a minor misdemeanour can be connived at; but without, by any means, permitting the child or youth to be aware of your connivance.

And again, this omission of punishment may take place when there is reason to believe, that the reproaches of conscience inflict a severer punishment than could be otherwise administered. External punishment often weakens the punitive inflictions of conscience. A wise plan of education, consistently pursued, will greatly diminish the necessity of punishment. It is notorious that those who have no plan or judgment are perpetually inflicting chastisement on their children, if they do not spoil them by indulgence. Sometimes we find both extremes strangely combined; and such a course of education usually produces monsters of wickedness. The golden mean is found only by the reflecting and wise.

C.

It should be the aim of the higher moral education gradually to lead the young to desire and to will the good solely for its own sake, and thus to acquire a truly virtuous character of their own.

Unconditional obedience should gradually cease, and the obedience of conviction take its place. Yet we must here repeat our protest against all premature reasoning and argumentation with the young on the subject of duties.

As soon as the child's understanding has attained a sufficient degree of maturity, sound moral *instruction* should be given, which should be directed against prevalent prejudices, and against any evil habits which the child may be forming: nothing but simple maxims, couched in concise and impressive language, should be given.

This instruction ought never to slide into a moralizing tone, but lay hold especially of living and historical examples. Direct discourses to the young, breathing a spirit of sound and exalted morality, can scarcely fail of accomplishing good; but, in order to this, the educator must possess a moral sense no less enlightened than quick. An instructer possessing these necessary qualifications will, of course, be exceedingly careful not to foist in wrong motives to virtue, be they ever so plausible and flattering, but to present it to the eyes of his pupil in all its exalted dignity, without seeking to invest it with any extraneous charms or artificial incitements to emotion.

In the more advanced years of youth, the example

of strict and exalted morality will exert an influence the more powerful, the more beautifully it illustrates all the instructions that have been previously given. The more mature, therefore, his pupils are, the more severe should be the educator's demands upon himself, the more rigid his examination and judgment of himself.

The reading of good treatises on morals, either of an argumentative or illustrative character, is much to be recommended; but the capacity of the reader, and the contents of the book to be read, should be carefully considered. Many books that profess to have a moral tendency are worse than worthless.

To this higher moral education belongs the direct culture of all those distinct virtues which combine in forming a just, in a word, a virtuous member of society, and for which the early preventive and habituating education must have laid the foundation. In stating the following points to be observed in this connexion, we are aware that we repeat what has already been said elsewhere; yet this brief recapitulation is necessary to complete the plan which it is here proposed to give. We remark, then, first, that, in order to fit man for social intercourse, his selfishness must be subdued. This is accomplished by the process which is styled the breaking of the temper; by abstaining from all flattery in the treatment of children; and by promoting a spirit of self-denial, in contradistinction from that eager egotism, which, even in the highest state of refinement, aims only at selfish enjoyments.

Again, on the foundation here supposed to be laid, modesty, as contradistinguished from arrogance, will spontaneously develop itself; yet it may be positively promoted by judicious instruction respecting its amiableness, especially in the young, and by directly cultivating such tempers as are essential to it.

Again, cultivate a love of truth in the young, on the plan already presented. It is a much to be lamented fact, that parents and others frequently dispose of the questions of children, or help themselves out of a difficulty which they may have with them, by telling them falsehoods. Words would fail us were we to attempt, in adequate language, to reprobate this practice, and to express our abhorrence of it. Apart from the sin itself, these falsehoods rarely fail of being eventually detected by the children; and what must be the effect of such discovery? Oh! that parents and other educators would, in all respects, walk before children as in the presence of the omniscient God, and cultivate in them a sense of his omnipresence and omniscience!

But, farther, in training the young to habits of good faith, their educators should themselves regard as inviolable any promise which they may have given their children or pupils, however inconvenient it may be to fulfil it; and then the pupil should be as inexorably required to be as good as his word; but no promise should be exacted from him which it would be difficult for him to fulfil.

Good faith in submitting to the laws manifests itself, in education, as obedience. This, then, the corrupt notions of our day to the contrary notwithstanding, is the child's, the pupil's first duty; the stem, as it were, out of which all others grow. Here the most tender moral sense can, and ought to, manifest itself, when the child obeys simply for the sake of obedience. But hence arises that most sacred duty of the educator, to require nothing that is not suitable and wise.

The young should be accustomed to respect the mutual claims which men have on each other, according to the principle, "Whatsoever ye would that men should do unto you, that do ye unto them." None are so mean that their kind offices should not deserve, at least, a grateful acknowledgment.

Lastly, the ideal of character, compounded of reflection, energy, action, and purity of soul, should be constantly kept in view by those intrusted with the business of moral education, and brought, more and more clearly, before the minds of the young. Historical and living examples are best calculated to illustrate it; though living examples may often have to be taken, in order to place the opposite of this ideal into strong relief. The development of this ideal in the soul of the pupil is the highest aim of moral education.

In conclusion, we add a few remarks in justification of the brevity with which we have treated the subject of the present chapter. We have been thus brief partly because much of what belongs here had already and unavoidably been considered elsewhere, in connexion with man's individual education; so that the reader, with the sketch here presented before him, need only refer to those pages where the subjects here specified are discussed in detail. But we have been thus brief on this head, chiefly because we are deeply convinced that moral character, without genuine, heartfelt piety, has, at best, only a relative value, and no absolute stability. We certainly do not mean to say, that the man of good moral principles and habits is not a better member of society than one who has no such pretensions; but we do intend to assert, and the history of our own time and country daily furnishes additional proofs of the fact, that moral character, without a real and deep religious basis, is not to be depended on in seasons of temptation, in circumstances which "try men's souls," and make it appear what is in man.

The very idea of pure and genuine cosmopolitism belongs to Christianity. It had no existence before the religion of Christ regenerated human life. Utterly fruitless must be every attempt to establish and carry out this grand idea, which unites all mankind in one great brotherhood, without the idea of one great destination, to which the human race is developing itself under the guidance of Providence; in a word, without the consciousness that we live and labour in the kingdom of God; without belonging to the Church of Christ. Without this, we should see nothing in the history of man but the constant repetition of that vast tragedy which we witnessed in the developments of the ancient world, and which, so far as his subjective stand-point is concerned, is still rolling along its dismal scenery before the eye of the unbeliever; and all the undertakings and doings of men, the work of education itself, would be idle and vain. Then would man only contrive a multiplicity of arts, in order to pass through life as agreeably as possible; then would parents have nothing better to do than to teach their children how to calculate accurately, how to think profoundly and acutely, and thus to make the shrewdest possible egotists; leaving, however, the prospect before them, that another, or ten, or a hundred, will outstrip them in the race, and leave them to mourn in despondency, or to sink into despair. What a miserable affair would be all human culture, if we had not Christianity! Without the belief that our labours will not, on the whole, fail of their high aim, all our educational institutions and efforts would be nothing but "vanity of vanities;" but, under the conviction that we are employed in prosecuting, in the kingdom of God, a work subservient to his purposes and praise, the business of education and instruction becomes a divine employment, and forms true citizens of the world.

To the Church of Christ, to its institutions and instrumentalities, we therefore leave the moral education of man as a member of the great human family.

The following chapter, which treats of the religious instruction of the young, is, in the main, derived from the work of Schwarz.

CHAPTER III.

RELIGIOUS EDUCATION.

It is the same with religion as with language, which is developed at once both from within and from without. As the child, in order to have any language, learns the language of its mother, its home, its country, the religion of man must also be evolved by tradition transmitted from the father to the son: its origin must always have a positive basis Doctrines must here always be communicated by the instructer, and be announced with a certain divine authority, because otherwise they would not gain admission into the child's mind, and because they would teach reflection, and not religion. We would not even arrive at any fixed moral precepts if we had not moral maxims and morals, and if not a voice of sacred authority from without first called forth the divine voice within. We would otherwise have to suffer the springtime of life to pass away unimproved, and to deny to the soul's most sacred impulse that light, without which it cannot burst into life. No: from the lips of their parents the language of virtue and religion must penetrate into the hearts of children, if all shall be well with them; something must in this way be given from without. We are therefore indebted to Providence for positive religion, as an essential element of education; consequently, there must be an important connexion between right instruction in religion and the religion actually possessed by the parents.

This instruction is, in the first place, domestic. As long as the child does not distinguish between things as good or evil, it is, as yet, incapable of religious thought. The first guides to this are the childlike feelings of confidence and gratitude; for in both the child can already perceive the good, and will in both affectionately strive upward to that Being from whom it derives what is good; in the first instance, therefore, to its parents. Thus we see the elements of piety unfold themselves with the development of the child's mind, and then, in due time, moral feeling and thinking.

Confidence, obedience, gratitude, and humility are the first and abiding religious feelings; these must be, first of all, awakened and animated, and through them the child must be drawn to the Father in heaven, if instruction in religion is to be thorough, truthful, and imperishable. As early as in the fourth year of life, the child begins to send its thoughts beyond the sensuous world, and to comprehend communications respecting God; it conceives of him with reverence as of a spiritual being, and the farther the child advances in intellectual development, the more will it worship the infinite Spirit. If now it be suitably instructed, it can, already in its seventh year, entertain the idea of an infinitely good, all-wise, and almighty Being, with the proper feelings and reasons, though the idea may only gradually become clear; and as it will now also form notions of the supersensuous, the ideas of heaven, and of the destination of man will, at this period already, connect themselves with that of God and the worship of God, and hence instruction must be given on this point also. The child of seven years of age must therefore be no stranger to the doctrines of God and of immortality. If any of Rousseau's disciples should here interpose his impertinent opinion, that, as yet, nothing should be said to the child respecting God, because it is not yet capable of comprehending him, they may be met with the question, "Do *ye* comprehend God?" and dismissed with that sacred word, "Become like unto children." The child that prays in its simplicity has more religion than the self-complacent philosopher. If, then, parents desire to bring up their children as true worshippers of God, they should begin early, on the basis of pious feeling, to give them instruction respecting God.

For this reason we have called this early religious instruction the domestic, and thus also pointed out the course which it should take. In the first instance, the child should occasionally hear something respecting the Father in heaven, but particularly on those occasions when it seeks aid in any matter, or rejoices at anything. Then the mother or the father may tell the child of God in heaven, as the Father of them all; and then their prayers should sometimes be offered up in the presence of the child, and the child itself be directed to pray ere it retires to rest. They need only give the child a few words, expressive of deep and lively feeling, to repeat, and give it frequently to understand that it may tell this Father whatsoever it pleases; that he hears and loves it, and is able to do whatever seemeth good to him Under the divine blessing, the parents will soon have reason to rejoice at the pious prayers of their child, and, in general, at the manner in which it will give utterance to what is passing within; and as the imagination will be ever employed in its plastic operations, the religious feelings of the child, which will frequently exhibit themselves in these productions of the imagination, should sometimes be noted, and gradually guided by the parents. But on this point no particular rules can be given, in addition to those given under the head of imagination.

It is, of course, a paramount requisite that the parents themselves be religious, and regarded with reverence by their children, otherwise the best instruction in religion which the child may receive will not be accompanied by the needful blessing.

When children are about the age of seven years, their regular instruction in religion should commence. This may be divided into three courses. The first should develop those feelings of confidence, obedience, gratitude, and humility, before spoken of; point to God, the Father of all men, and show how all men are intended to be the children of God, and to become eternally happy. This course should also give instruction concerning Jesus as the best of men, but as one come from heaven, by whom the Father himself instructs men. All historical statements in relation to religion must be made authoritatively, without superadded reflections and proofs, because for these the child is, as yet, far from being prepared; and the supposed truth which it might be expected to receive on these subjects would not really be truth, but would, in the soul of the child, be untruth: it is sufficient if its heart receives all this; for then it will, at this period already, hold it as truth, and become more and more confirmed in its convictions; and thus it becomes truly sanctified in the truth of the divine word. It is necessary to take the child aside from other witnesses, and to devote, at most, half an hour at a time to this subject, or, rather, no longer time than while its religious feelings manifest activity; for these are here principally concerned, because without them the ideas presented would become mere empty formulas, and consequently be a desecration of the divine name; but, whenever they are received by the heart, let them be expressed in definite terms or propositions. Occasionally a passage of Scripture, or a stanza of a hymn, should be repeated to children, which may serve in the place of such a proposition, and will now be understood by the young heart.

The second course, opening with about the ninth year, will apparently again commence at the beginning, inasmuch as it will more fully analyze and elucidate all these doctrines, and particularly, also, give more distinct instruction respecting the divine Redeemer. The morals of Christianity must also be more extensively treated; but always, of course, with reference to the doctrines of faith, and with special reference to the childlike mind, adapting instruction to its state of development. At the same time, more passages of Scripture and hymns ought to be committed to memory.

The third course, which cannot begin before the twelfth year, will embrace a review of the preceding, and bring everything into due connexion, while it is, as it were, a repetition of the first, completed by the second. This course will give unity to the finished whole.

The consideration of the farther prosecution of this domestic religious instruction does not belong to our present undertaking; for those who would communicate such instruction according to the plan here presented, and with a religious spirit, must themselves possess that spirit, and will then readily mark out the subsequent course for themselves. Every father ought to do this. We merely remark, that only one child alone, or, at most, a few brothers and sisters, can be thus instructed at a time, because there must be no restraint; because everything should be directly received by the heart, and by the heart also freely expressed. If this religious instruction is to produce all its intended and happy results, three important influences (subordinate, of course, to the spirit of grace) must combine in one harmonious operation: the father's instruction, the mother's tenderness, and, in general, the love of the parents and the pious spirit of the family, exhibited in the good deportment of every member of the household. Whenever one of these influences is absent in any family, religion will not flourish as it ought, and what is there that could make up for such a deficiency?

Domestic religious instruction is followed by that of the Church. In a manner corresponding to the former, there must here also be a union of three sources or influences: the instruction of the pastor, the influence of the Christian spirit in the Church, especially through the sacred Scriptures, and the good tone of public morals. Important means of religious education are devotional exercises in the family, and the solemn days of the Church.

It is not our province to enter farther into this subject, and to show the happy influence which, in our country, Sabbath-schools may and generally do exert, or to speak of the necessity of Bible-classes, and other important means of religious instruction; but we may observe that the teachers of Sabbath-schools ought to be selected with more attention to their qualifications to instruct in sacred things, than we have reason to believe is always the case. They should not only be decidedly pious, but capable of speaking to the young, wisely and well, of those things that belong unto man's everlasting peace.

And we would add that we consider the practice of our churches, as regards religious instruction, to be defective in a considerable degree. There is too little done to develop religious character in children, and hence arises a necessity for extraordinary efforts to bring the youth and adults into the Church; and we recommend the above discussion to the attention of parents and others, in the hope that they will be induced to sow early that divine seed, which, when early sown, may be expected to bear rich and copious harvests ; for such are the promises of Holy Writ.

We are quite sensible that what we have given above is but a brief sketch, unaccompanied by those earnest and fervent admonitions which many will probably look for in connexion with the solemn concern under consideration ; but the subject is so great in itself, and of such vast importance, that it demands a literature of its own, and of such a literature our country possesses much that is truly valuable and excellent. Our present purpose could only be to present a simple plan of religious education for that period of life, in which it is most generally neglected, in that very sphere where most can be effected for it: we speak of home. And if the brief treatise given above should be effectual in enlightening hitherto neglectful parents respecting their duty, and in guiding them in its faithful performance, our purpose will be attained.

THE END

www.ingramcontent.com/pod-product-compliance
Lightning Source LLC
LaVergne TN
LVHW010209110826
845151LV00002B/645
* 9 7 8 1 4 2 5 5 3 4 2 1 9 *